COUNTERTERRORISM

STRATEGIES

FOR

CORPORATIONS

THE
ACKERMAN PRINCIPLES

To Michael Groeten
J The my best
wishes

Mi A

COUNTERTERRORISM

STRATEGIES

FOR

CORPORATIONS

THE
ACKERMAN PRINCIPLES

MIKE ACKERMAN

Foreword by
DR. ARIEL MERARI
Founder of the Hostage Negotiation and
Crisis Management Team of the Israeli Defense Forces

Prometheus Books
59 John Glenn Drive
Amherst, New York 14228-2119

Published 2008 by Prometheus Books

Inquiries should be addressed to
Prometheus Books
59 John Glenn Drive
Amherst, New York 14228–2119
VOICE: 716–691–0133, ext. 210
FAX: 716–691–0137
WWW.PROMETHEUSBOOKS.COM

12 11 10 09 08   5 4 3 2 1

Library of Congress Cataloging-in-Publication Data pending

Ackerman, Mike.
    Counterterrorism Strategies for Corporations: The Ackerman Principles.
        p. cm.
    Includes index.
    ISBN 978–1–59102–654–9
    1. Corporations—Security measures. 2. Security systems. 3. Terrorism—
Prevention. I. Title.

HV8290.A35 2008
658.4/77—dc22

2008030588

Printed in the United States on acid-free paper

DEDICATION

In memory of my beloved parents, John and Dorothy Ackerman.

ACKNOWLEDGMENTS

I t would be impossible for me to acknowledge everyone who has schooled me in the principles of security and counterterrorism since 1963, when, as a brand-new second lieutenant, I took responsibility for a midnight shift of air policemen guarding nuclear-laden B-52s in the Strategic Air Command (SAC). I do, however, want to thank friends and colleagues who have read and contributed to my manuscript. These include Ackerman Group colleagues Bill Reynolds, Wes Odom, Eamonn O'Brien, and George Dew. Frank Pedrozo, Marshal Valentine, and Rick Ford also made valuable suggestions.

I also want to take special note of former corporate security directors and good friends Ernie Conrads, Jim Geer, and Pat Keefe, who not only read the manuscript but collaborated on the chapters addressing corporate security.

Other readers to whom I am indebted include Mark Rush, the Robert G. Brown Professor of Politics and Law, head of the Department of Politics and director of the Program in International Finance and Commerce at the Williams School of Commerce, Economics and Politics of Washington and Lee University; David Overton, my classmate at Dartmouth, a former senior economist at the CIA and a former senior lecturer at Dartmouth's Amos Tuck School of Business Administration; Morton M. Palmer III (Pete), a former colleague at both the CIA and The Ackerman Group; and last but not least, Jack Stein, my attorney for twenty-eight years and friend for even longer than that.

It should not be assumed that the collaborators and readers agreed with all aspects of the book. Indeed, several took strong exception to some points. Much that is worthwhile in the book, however, I owe to them. Responsibility for the shortcomings, of course, rests with me alone.

I also want to acknowledge Jan F. Larsen, the former director of corporate security at Pfizer, who embraced the project early on and provided an introduction to my literary agent, Peter Riva. Peter's championship of the book and useful suggestions were instrumental to its publication.

Also, I want to express my sincere appreciation to Arleene Avila, my research assistant, and especially to Yolanda Merced, who not only proofread the manuscript but took much of the burden off my shoulders in preparing it for publication. I also am indebted to Steven L. Mitchell, my editor at Prometheus, for patiently shepherding the project to its conclusion.

Lastly, I am indebted to my wife, Lauren, and children, John, Josh, Jenna, and Arielle, for inspiring and delighting me every day and especially for putting up with the sudden absences that come with my job.

CONTENTS

FOREWORD   13

THE ACKERMAN PRINCIPLES   17

SECTION 1. PROLOGUE
1. The Great Asparagus Caper   21
2. The Critical Need for Intelligence   27

SECTION 2. CONTENDING WITH GLOBAL JIHAD
3. The Character of Global Jihad   37
4. The Aims of Global Jihad   43
5. Al-Qaida Goes for the Jugular: The Pakistani Aberration 47
6. Specific and Class Attacks: Algeria and Egypt   53
7. Attacks against Specific Economic Targets   65
8. Class Attacks: Commercial Aviation   75
9. Class Attacks: Trains and Subways   83
10. Class Attacks: Hotels and Hangouts   91
11. Class Attacks: Tourism   97

SECTION 3. DEALING WITH KIDNAPPINGS, EXTORTIONS, THREATS
12. Chaos Breeds Kidnapping   105
13. Kidnapping: The Ultimate Corporate Nightmare   113
14. Cases from Hell   131
15. Dealing with Extortion   137
16. Dealing with Threats   145

SECTION 4. CONVENTIONAL CRIME PROBLEMS

17. Express Kidnapping   155
18. Other Violent Street Crime   161
19. Entertainment Venues   167
20. Residential Crime   169

SECTION 5. PROTECTING EMPLOYEES FROM SPECIFIC ATTACKS

21. Modifying Behavior   181
22. Armored Cars   189
23. Bodyguards   195

SECTION 6. INTERACTING WITH CORPORATE SECURITY

24. The Corporate Security Function   207
25. What to Look for in a Corporate Security Director   211
26. Success Depends Upon:
     Credibility, Authority, Business Acumen   215

SECTION 7. EPILOGUE: A LOOK BACK AND A LOOK AHEAD

27. A Look Back at My Career   223
28. A Look Ahead   241

ADDENDA

MAJOR GLOBAL JIHAD ATTACKS AND ATTEMPTS POST-9/11

A. Direct Attacks on Commercial Targets   249
B. Commercial Aviation Targets   251
C. Train and Subway Targets   252
D. Hotels   253

E. Tourism-Related Targets   254
F. Governmental and Military Targets   255

TRAVEL GUIDES
1. Air Travel   257
2. Travel by Senior Officers with Protective Details   263
3. Solo Travel to Countries with
   High Terrorism or Crime Risks   267
4. Travel to Moderate-Risk Destinations   272
5. Travel to the Muslim World   275
6. Travel to Hostile Countries   278
7. Travel to Unstable Countries   281
8. Travel Tips for Women   282
9. Travel Tips for Nonwhites   283
10. Surviving an Abduction   283

RESIDENTIAL SECURITY CHECKLISTS
1. Apartment—High-Risk Area   285
2. Apartment—Moderate-Risk Area   290
3. Single-Family Dwelling in Walled,
   Gated Community—High-Risk Area   294
4. Single-Family Dwelling on Public Street—
   High-Risk Area   299
5. Single-Family Dwelling—Moderate-Risk Area   305

INDEX   309

FOREWORD

My friendship with Mike Ackerman goes back about a quarter of a century. I first met Mike when he came to Israel in the early 1980s to get a firsthand impression of the terrorism situation in the country and to identify sources of information for preparing risk-analysis reporting for his clients. At that time I served as the director of the Terrorism and Low Intensity Warfare Project, which I founded at Tel Aviv University's Center for Strategic Studies. I also commanded Israel's Hostage Negotiations Unit. Naturally, we had much common ground to talk about.

In the ensuing years, I have met Mike many times in the United States and again in Israel. I participated in several of the conferences Mike has held annually to brief his clients about the risks of terrorism and crime around the globe. In all these meetings I was struck by Mike's outstanding professionalism and his thorough knowledge of situations in all parts of the world where terrorism developments took place. His knowledge and forecasts were no less accurate and penetrating than those of the best government intelligence organizations. In contrast to government agencies, however, Mike's emphasis was on the defense of the business community rather than on state interests.

This difference is best illustrated in the area of hostage recovery: The Ackerman Group's central concern is the safe return of hostages, whereas a government's prime interest is in arresting kidnappers. In conducting negotiations with terrorist hostage-takers in Israel, I have seen these conflicting interests at play.

Understandably, families want their dear ones to be released at any cost. Governments, on the other hand, have other considerations in addition to the safe release of hostages. Most important among these considerations is the question of whether the conclusion of the event

13

will deter terrorists from this course of action or will encourage them to repeat it. For this reason, Israel has always opted for a rescue operation whenever such an assault was feasible. Typically, rescue operations are possible in hostage-barricade situations, wherein terrorists barricade themselves along with hostages at locations inside Israel, posing an immediate and direct challenge to the government.

Since in most cases the hostage's location has been known and is accessible, and the deadlines posed by the terrorists are very short—usually a few hours—Israel invariably has used special forces in rescue operations. In cases wherein the hostages have been held outside Israel's borders, however, an assault has been out of the question, and the government has been obliged to negotiate. The sole exception to this rule was the hostage rescue at Entebbe, Uganda, in July 1976.

Since 1978, Israel's record of success in negotiations with hostage-takers outside its territory has left much to be desired. In order to secure the release of a few hostages, Israel in several cases has freed thousands of convicted terrorists. Its poor negotiating record in these cases can be attributed to several factors, among them flawed tactics. I have often thought that these miserable results would not have occurred if Mike Ackerman had conducted the negotiations.

In the 1980s, two main types of groups carried out most of the international terrorist attacks. One category consisted of nationalist groups, which operated mainly in the Middle East and Western Europe and included the Palestinian organizations, the IRA, the Basque ETA, Armenia's ASALA and Justice Commandos, and several other similar groups. The other type were radical leftist groups that operated mainly in Latin America and Western Europe, such as the FARC and the ELN in Colombia, Shining Path in Peru, and the Farabundo Marti National Liberation Front (FMLN) in El Salvador. Both types of groups carried out attacks against American targets; by State Department statistics, attacks on US nationals and property amounted to more than one-third of the total number of international attacks during the 1970s and 1980s.

Today's main perpetrators of international terrorism are quite different from those of the past. In the current century, the salient groups that have attacked Western targets have been militant Islamic organizations. In contrast to nationalist groups but similar to leftist movements, they represent a global, internationalist ideology and are therefore inclined to maintain links with like-minded groups beyond their national boundaries, a fact that facilitates their global reach.

These new actors have introduced significant changes in the nature of terrorism. Most important, their attacks have been much deadlier than those of their predecessors. They seek to kill large numbers of people rather than to merely make a statement. The average number of casualties of a terrorist attack in the present decade is considerably greater than the average number per attack before the turn of the century. The 9/11 attacks are, of course, the starkest example, but many other incidents come to mind, such as the October 12, 2002, attack on a nightclub in Bali, which killed 193 people, the attack on the trains in Madrid on March 11, 2004, which killed 191 people, and the attacks on the London transportation system on July 7, 2005, which resulted in the deaths of 52 people.

Associated with the increased lethality is the growing indiscrimination of the attacks. As early as 1996, Usama bin Ladin issued a "declaration of war against the Americans" in which he advocated attacks against Americans—combatants and civilians alike—around the world. This call has subsequently been implemented in numerous attacks.

The tendency to resort to indiscriminate, high-casualty attacks translates into readiness to use weapons of mass destruction (WMDs). Long before 9/11, terrorist groups could produce at least crude chemical weapons and perhaps some biological weapons as well. Presumably, they refrained from employing them because they feared the repercussions that were likely to result from breaking what the world community generally perceived as a taboo. The 9/11 high-casualty attacks on civilian targets broke this taboo, however. There is evidence that al-Qaida leaders have attempted to obtain weapons of mass destruction, and their efforts to do so are likely to continue. If and when these efforts materialize, the implications concerning defensive measures are going to be immense.

Unlike the endemic form of terrorism and common crime in certain countries and regions, such as Latin America, the militant salafi-jihadi Islamic ideology is inherently international and therefore tends to spread geographically. During the Soviet-Afghan War (1979–1989), Muslim militants from many countries went to Afghanistan to fight against the infidels. Once the war was over, most of these volunteers returned to their home countries, where they became an important factor in the strengthening of local Islamic extremist groups. Their zeal and the fighting skills that they acquired in Afghanistan radicalized local groups and augmented their terrorist capabilities. This so-called Afghan effect is likely to be replicated on a larger scale once the war in Iraq is over. Recent studies show that foreign jihadi volunteers came to Iraq from all Arab countries, as well as from immigrant communities in Europe. Their return home will certainly boost the intensity of terrorism in a large number of countries.

Despite the changes in the nature of terrorism that have taken place in the recent two decades, business personnel and facilities have remained a prime target of terrorist groups around the globe. As Mike Ackerman amply demonstrates in this book, the salafi-jihadi militants, who dominate today's scene of international terrorism, have attacked a variety of business personnel and facilities around the world, both directly and indirectly, and will probably continue to do so in the foreseeable future. That is what makes this book so important.

Dr. Ariel Merari

THE ACKERMAN
PRINCIPLES

1. Expect Global Jihad to confront us for decades and to target Western economic interests, especially those related to oil. Other terrorist groups will also attack commercial interests. Terrorists will be the skunk at the globalization lawn party.

2. Do your best to acquire a solid grasp of the risks that pertain in areas in which you are doing business or intend to do business—ideally from several sources. Corporations in general undervalue risk analysis. The informed manager has a distinct advantage over competitors.

3. Don't be intimidated by those risks. In most cases, you can bolster your defenses and go about your business. Remember the Jim Flannery dictum: "Perfect security means doing nothing in a vacuum."

4. On the other hand, always weigh the risks against the potential rewards of a given project. Devise strategies for curtailing risks. Certainly avoid unnecessary risks.

5. Investigate thoroughly key employees, distributors, vendors, joint-venture partners, and domestics. You will have your hands full with external forces and you don't need problems inside your tent.

6. Train personnel bound for high-risk areas in protective tactics. Training is the most cost-effective means of enhancing their safety. Even senior managers should develop a thorough understanding of their security arrangements.

7. Don't fall in love with security technology. It is an aide, not an answer. Armored cars, for example, though a useful part of a security program, should not be considered impenetrable cocoons.

8. Well-trained bodyguards also have a role to play in protecting senior personnel, but their value lies more in deterring attacks and forestalling them by spotting early-warning signs than in responding with lethal force.

9. If confronted by assailants, choose reason over heroism. If unarmed, follow the assailants' instructions. If armed, consider that you might be outgunned.

10. Prepare diligently for crises. Expect the unexpected, and when emergencies arise, respond thoughtfully, and not by rote or reflex. For example, it is often best to stay put instead of heading for the exits in the immediate aftermath of a coup or an uprising.

SECTION 1

■

PROLOGUE

■

Chapter One

THE GREAT ASPARAGUS CAPER

T he year was 1985. Ronald Reagan had just begun his second presidential term, and Americans in general were feeling pretty good about themselves and about the world at large.

Terrorism on the scale of 9/11 was still unimaginable. Indeed, most of what passed for terrorism in those days was perpetrated by leftist groups with ties to the Soviet Bloc. Most were subnational, as opposed to transnational, but several Palestinian Marxist groups had begun to operate across international boundaries, in several cases attacking commercial aviation. Hizbollah, the Iranian-backed Lebanese Shia extremist movement, had burst onto the scene two years earlier with a suicide bombing of the US Marine barracks in Beirut, but its first transnational operation, the hijacking of TWA Flight 847 from Athens to Rome, was still months away.

I was summoned to the headquarters of a major US food processor. The corporate security director, a former special agent of the FBI, had managed to convince senior managers that they would benefit from hearing my views on a prospective overseas investment. The security director was quite surprised and delighted by management's decision to invite me to the meeting, since it was rare in those days to grant security a place at the august table at which a new investment was being considered.

The corporate security director had been successful in getting me entree, I learned during that initial conversation, because the prospective investment target was Colombia. Leftist insurgents had staged several highly publicized kidnappings of American managers in that country in the preceding two or three years.

The matter at hand was the wisdom of a substantial investment in Colombia's agricultural sector, specifically in the fertile Cauca Valley, where the country's senior guerrilla movement, the Colombian Revolutionary Armed Forces, normally known by the Spanish acronym FARC, was known to be operating. I was being asked to assess risks from FARC and estimate how much it would cost to protect the technical personnel who would need to visit production sites, if, indeed, special protection measures were warranted.

The meeting was held in what clearly was a high-rent conference room and was chaired by the senior vice president, international.

First up was the marketing vice president; he made the case that we would see in the coming years a substantial increase in world demand for asparagus, which, I learned for the first time, was the product under consideration. The SVP reinforced his case with a series of charts supporting the proposition that as people around the world became more affluent, their taste for asparagus would grow proportionally. Perhaps more than proportionally! Who knew?

I had, in the course of my eight years in the private sector, sat through a number of presentations dealing with economic forecasts of various types, but it had never dawned on me that one by-product of a rising standard of living was a hunger for asparagus. Nor did it ever occur to me that large agribusinesses plotted the demand curve for their vegetables, though, sitting there, it made perfect sense that they would.

Next came the chief agronomist, who reported that, although many places in the world were well suited for the production of asparagus, few were as ideal as the Cauca Valley. Again, his point was illustrated with a series of charts dealing with soil content, weather, and the like.

The third speaker was the vice president for business development, and his point was that a Colombian agricultural association bent on diversification beyond coffee and other traditional crops was offering the company extraordinary terms for what would amount to a joint venture in asparagus production. Investment would be minimal, and the profits potentially handsome. The company's principal contributions to the project would be seed stock and technical expertise. Local farmers would be counting on American technicians to teach them asparagus cultivation and ensure quality control.

I was up last, and clearly I had been assigned the role of skeptic. Security people are expected to find fault with prospective projects—to be naysayers, which may explain in part their limited role in decision making on investments. I had always fought hard against this inclination, mindful of the dictum of Jim Flannery, one of my early bosses at the CIA, who equated perfect security with "doing nothing in a vacuum." In almost all instances, I believe, it is possible to find practical ways for dealing with risk. But there were a lot of good reasons to be negative about this particular project.

I cited them, one by one. FARC and other Colombian guerrilla groups were inveterate kidnappers, ransom abductions, along with narcotrafficking, being their principal means of raising operating funds. Moreover, FARC had a heavy presence in the Cauca Valley, where it frequently kidnapped well-to-do farmers and ranchers and members of their families. Few foreigners had been taken in the valley, but only because there were few available. FARC and the other groups were not at all hesitant to kidnap foreigners. Indeed, they appeared to take special satisfaction in abducting Americans and other foreigners, especially those from "exploitive" multinational corporations.

Risks in the Cauca Valley were so acute, I contended, that American technicians could not safely go there without costly protective arrangements. Oil companies operating in other parts of Colombia, in deference to similar risks, had taken to shuttling personnel by helicopter between major cities, where kidnapping levels were substantially lower than rural areas, and highly fortified compounds. The food processor's technicians, by definition, would not be headed for protected compounds, so it would be necessary not only to transport them by helicopter but also to furnish them with heavily armed bodyguard complements. A less expensive—but far more dangerous—alternative would involve transporting the technicians in convoys of at least three vehicles, again manned by heavily armed bodyguards.

Expressions around the table grew sour. The security director asked me to estimate the hourly cost of a helicopter. At the time, it was about $850. No one asked me to cost out the bodyguards. There was a lot of shuffling of papers, and some participants began to show a lot of interest in their wristwatches.

I went on to my final point. A major US airline had been fined on more than one occasion because ground crews had secreted cocaine aboard planes bound for Miami. Flower growers and manufacturing concerns were encountering similar problems: Traffickers had little trouble bribing shipping clerks to place drugs in containers bound for the United States. Presumably, asparagus crates also would serve their nefarious aims. Robust cargo-security measures would have to be put in place, and, given the traffickers' enormous capacity to suborn low-paid personnel, there would be no certainty even then that shipments would not be compromised—with disastrous consequences for the integrity of the brand.

At this point, the senior vice president cut me off with the words, "Whose f_____ idea was this anyway?" The meeting ended on that note.

When last I heard, the program was being undertaken in Chile, then and now Latin America's safest country. Perhaps the soil and climatologic conditions were not as ideal, and perhaps the terms were not as attractive, but the relative absence of security concerns more than offset these shortcomings.

Indeed, had my client ventured to Colombia against my advice, it might have found itself in the same dilemma as Chiquita Brands, which recently paid a $25 million fine to US authorities for doling out $1.8 million in protection money over a seven-year period ending in 2004 to the United Self-Defense Forces of Colombia, known as the AUC, a rightist paramilitary group, ostensibly to protect its banana plantations in northwestern Colombia from FARC. Previously, the Justice Department alleged, Chiquita had made similar payments to the leftist movement.

The AUC was established in the 1990s with encouragement from Colombian elites, who had become frustrated with the inability of a succession of weak presidents to protect them from leftist kidnappings and extortions. The army in fact did not really begin to engage FARC until hard-nosed Alvaro Uribe was elected president in 2002. In the interim, the AUC had turned just as thuggish as the leftist movement, levying "war taxes" on companies operating on its turf and even following FARC into narcotrafficking.

Chiquita's situation, I must point out, was distinctly different from that of my client. Descended from the United Fruit Company and United Brands, it had operated banana plantations in Colombia for decades, long before the development of the guerrilla problem.

I'm certain that senior Chiquita executives felt that they had little recourse but to pay up if they wished to keep those plantations productive. Certainly, a banana concern could not afford to establish the kind of private security force needed to protect its interests from either FARC or the AUC. Only oil companies and mining concerns, which by definition must go where the resources are, could anticipate the kind of economic rewards that would justify the heavy costs of providing comprehensive protection for their personnel and property.

Corporate leaders today are faced with unpalatable choices and are obliged to make tough calls on matters relating to terrorism, crime, and political stability matters, for which many, frankly, are ill-prepared. **Certainly, business schools have not prepared them. By and large, their focus is on more traditional management concerns.**

Employees in more than a few countries face serious kidnap risks. Insurrections force snap decisions on whether to hold tight or evacuate. Jihadists threaten personnel and operations in several Muslim lands.

Indeed, companies operating globally face an abundance of risks, and even firms working within US borders should not antic-

ipate a pass. Al-Qaida lurks on the Pakistan-Afghan frontier, spoiling for the opportunity to wreak even greater havoc in the United States than it did on 9/11.

Decision makers who discount these risks do so at their peril.

Chapter Two

THE CRITICAL NEED FOR INTELLIGENCE

M y involvement with corporate security matters began in 1977. I was two years out of the Central Intelligence Agency, where I had spent eleven years hopscotching the world as an operations officer, what the public calls a spy. Together with a partner, Lou Palumbo, a retired CIA security officer, I was trying to establish a Miami-based international security consultancy. It wasn't easy. Jimmy Carter, no fan of the Agency, had just been inaugurated as president, and congressional investigations into CIA misdeeds were fresh in everyone's mind. Former CIA officers were not in great demand.

I traveled to Dallas one very hot July day to try to sell our training seminars to, among others, the security director of a major oil-service company. I didn't get very far into my presentation when he interrupted with the following observation: "I'm sure your programs are worthwhile, Mike, but I don't have the slightest idea where they're needed. I'm a former naval officer, and I'm used to making decisions on the basis of intelligence. If you want to make a real contribution to the corporate security field, fill that need."

I wrote off the meeting as another in a string of failures. Indeed, when I returned to Miami, Lou and I had a good laugh about how this former naval officer was pressing us to establish a worldwide, corporate-directed intelligence-gathering operation. The project seemed far beyond our capabilities, to say nothing of our means.

Deep down, both of us understood where the navy man was coming from. Still, how could we possibly fulfill his request? It took us several more months to figure out the answer, and we arrived at it only out of desperation—because we were having so little success selling other services.

In October, American labor lawyer Alan Randall was shot to death outside his home in the exclusive Condado district of San Juan, Puerto Rico. Shortly after the murder, a reporter was directed by a telephone caller to a San Juan phone booth, where he found a manifesto. The screed declared that Randall had been executed by "labor commandos" because he had sought to eliminate the hard-won gains of Puerto Rican workers.

There was concern among many in the corporate community, especially managers from the US mainland, that the murder was the first strike in a wave of terrorism, and several people departed Puerto Rico with their families. A couple of security directors phoned us and asked for our assessment of the situation.

Sensing a business opportunity, I traveled to Puerto Rico to research the matter and, upon my return to Miami, wrote a report on the murder and the island's security climate in general. My conclusion was that the "hit" was not the harbinger of a terror campaign but, instead, was something of an aberration. It most likely had been ordered by one of several labor leaders with whom the victim had clashed. Puerto Rican trade unionists had a long history of playing hardball with management, though they had never taken it quite that far. The bottom line was that managers involved in labor disputes needed to take special precautions. Others could be at ease.

We sold the report to several security directors, and a couple of weeks later, one of them called and asked if we had similar reporting on Mexico. That prompted a visit to Mexico City, and we were on our way.

After an initial round of visits to about twenty countries, there were requests for follow-on reporting. After all, no situation was static.

Our first big score was a September 1978 analysis of Iran, in which we foresaw the imminent departure from power of Shah

Mohammed Reza Pahlavi. We were hoping that the shah, teetering in the face of a popular uprising, would turn over the reins of government to a military junta as a means of staving off a seizure of power by radical Islamists loyal to the Ayatollah Khomeini. But Washington was dead set against a solution of this sort. Indeed, President Jimmy Carter, in the last days of the shah's regime, sent to Tehran General Robert Huyser, then deputy commander of the European Command, with the express purpose of dissuading the Iranian military from seizing power.

In late November, two months before the departure of the shah and the return to Tehran of Khomeini, we urged clients to evacuate their expatriate personnel in an orderly manner aboard commercial aircraft.

Virtually all of them did so. Electronic Data Systems (EDS), which was not a client, evacuated some of its foreign personnel but left two in place to complete a government project for which the company was still owed a considerable sum of money. They were arrested, and EDS CEO Ross Perot was obliged to resort to extraordinary, ultra-high-risk means to rescue them from the prison to which they had been taken. Perot seized on the episode to generate a good deal of publicity, making himself into something of a hero. Corporate security directors, by and large, knew better.

In the years since 1978, our intelligence effort, which we now call *Risknet*, has grown to cover one hundred countries. It is now Internet based and is updated every business day. Several competitors have arisen, some of them quite competent, which is all to the good. In my opinion, corporations should subscribe to at least two, and possibly three, services to ensure that they are receiving the very best information available.

In reality, however, few corporate security or international operations staffs have sufficient personnel available to follow more than one risk-analysis service, or even to follow one service in any depth. We live in an age in which everyone wants to get to the point as quickly as possible. Few have the patience to read in-depth risk analysis.

To my mind, this is unwise. **A sizeable multinational corporation is mistaken if it does not assign at least one mid-level**

employee on at least a part-time basis the task of keeping abreast of overseas developments affecting the security of its personnel and viability of its investments.

Handicapping risk-analysis services can be challenging. In my view, there are five critical criteria:

First, the service should address a broad spectrum of risks: terrorism, crime, and political stability.

Second, it should employ at least some analysts who have an intelligence background, either civilian or military, or who have been trained exhaustively by someone with that background. It's fine to use journalists to improve readability, but there is no substitute for experience in analyzing intelligence.

Third, the service should dispatch its analysts to every country that it covers at least once a year. Several lower-end services obtain their information from the Internet, which is much less expensive than dispatching analysts but doesn't get the job done.

Fourth, the service's tilt should be forecasting future developments. Anyone can tell you what happened yesterday. Foreseeing what is likely to happen tomorrow is infinitely more challenging.

Finally, analysts should be readily available to answer subscribers' questions.

Forecasting future actions by criminal gangs and terrorist groups is made possible by their propensity to follow established methodologies.

Criminals in particular tend to adopt a particular modus operandi, or MO, making it relatively easy to predict their future targeting, but terrorist movements, too, tend to develop patterns of behavior. It is well known, for example, that al-Qaida and Islamic extremists linked even loosely to it favor multiple, simultaneous attacks. Somewhat less attention has been paid to the fact that radical Islam has a penchant for striking at particular kinds of targets, and that many of these are commercial in nature. Indeed, of militant Islam's six top target categories—commercial airliners; hotels; railroads/subways; resorts and tourist attractions; corporate properties, such as oil installations; and governmental/military entities—only the latter lacks direct commercial connections.

The fixation of Islamic extremists with attacking particular aspects of international commerce has enabled analysts to predict, with some degree of accuracy, the targets they are likely to strike.

Perhaps the most daunting challenge for analysts is dealing with questions of political stability. While it is often possible to foresee revolutions, such as Iran's, which tend to gather momentum over a period of months, military coups, because of their conspiratorial nature, are almost impossible to forecast. And it is also impossible to foresee the impulsive acts of despotic leaders, such as Saddam Hussein's August 1990 invasion of Kuwait or Sheikh Hassan Nasrallah's decision in July 2006 to kidnap Israeli soldiers—and trigger a thirty-four-day conflict across the Israeli-Lebanese frontier.

Even evacuations prompted by foreseeable crises, such as revolutions, are not easy to deal with. Normally, they involve pulling the plug on profitable operations. Sure, personnel can be sent back into the area if the crisis recedes, but the host government is apt to have been offended by the evacuation and cannot be counted upon to lay down the welcome mat. Ministers on more than one occasion have told our clients that they will not forget corporate partners who stick with them in hard times, and they will not forgive those who flee in the face of peril.

Coups and sudden military flare-ups present even greater challenges. In most cases, our advice to companies faced with these situations is to have their people stay put indoors until the crisis passes or a lull in the violence permits a safe evacuation by an embassy or by private means. The first inclination of corporate managers often is to act quickly and try to get people out of danger by hook or by crook. Although the instinct "to do some-

thing" is fully understandable, it is best to suppress it. Indeed, an attempt at an evacuation might well put personnel in harm's way. Airports are apt to be shut down as soon as the crisis erupts, and roads leading to them, in any event, are probably going to be manned by nervous, trigger-happy troops.

Attempting to evacuate personnel overland can be even more harrowing. Several corporations removed foreign personnel overland from Beirut to Damascus during the July-August 2006 conflict between Israel and Hizbollah, and, as far as can be determined, they were able to do so without sustaining casualties. But, with Israeli fighters strafing roads and bombing bridges in an effort to shut down Syria's resupply of rockets to Hizbollah, personnel were placed in a substantially more dangerous situation than they would have been if they stayed put and waited to be taken out aboard embassy-sponsored passenger ships. Corporate managers in almost all cases resided in Christian districts and suburbs of northern Beirut, areas well removed from the southern Shia suburbs that bore the brunt of Israeli bombing raids.

Good intelligence, based on the careful study of political trends and relative predictability of both terrorist and criminal groups, is an indispensable tool for managers of overseas operations. Astute managers consider security issues not only in weighing investment decisions, as the food processor did in the opening chapter, but also in their day-to-day operational decision making.

Do the potential rewards justify the risks involved in sending an American technician into a war zone or a country rife with kidnapping? Are the rewards such that they justify laying on extensive security for the technician, or is there some other way to get the job done? Could the American train a local to accomplish the task at hand, either in the United States or a safe third country? Should the corporation protect itself against a kidnapping or extortion through the purchase of Kidnap, Ransom, and Extortion insurance, generally known as KR&E?

KR&E insurance is itself quite controversial. Some argue that it fosters kidnapping by encouraging the payment of ransoms. Indeed, some countries—Italy, for example—prohibit its sale. I for one do not believe that KR&E insurance encourages ransom payments. Indeed, most of the large corporations and wealthy individuals who purchase the insurance would be prepared to ransom their employees or the employees' loved ones even if they did not have coverage. What KR&E does is protect them from the financial damages arising from a kidnapping or extortion. In this sense, it is exactly like other types of insurance.

The downside of KR&E is the fact that many companies use it as a substitute for costly upgrades to security arrangements. In other words, they find it more cost-effective to purchase insurance than to put comprehensive defenses in place in high-risk countries. Normally, this strategy is effective only in the short term. If kidnapping levels rise to a critical level, they will feel themselves obliged to choose between undertaking costly security programs and discontinuing operations. If they try to soldier on without instituting comprehensive security arrangements, their employees will take the decision out of their hands by refusing to go to the area in question.

A case in point is the current situation in Nigeria's oil-rich Niger Delta, where ineffectiveness of security forces has led to the development of a kidnapping and general terrorism problem that has gotten out of hand. Tribal-based gangs, some masquerading as separatist organizations and some perhaps with real separatist agendas, abducted more than one hundred and fifty foreign oil and oil-service workers in 2007.

Some companies suspended operations in the highest-risk portions of the delta, while others, with huge oil revenues at stake, elected to stand their ground and establish comprehensive security programs to safeguard their personnel. A third category, unfortunately, stayed on but failed to bolster security, banking on their insurance arrangements to protect them from the financial exposure from kidnappings.

All companies operating in the Niger Delta have experienced

problems in recruiting foreign technicians, but this last category has had particular difficulties, and deservedly so.

Does the establishment of comprehensive security programs mitigate risks entirely? Of course not! No course of action is ever without risk, and refusing to accept reasonable risks is a surefire formula for failure. Perfect security, you will recall, involves "doing nothing in a vacuum." But surely such programs would reduce risks to an "acceptable" level. Short of a situation involving open conflict, as in Iraq or Afghanistan, there is always a way to get the job done.

SECTION 2

■

CONTENDING WITH GLOBAL JIHAD

■

Chapter Three

THE CHARACTER OF GLOBAL JIHAD

Al-Qaida, which is best translated as the "base," or "foundation," was founded in the late 1980s by Usama bin Ladin and other Arabs who had gone to Afghanistan to wage jihad, or holy war, against the Soviets and wished to utilize the skills they had acquired to confront other "oppressors of Islam." The movement preaches a strongly fundamentalist brand of Sunni Islam known as *salafism*, adherents of which seek to emulate the lifestyle of the Prophet Muhammad and his contemporaneous followers. Its orientation also is *takfiri*, meaning that it espouses not only the murder of non-Muslims in the cause of jihad but also the killing of Muslims who follow other currents of Islam.

Al-Qaida, through a web of relationships with the Taliban, a fanatically Islamist local militia, turned Afghanistan into a safe haven in the late 1990s. Not only was its core leadership based there, but it also had developed a complex of training facilities from which operatives were deployed worldwide. **After 9/11 prompted the United States to invade Afghanistan, the movement evolved into a much more amorphous terrorist complex, which Yuval Diskin, the head of Shin Bet, Israel's internal security agency, has termed Global Jihad.**

Global Jihad, it has become increasingly clear, has four components: what remains of the al-Qaida core; regional affiliates; self-generated cells that manage to develop direct links to the al-Qaida core or to subsidiaries; and self-generated cells that remain independent.

The al-Qaida core remains, for the most part, bottled up in the farthest reaches of northwestern Pakistan and is preoccupied mainly with self-preservation. It is no longer able to deploy abroad operatives for attacks on the scale of 9/11, though it would be premature to discount entirely the possibility that it will regenerate this capability, especially if Pakistani forces do not prevail against al-Qaida and its tribal allies in North West Frontier Province (NWFP). Indeed, Western intelligence agencies are increasingly preoccupied with the prospective development of NWFP into a new al-Qaida safe haven.

There are at present six regional affiliates. Two, the Taliban and the al-Qaida Organization for Jihad in Iraq (QJI), are consumed with waging insurgencies in their home countries, though QJI also has attempted to strike outside Iraq, mainly in Jordan.

The other four are: al-Qaida in the Arabian Peninsula (QAP), which operates mainly in Saudi Arabia; the al-Qaida Organization of the Islamic Maghreb (QIM), which strikes mainly in Algeria, although it aspires to extend its reach to all of North Africa; Southeast Asia–based Jemaah Islamiyah (JI—Islamic Group); and a complex of Pakistani jihadist groups.

The Pakistani complex includes Lashkar-e-Tayyaba (LT—Army of the Pure), which arose from the struggle to separate Kashmir from India and strikes exclusively in Pakistan and India, and a coalition of tribal militants from NWFP headed by Baitullah Mahsud that has taken to calling itself the Pakistani Taliban. The Pakistani Taliban in recent months has supplanted LT and other Kashmiri jihadist groups as the principal perpetrator of terrorist attacks in Pakistan proper.

Regional affiliates operate in the Muslim world and in countries, such as India, with large Muslim minorities. QIM in recent months has been attacking multinationals in Algeria, while LT menaces India's IT triangle of Hyderabad, Bangalore, and Chennai (Madras). More will be said about these situations later.

Perhaps the most dramatic post-9/11 development has been the rise of self-generated groups of Islamic extremists inspired by al-Qaida. In most cases, local imams play a key role in forming

these self-generated cells. In others, militants are called to action by Islamist Internet sites.

There are two classes of self-generated cells. The first manages to establish contact with the al-Qaida core, usually in Pakistan, or with regional affiliates, and receives training and, in some cases, terrorist gear and financial support. The second remains independent of al-Qaida and its affiliates, depending entirely on the Internet for its operational know-how and relying on members or local sympathizers to supply funds and materiel.

An example of a self-generated cell with linkage to al-Qaida is the one that staged the suicide bombings aboard three London subway trains and a bus in July 2005, killing fifty-two innocents. Another is the British-based cell that plotted in 2006 to bomb multiple commercial flights to the United States, using liquid explosives concealed in beverage containers and detonators disguised as common electronic devices. A third example is the cell consisting of at least six German citizens and residents, including two ethnically German converts to Islam, that was caught in 2007 planning bombings against US troops at Ramstein Air Base and at Frankfurt International Airport. A fourth, a cell made up of six Muslim citizens of Denmark and two foreign residents, was rolled up the same year in Copenhagen and charged with plotting attacks with explosives.

Of the independent, or "do-it-yourself," cells, perhaps the quintessential specimen is the one led by an Indian doctor and an Iraqi engineer that on June 29, 2007, tried unsuccessfully to stage a pair of car bombings in London's theater district and the next day failed in an attempt to ram an explosives-laden vehicle into Glasgow airport. Only the Indian doctor, the driver of the attack vehicle, was killed in the Glasgow incident, and he had to douse himself with gasoline to accomplish even his suicide.

The London car bombing attempts failed because of inoperable cell phone detonators, while the airport attack collapsed because inadequate reconnaissance had failed to take into account the bollards that blocked vehicular access to the airport entrance. Finally, the cell was quickly apprehended because of dreadful operational security. Operatives left behind a wealth of material that police harvested to quickly identify all members of the cell.

It is interesting to note that even though the attempts in London and Glasgow failed, they were the focus of Western media attention for days, even weeks. This was because they took place in the heart of Western Europe. Conversely, a near-contemporaneous attack at the Queen of Sheba Temple, a tourist attraction in Yemen, attracted relatively little notice from the media, even though nine people, including seven Spaniards, were killed.

Several do-it-yourself cells attempted to strike in the United States in 2007. Among them were two Egyptian students who appear to have attempted to stage pipe bombings in the vicinity of naval installations in Goose Creek, South Carolina, a group of Guyanese and Trinidadian Muslims who originated an amateurish plot to blow up a fuel pipeline at New York's John F. Kennedy International Airport, and a small group of mostly Albanian Muslims who plotted to attack soldiers at New Jersey's Fort Dix army base with rocket-propelled grenades and assault rifles. The last plot came a cropper after cell members took a video of their training exercises to a commercial outlet for transfer to a DVD.

Al-Qaida-linked cells clearly benefit from the input they receive from the al-Qaida core and from regional affiliates, but at considerable cost. The cell responsible for the London transit bombings went unnoticed before it struck. But the other three discussed above were all detected because at least one member had traveled to Pakistan to undergo training and had come to the attention of the oft-maligned (unjustly so) Pakistani intelligence services and their Western counterparts. It is the nexus with al-Qaida or its subsidiaries that brought them down.

Conversely, independent cells are better able to fly under the radar of intelligence services but at considerable cost in operating capability. The do-it-yourselfers in most cases just do not get it right.

The conclusion is clear: It has been al-Qaida's inability to solve the problem of infusing far-flung cells with operational know-how that has helped insulate the West from serious attack.

Will al-Qaida develop this capability? Almost certainly it will—eventually. While local and Western intelligence services have been remarkably successful in tracking Western-based extremists who make contact with jihadist elements in Pakistan, they cannot be expected to snag every one. Also, it is difficult to be confident that the dispersion of operational know-how and bomb-making expertise stemming from the war in Iraq will not result in an escalation of jihadist activity in both the Middle East and, eventually, the West, the United States included.

The Iraq War has been a quintessential double-edged sword. The Bush administration's contention that it has attracted—and neutralized—jihadists of many nationalities who otherwise would have put their revolutionary zeal to use against Western targets in their home countries has considerable merit. Not all the jihadists who went to Iraq have been killed or captured, however, and the dispersion of operating experience and explosives know-how is never a good thing.

Chapter Four

THE AIMS OF GLOBAL JIHAD

Most casual observers of Islamic extremism, and some not-so-casual observers, if pressed to name the principal objective of al-Qaida's terror campaign would cite the wholesale slaughter of nonbelievers. There is no question that the movement has killed thousands of Christians and Jews, and it certainly can be argued that some of Global Jihad's more primitive cells are simply out to spill the blood of infidels. In most cases, however, and certainly in those cases in which al-Qaida leaders have input, the slaughter is a mere by-product of a much more ambitious objective—to bring down the West and its Muslim allies and, ultimately, to build a new, expansive caliphate (Islamic state) as a political manifestation of their religious ideals.

How does Global Jihad intend to bring down the West? Its approach is two-pronged. It seeks both to sow political chaos and to disrupt economic activity. Few would deny that one of Global Jihad's aims is to sow political chaos, but its parallel emphasis on economic disruption has been underreported and is not as well understood.

Indeed, the 9/11 attacks stand as a quintessential example of al-Qaida's two-pronged targeting. Two of the aircraft commandeered by the assailants clearly were intended to strike at political targets in Washington, with one hitting the Pentagon. The second plane, which most likely was destined for the Capitol, was forced by heroic passengers to crash in a Pennsylvania field.

The other two aircraft, of course, struck the twin towers of the

World Trade Center, the wheelhouse of American capitalism, killing nearly three thousand people, among them senior managers of some of the West's most prestigious financial institutions. Moreover, in addition to grounding American commercial aviation for four full days, with devastating economic impact, the attack closed the New York Stock Exchange for the better part of five trading days and triggered a 14.3 percent slide in the Dow Jones Industrial Average in the week the exchange reopened, the steepest one-week drop in sixty-one years. The GDP also fell in September and October 2001, though it began to show growth again by November.

Usama bin Ladin hails from an immensely wealthy Saudi family and knows his economics. In a videotape aired by al-Jazeera in October 2004, he boasted that the attack and its aftermath cost America "according to the lowest estimate, more than $500 billion." He sounded like Neil Cavuto turned upside down!

In reviewing attacks since 9/11, Global Jihad's emphasis on economics is strikingly clear. A survey of major attempts and attacks by the al-Qaida core, its regional affiliates, and directly linked cells (outside the war zones of Iraq and Afghanistan) reveals the following: thirteen attacks were aimed directly at economic targets, while twenty-five were directed at commerce-related targets (six at commercial aviation; five at trains and subways; seven at hotels; seven at tourism-related targets), for a total of thirty-eight.

Seventeen, on the other hand, were directed at governmental and military targets, and ten of those—more than half—involved assassination attempts against Pakistani president Pervez Musharraf and his political allies; Benazir Bhutto, another secularist, although a political opponent of Musharraf; and members of the Pakistani security establishment.

Five major attacks, two against Istanbul synagogues and three against crowded venues in Islamabad, Pakistan, and Hyderabad, India, cannot be classified as either economic or governmental. See addenda A through F for a list of major attacks against both economic and governmental targets.

The reasons that al-Qaida has focused so many of its political attacks in Pakistan will be discussed in the next chapter. I will argue that these attacks were something of an aberration, however. If al-Qaida is successful in overthrowing that country's secular government and installing in its place a radical Islamic regime, which I believe is unlikely, it may turn increasingly to political attacks, in the Muslim world at least. But if that effort is unsuccessful, Global Jihad almost certainly will refocus on the economy.

It could be argued, one supposes, that Islamic extremists have keyed on commerce-related targets rather than military and governmental entities because they are easier to get at, but the numbers (thirty-eight economic versus, at best, seventeen governmental) suggest another explanation: that Western economies—and by extension multinational corporations—are solidly in their crosshairs.

Perhaps the most striking evidence of al-Qaida's focus on commerce was core operative Abu Issa al-Hindi's admission to a British court in October 2006 that he had been dispatched to the United States in 2000 and 2001 by Khalid Sheikh Mohammed, the mastermind of the 9/11 attacks, to case the New York Stock Exchange and Citigroup Manhattan headquarters, the Prudential insurance complex in Newark, and the International Monetary Fund and World Bank headquarters in Washington. And Mohammed himself has admitted to planning an attack on Chicago's Sears Tower.

Hindi, a Hindu convert to Islam, was born in India and raised in the United Kingdom. His British passport allowed him repeated entry into the United States, and he was able to produce meticulous maps and security studies of the targeted institutions. His detailed casings were discovered in the database of an al-Qaida computer and communications expert captured in Pakistan in July 2003, and he was arrested by British police the following year.

Hindi's activities, and the track record of Islamic extremists around the world since 9/11, support the argument that a new attack in the United States would key on the American economy. I am haunted by concerns that it will target New York City, our country's

financial fulcrum, and that it will involve the explosion of a bomb that combines radioactive materials with conventional explosives, a so-called dirty bomb and not necessarily a nuclear device, on Wall Street or a nearby district. Another strong possibility is a series of explosions in transport hubs or the New York subways.

We Americans should steel ourselves for this eventuality, resolving to sustain the blow and carry on with business, as we did after 9/11. New York–based corporations should pay special attention to disaster-recovery planning.

At the same time, we need to prepare ourselves even more immediately for smaller-scale attacks by do-it-yourselfers in the population centers in which they reside. United States intelligence and law-enforcement agencies have been remarkably successful in penetrating and neutralizing those cells, but sooner or later one of them will bring to fruition an attack or spate of attacks, and recent history suggests that the US media will jump on even minor attacks and pump them up to the point that they take on monumental significance. Witness the media coverage of the attacks in 2002 by the Washington Beltway snipers and the more recent killings at Virginia Tech. Imagine the hype if they had been staged by jihadists!

There is no telling what kind of panic would be set off by even small-scale attacks, and how grave the economic consequences might be. One of my concerns is that media coverage of even a small-scale attack would be such that it would inspire other do-it-yourselfers to stage copycat strikes, with the result that we would indeed be confronted with a major problem.

One would hope that when small-scale attacks do take place, the media will be able to restrain their understandable but nevertheless unfortunate proclivity to beat the drum, but I wouldn't count on it. Almost certainly, the burden of putting the attacks into perspective will fall on our political leaders. Corporate leaders, too, will have an important role to play in keeping their companies—and the economy—productive.

Chapter Five

AL-QAIDA GOES FOR THE JUGULAR: THE PAKISTANI ABERRATION

Al-Qaida, I believe, went "political" in Pakistan for two reasons. The first was defensive: President Pervez Musharraf since 9/11 had made himself the jihadist movement's nemesis, first by ordering his intelligence services to cooperate with their Western counterparts in arresting both core al-Qaida operatives and members of self-generated foreign cells who had gone to Pakistan to attempt to link up with core operatives. In addition, he intermittently had sent his armed forces to battle frontier tribes sheltering al-Qaida leaders, or at least turned a blind eye to American strikes against those leaders.

The second reason was opportunistic. Musharraf had acquired considerable popularity in the years after his 1999 coup by enforcing stability and fomenting economic growth. But the longer he stayed in power, the more his countrymen wearied of him. Indeed, his failure to prepare for a reasonable succession and depart the stage placed Pakistan in play—nuclear arsenal and all. It was just too much for al-Qaida to resist.

Musharraf in the early months of 2007 made matters worse by attempting to browbeat the Pakistani Supreme Court into permitting him to extend his presidency while continuing to serve as armed forces commander. When he could not do so, he suspended Chief Justice Iftikhar Chaudry for allegedly abusing his power. The suspension sparked a series of protests by a group of lawyers led by Aitzaz Ahsan, and the president's popularity plummeted.

Meanwhile, frontier tribesmen led by Baitullah Mahsud, whom Musharraf alternately had pursued and attempted to appease, sensing the president's weakness, had turned increasingly strident, and extremists associated with them had taken over Islamabad's Lal Masjid (Red Mosque). In open defiance of the president, students associated with the mosque attacked a nearby police post on July 3, 2007, taking hostages and seizing firearms. Musharraf responded by ordering his commandos to storm the mosque, a daylong operation in which at least seventy militants were killed or captured, and resuming military operations against the tribesmen.

Baitullah's followers were quick to strike back, attacking not only the security forces but also the lawyers, who had placed themselves at the forefront of the secular opposition. On July 17, a suicide-bomber killed sixteen people and wounded sixty at an Islamabad rally for Chaudry. The former chief justice himself was supposed to address the rally but had yet to arrive when the explosion took place. Three days after the bombing, with Musharraf visibly weakened by the three-cornered struggle, the Supreme Court reinstated Chaudry.

The jihadists' frontal assault on the Pakistani strongman was initially promoted by Ayman al-Zawahiri, bin Ladin's deputy, and in September 2007 was blessed by bin Ladin himself. Its principal instrumentality has been Baitullah's tribesmen, calling themselves Pakistani Taliban, who by this time had replaced the Kashmiri jihadist group LT as al-Qaida's main Pakistani surrogate.

Ensuing months witnessed a drumbeat of attacks against the Pakistani military and its intelligence service, many in NWFP, and others in Rawalpindi, the garrison city just outside Islamabad. Then, on October 18, 2007, jihadists staged their most ambitious attack of the campaign, a suicide bombing in Karachi against a motorcade welcoming back from several years of exile former prime minister Benazir Bhutto. Bhutto survived the explosion, but some one hundred and thirty people were killed, most of them innocents.

Bhutto's return to Pakistan had been facilitated by Washington, which had pressed Musharraf to drop corruption charges against her stemming from two stints as prime minister, in the hope—unrealistic in my view—that dropping the charges would foster a secular alliance between the faltering strongman and the still popular opposition leader. Two weeks after the attempt against Bhutto, Musharraf declared a state of emergency, removing Chaudry from his post once again and scuttling any chance for a secular alliance. He was reelected president by a parliament dominated by his followers, but soon after his election he gave in to pressure, both domestic and international, and turned over command of the military to General Ashfaq Parvez Kiyani.

Baitullah was far from finished. On November 24, his militants staged simultaneous suicide car bombings against military and intelligence targets in Rawalpindi, killing fifteen. Then, on December 21, a suicide-bomber attempted to murder former interior minister Aftab Ahmed Khan Sherpao, a close Musharraf ally, by blowing himself up in a mosque near Peshawar, in NWFP. Sherpao was not injured in the attack, but forty other worshippers were killed.

A week later came Baitullah's coup de grâce, indeed Global Jihad's most significant strike since 9/11. A suicide-assailant murdered Bhutto as she departed a campaign rally at a park in Rawalpindi in advance of elections scheduled for early January, first firing a handgun and then setting off an explosives vest. Twenty-three others also died in the attack.

The assassination touched off severe rioting in Bhutto's home province of Sindh by members of her Pakistan People's Party (PPP) and took the country to the brink of political chaos. PPP leaders laid the blame for the murder on Musharraf, with some insisting that he masterminded the attack, while others faulted him only for inadequate security arrangements. The slain leader's husband, Asif Ali Zardari, refused to permit an autopsy, sparking controversy over the cause of death. Officials deduced that Bhutto had died from the impact of the explosion, but videotapes of the assassination clearly demonstrated that a handgun had been fired. The regime's credibility was so low that Musharraf was obliged to invite a team of detectives from Scotland Yard to confirm its finding.

The PPP leaders also discounted the government's publication of a purported intercept of a conversation in which Baitullah congratulated a lieutenant for the assassination, though US intelligence subsequently confirmed Baitullah's involvement.

Permit me an aside on Bhutto's security arrangements. While the government may have been deficient in protecting Bhutto, her own arrangements clearly were lacking. I was particularly struck by the limitations of her armored Toyota Land Cruiser (the fact that it had a sunroof) and by her decision to stand in the vehicle—with her head outside the sunroof—to greet her supporters. Major political figures simply cannot ride exposed in vehicles, certainly not in places as dangerous as Pakistan. American presidents haven't done so since the assassination of President John F. Kennedy.

While it is worth noting that no one inside the car was injured in the explosion, this circumstance should not be taken as an endorsement of utilizing armored cars with sunroofs. Indeed, to my mind, a sunroof-equipped armored car is an oxymoron, since the sunroof by definition weakens the structural integrity of the roof. Car-armoring companies, when faced with the need to armor vehicles with sunroofs, invariably disable and armor over them. Much more will be said about armored cars, and their strengths and limitations, in chapter 22.

In any event, while Musharraf made misstep after misstep in the final months of 2007, the opposition also missed the bell. Bhutto, who had never been the democratic paragon she made herself out to be, bequeathed the PPP leadership to her nineteen-year-old son, Bilawal, with Zardari, her widower, assuming control of the party while Bilawal continues his studies at Oxford. Zardari, who has a well-deserved reputation for corruption and has spent eleven years in jail on corruption-related charges, is no inspirational leader. A splendid opportunity to pass the PPP mantle to Aitzaz Ahsan, who had so ably led the lawyers' movement against Musharraf, was missed.

The PPP did indeed win a plurality in the February 2008 parliamentary elections and now leads a coalition government made up of traditional parties and excluding groups linked to Musharraf. Indeed, the new government is expected to restore Supreme Court justices fired by Musharraf, who may invalidate his election as president on the grounds that he was serving as armed forces commander at the time of his election.

Still to be determined is the effectiveness of PPP governance. Will it negotiate a peace agreement with Baitullah's tribesmen in NWFP? Will the Pakistani government permit US forces to pursue foreign jihadists? Will the agreement in effect concede a safe haven to al-Qaida? Will Baitullah take advantage of the prospective truce to prepare a new frontal assault on Pakistani democracy? Will the armed forces and intelligence services under the pro-American Kiyani have permission to pursue extremists transiting Pakistan?

While Pakistan has been taken to the brink of chaos, Islamic radicals have been unable to push it over the edge. The reason is simple. The secular opposition has no incentive whatsoever to make common cause with the jihadists.

Indeed, we take some hope in the long term from the fact that Baitullah's attacks have exposed to Pakistani Muslims the militants' brutal *takfiri* doctrine. Only *takfiris* could justify killing one hundred and thirty people, most of them innocents, in the first assassination attempt against Bhutto, and at least twenty-three in the second. Only they would have set their sights on killing a woman. Only they would have gone after Sherpao as he prayed in a mosque, murdering fifty other worshippers in the process.

It is telling that in the February 2008 election, parties associated with the Islamic radicals were defeated by secular opponents, causing them to lose control of a province they had governed since 2002.

Why, then, do the radicals continue to uphold *takfiri* principles?

One would have thought that al-Qaida would have learned its lesson from Iraq, where the savagery of QJI, its regional affiliate, turned against it even Sunni insurgents terrified by the prospect of being governed by the country's Shia majority. Indeed, no less an al-Qaida figure than Zawahiri in June 2005 seemed to pull back from *takfiri* doctrine. In a letter to Abu Musab al-Zarqawi, the founder of QJI, Zawahiri urged him to cease his relentless bombings against Iraqi Shia, warning him that such attacks "will not be acceptable to Muslims, no matter how much you try to explain them."

Why is the killing of Pakistani Muslims acceptable to Zawahiri, while the slaughter of Iraqi Muslims is not? Apparently, tactical considerations determine the limits of permissible brutality.

It is my hope and my prayer that mainstream Pakistanis, despite their ineffectual political leadership, will continue to reject the *takfiri*.

It is my expectation that al-Qaida, sooner or later, will draw back from its current offensive in Pakistan into a more defensive posture inside that country. A tactical shift of this sort, however, would have an important downside: The rejection of *takfiri* doctrine inevitably would redirect Global Jihad back to its stock-in-trade economic attacks against Western infidels—meaning us.

Chapter Six

SPECIFIC AND CLASS ATTACKS: ALGERIA AND EGYPT

I n its economic attacks, Global Jihad mainly targets classes of victims: businesspeople working at the Twin Towers, aircraft passengers, train and subway passengers, hotel guests, tourists. On occasion, however, jihadists have staged specific attacks against individual businesspersons or technicians; corporate facilities, such as the Istanbul office of London-based HSBC bank; and oil refineries, including Saudi Arabia's giant Abqaiq refinery. Corporate personnel are at risk from both specific and class attacks. The distinction is important, however, because it affects security planning.

It is important to know whether a particular manager is at specific risk because of who he or she is and where he or she works, or at general risk because his or her office is located in a landmark, or because he or she flies commercially, takes trains, stays at hotels, or visits tourist sites. In general, specific risks are more difficult for corporations to confront than class risks, though the latter also have their challenges.

It is relatively easy to deal with risks to landmark buildings—by locating elsewhere. Similarly, tourist sites can simply be avoided. Though they can be great fun and are a significant incentive for overseas travel, visits to tourist attractions are rarely essential to the conduct of business.

Class risks to commercial air carriers, trains and subways, and hotels are more difficult to confront, since it is impractical for most corporate employees to avoid flying commercially, taking commuter trains or subways, or staying at hotels.

Subnational movements of Islamic extremists began to focus on attacking commerce in the early 1990s, when al-Qaida was still in the early stages of organization. One movement, Egypt's al-Gama'a al-Islamiya (Islamic Group), staged only class attacks, while another, Algeria's Armed Islamic Movement—which is known by its French acronym, MIA, with one significant exception—stressed specific attacks. The two campaigns are worth a detailed look because they impart important lessons in risk analysis and risk avoidance.

In both Egypt and Algeria, Islamic extremists initially set about to bring down their countries' respective secular regimes by attacking them head-on. In both instances, they shifted their focus to the regimes' economic underpinnings only after direct attacks against government leaders and the security forces failed to achieve their objective.

Egyptian zealots set their sights upon the crucial tourism industry, their country's greatest source of foreign exchange, while their counterparts in Algeria, which does not have signifi-cant tourism, hit upon the idea of sowing economic chaos through specific attacks—serial murders of non-Muslim foreigners. (In neither case, it is presumed, were the extremists' motives purely eco-nomic. In both instances, the attacks on the Westerners also satisfied the zealots' basic xenophobia.)

Both campaigns exacted serious economic tolls, at least until the secular regimes in the two countries rallied their forces for successful counteroffensives. But their different natures elicited different private-sector responses. In Algeria, as soon as the thrust of the terrorist campaign became clear, we were quick to counsel foreigners who were not heavily protected to depart. In Egypt, on the other hand, we were comfortable in telling foreign managers that they could remain in-country as long as they avoided tourist sites and the heavily fundamentalist south.

Of course, the paths to these conclusions were not clear-cut. They never are, so allow me to provide some historical perspective.

Islamic extremism, which had festered in Egypt for three decades, scored a major hit in November 1981, when a group calling itself al-Jihad, furious with President Anwar Sadat for making peace with Israel, murdered him at a military parade. Hosni Mubarak, who succeeded Sadat, ordered the security forces to come down hard on that fundamentalist movement. Among the three hundred militants arrested in the initial crackdown was a young physician named Ayman al-Zawahiri who had risen quickly in the ranks of the terrorist movement. Zawahiri, though he could not be linked directly to the plot, served nearly three years in prison. Upon his release, he journeyed to Saudi Arabia and then Afghanistan, becoming Usama bin Ladin's doctor and, eventually, his deputy.

Another of those arrested was Sheikh Umar Abd-al-Rahman, whose radical teachings influenced both al-Jihad and the parallel movement al-Gama'a al-Islamiya (Gama'a). Rahman, known as the blind sheikh, was released from prison after six months and made his way to Afghanistan, Sudan, and, ultimately, thanks to America's unbelievably lax pre-9/11 immigration system, Jersey City. He was the spiritual godfather of the 1993 attack upon New York's World Trade Center and is serving a life sentence for his involvement in that plot.

The crackdown, which continued through the 1980s and involved the imprisonment of some twenty-five hundred militants, kept the Islamic terrorist movement on the defensive through most of that decade, though adherents of a splinter group tried unsuccessfully to assassinate several government officials. Still, al-Jihad and Gama'a continued to proselytize and recruit young militants, and they were especially successful in Ain Shams and other slum districts of Cairo and the southern governates of Asyut, Mina, and Fayoum.

On October 12, 1990, nine years after the Sadat assassination, al-Jihad tasted success again. In a meticulously planned and flawlessly executed attack on Cairo's nearly gridlocked Nile Corniche, a team of motorcycle-borne assassins armed with AK-47s and grenades murdered Rifaat al-Mahjoub, the speaker of Egypt's parliament, and four of his bodyguards. Scores of arrests followed. Islamic extremists were back on the defensive, but not for very long.

By 1992, Gama'a had become far stronger than its radical sibling, and it soon became clear that the group had decided to key on tourism instead of government leaders.

The campaign began in early June in southern Egypt, when Islamic extremists set off four small bombs near the Temple of Karnak. Next came a series of attacks upon tourist buses in the south. There were only a few minor casualties, but Gama'a threatened more serious attacks. In July, four of its militants gave a clandestine press conference in Imbaba, a working-class suburb of Cairo and one of its strongholds, demanding an end to tourism and the destruction of the "pagan" pharaonic statues and temples in the south.

In September, on the eve of a convention of the American Society of Travel Agents (ASTA), which the Egyptian government had worked feverishly to bring to Cairo, Gama'a issued another statement, warning tourists to stay out of the southern Egypt tourism centers of Qena and Luxor.

Nothing untoward happened during the ASTA meeting, but in early October shots were fired at a Nile River tourist boat carrying German tourists to Luxor and Aswan. Later the same month, gunmen ambushed a tourist bus near Dayrut, which is also in southern Egypt, killing one Briton—the first fatality of the campaign against tourism—and wounding two others. In November, Gama'a members sprayed a minibus carrying German tourists through southern Egypt with automatic-weapons fire, injuring five passengers. Despite the relatively small number of casualties, publicity generated by the attacks savaged the 1992–93 winter tourist season, especially in the south, costing Egypt at least $1 billion in revenues.

Next, the extremists turned their attention northward to Cairo. In January 1993, they threw a firebomb at a bus carrying German tourists to the Pyramids, and, in a communiqué taking responsibility for the attack, Gama'a announced that "from this date Cairo has become a stage for legitimate jihad operations." A similar attack took place in the capital in early February, this one involving South Korean tourists.

It was in early 1993 that Gama'a registered the first in a series of threats to expand its terror campaign beyond tourism to all Western interests, and by February 1994 the Islamist terrorist movement issued a "final warning to foreigners" to depart Egypt immediately.

Our *Risknet* service already had been advising corporate personnel to avoid tourist sites and to forego travel to points south. The new threats caused our analysts to consider warning clients to avoid Egypt altogether or at least lay on serious protection when in-country, but it was decided to put off this call until Gama'a demonstrated an intention to make good on its fulminations. In general, you cannot allow yourself to be intimidated by mere threats: Sometimes, you have to give the dog the first bite.

Gama'a never did expand the commercial aspect of its campaign beyond tourism, and we never did recommend against travel to Egypt on essential business. Indeed, the only corporate casualties during Gama'a's campaign were two American engineers who were shot to death along with a French jurist in October 1993 in a restaurant in Cairo's prestigious Semiramis InterContinental Hotel by a mental case named Sabir Abu al-Ila. The shooter, it was determined, had no affiliation with Gama'a or any other terrorist group, though he may have been inspired by Gama'a's campaign against tourism. He described his attack as a protest against the West's failure to halt the killing of Muslims in Bosnia.

The security forces struck back hard at the extremists during the summer of 1993, killing several dozen, arresting hundreds, and hanging at least fifteen. Gama'a retaliated with attacks against senior military and police officials, and by the winter season they once again were striking regularly at tourist targets.

There was an automatic-weapons attack in December 1993 on a bus carrying Austrian sightseers in Cairo, where tourism was down at least 35 percent. In February 1994, a powerful bomb devastated a train car carrying foreigners near the southern fundamentalist hotbed of

Asyut, wounding six people. There were also two attacks on riverboats in southern Egypt in February and March of 1994, one of which resulted in serious injury to a German tourist. Also, there were eight attacks against trains carrying foreign tourists from Cairo to Luxor in the first four months of 1994, most of them near the fundamentalist stronghold of Abu Tig.

In late August, gunmen hiding in southern Egypt sugarcane fields fired automatic weapons at a minibus carrying Spanish visitors. A thirteen-year-old boy was killed, and several other passengers were wounded. The tour company had failed to request a police escort, which by this time was de rigueur.

In September, militants struck for the first time against a Red Sea resort, spraying a crowd of German tourists with automatic-weapons fire in Hurghada as they shopped for souvenirs in the town's bazaar. A German and two Egyptians were killed, and a second German was wounded.

In October, a minibus carrying British tourists in the southern town of Neqeda was strafed with automatic-weapons fire. One of the tourists was killed and several were wounded. In January 1995, two Argentine tourists were wounded when their train was strafed in the same area. In ensuing months, however, attacks fell off as the government offensive took its toll on the extremists.

With the government touting its successes, tourism bounced back, with the 1995–96 winter season attracting a record 3.6 million tourists who spent more than $3 billion. The security situation turned decidedly sour in April, however, when a Gama'a hit squad massacred seventeen Greek tourists waiting to board a bus outside the Europa Hotel on Cairo's Pyramids Road. The assailants may have mistaken the Greeks for Israelis. In any event, the body count was by far the largest of the campaign, suggesting that Gama'a operatives were becoming both more brutal and more efficient.

In September 1996, none other than Sabir Abu al-Ila, this time aided by his brother, forced his way onto a tour bus carrying German tourists in Cairo's Tahrir Square, shot the driver in the head, and threw Molotov cocktails into the bus's crowded interior, killing nine passengers. It turned out that Abu al-Ila had escaped from the mental hospital to which he had been confined after his October 1993 fatal attack upon diners at the Semiramis InterContinental. Again, there was no indication that Abu al-Ila had ties to Gama'a, though he appears to have been inspired by its atrocities. (Singleton head cases like Abu al-Ila, because their behavior is not predictable, give fits to both police services and risk analysts.)

By 1997, Egyptian authorities were boasting that they had broken Gama'a's back. Indeed, they had made substantial progress against the movement, but it was not ready to be counted out. In November, a weakened Gama'a managed a last hurrah, its signature massacre of fifty-eight foreigners and four Egyptians at one of Luxor's preeminent attractions, the temple of Queen Hatshepsut. Six heavily armed militants arrived at the temple gate in a commandeered taxi, overpowered police guards at the entrance, stormed inside, and embarked on a ninety-minute killing spree, slitting the throats of many victims as they begged for mercy. They committed suicide when police reinforcements arrived.

The Gama'a leadership initially claimed credit for the massacre, then, sensing the revulsion of the Egyptian man on the street, tried to distance itself from the attack, affirming that it had intended to take hostages rather than kill.

The Luxor atrocity stiffened the resolve of the Mubarak regime to do away with Gama'a once and for all. Its no-holds-barred counterterrorist campaign was remarkably successful, and on March 26, 1999, Gama'a's leadership in exile announced an end to its terrorist campaign. Thereafter, little has been heard from the group, though Zawahiri in an August 2006 statement claimed that Gama'a had decided to formally affiliate with al-Qaida.

Though Gama'a clearly has been in remission, if not completely neutralized, both its zealotry and its attack methodology has been embraced by independent jihadist cells and by an organization of strongly Islamist Sinai Bedouins. (Their operations will be discussed along with other post-9/11 attacks against tourist targets in chapter 11.)

The Mubarak regime's suppression of Gama'a, incidentally, heralded similar successful crackdowns against Islamic-extremist insurgencies in other Muslim countries, including Jordan, Saudi Arabia, Yemen, and, to some degree, Pakistan and Algeria, though, as of this writing, the latter two countries remain in play. In no instance has a determined Sunni Muslim regime been unable to deal effectively with al-Qaida-style Islamic extremism.

Algeria's Islamic terrorism campaign was markedly different from Egypt's.

A brief uprising by Islamic fundamentalists in 1985 was put down quickly by Algeria's security forces, but the secular nationalists who had ruled the country since winning independence from France in 1962 were unable to deal with a political offensive waged in the late 1980s by the fundamentalist Islamic Salvation Front, known by its French acronym, FIS. FIS, in 1990, shocked the establishment by riding widespread dissatisfaction with the heavy-handed, corrupt rule of the nationalists and their inability to spur economic development to electoral victories in more than half of Algeria's municipal governments.

In June 1991, the government, faced with the prospect of a FIS victory in December parliamentary elections, changed the voting ground rules. For one thing, it decreed that successful candidates would have to win a majority of votes in their districts instead of a mere plurality, thus giving secular parties the opportunity to combine forces in prospective runoffs. It also diluted the voting power of religious conservatives by taking away from the heads of families their right to vote for their wives and children.

FIS drubbed the secular parties in the first round of voting in December and was poised to win a strong majority in January runoff elections when military leaders staged a palace coup, but that is getting ahead of our story.

FIS protested the changes in electoral rules in June by staging a strike and then promoting raucous demonstrations in Algiers that quickly turned violent, with militants exchanging gunfire with police.

When the smoke cleared, two hundred people had been killed and several thousand FIS militants, including the movement's two top leaders, had been arrested.

It seems that FIS had had in its ranks about one hundred and fifty militants who had received guerrilla training in Afghanistan in the mid-1980s and who subsequently trained younger adherents in the tactics employed during the protests. These militants formed the core of FIS's military wing, the Armed Islamic Movement, or MIA.

The first stirrings of the MIA terror campaign followed quickly on the heels of those protests. There were attacks against government officials and raids against military and police units in Algiers and the interior, and, on the night of January 30, 1992, approximately three weeks after the coup, bombs were hurled into the compounds of the US and French embassies and at the ministry of justice.

By August, the terrorist campaign had ripened, with foreign commercial interests joining embassies in the militants' sights. On August 26, a powerful bomb planted near a crowded Air France counter at Algiers's Houari Boumedienne International Airport killed 9 people and injured 124. Another bomb exploded that day at an Air France ticket office in downtown Algiers, and a third device was defused at a Swissair office in the capital. On September 23, the same Swissair office was targeted again, this time successfully.

In early 1993, MIA, though still attacking government officials and engaging rural units of the security forces, began an assassination campaign against Algerian intellectuals. More than a dozen secular writers and educators were killed in the span of a few months.

By September 1993, the campaign against intellectuals had given way to a determined effort to murder foreigners, with the objective of driving from the country multinational corporations and aid organizations, public and private, and thus undermining the economy. In late September, two French surveyors were kidnapped and butchered in an isolated mountainous area. In October, two Russian military advisers were shot to death, and a Colombian, a Peruvian, and a Filipino working for an Italian construction company were abducted and murdered.

Those attacks took place in rural areas, but on October 24 three consular employees of the French Embassy were kidnapped as they left their Algiers residence. Two of the victims, both men, were rescued several days later from a mosque in an Algiers suburb, while the third, a woman, was released by her captors with a handwritten note warning that all foreigners remaining in Algeria after November 30 would be killed. "This will be more violent than Egypt," the note said, "leave the country."

Our *Risknet* analysts did not have to ponder long our recommended response. The Algerian campaign was not focused on tourism or a particular economic sector. Instead, it was aimed at all non-Muslim foreigners. Without heavy complements of bodyguards, which most enterprises could not justify, foreigners could not be safe.

On October 25, we recommended that all non-Arab, non-Muslim foreigners be evacuated from the country no later than the November 30 MIA deadline. The only exceptions were personnel employed at the heavily fortified gas fields at Hassi Messaoud in the deep south, which remained reasonably safe, provided that charter aircraft were used to get there. This advice remained in effect, and in general was heeded by our clients, for the next six years.

Twelve Croatian and Bosnian Christians were slain in a December 14, 1993, massacre at a construction camp thirty-eight miles southwest of Algiers. Several Bosnian technicians were spared because they said they were Muslims.

In January 1994, a low-level employee of the French Consulate, a woman, was shot twice in the head by a fundamentalist gunman as she walked to her car in a downtown Algiers parking lot. Two months later, a French businessman and his son were stabbed to death in their home in a suburb of the capital.

The Islamists' campaign against foreigners had the desired effect. By early 1994, most non-Arab, non-Muslim foreigners had fled the country, though from time to time the zealots came upon—and executed—holdouts.

In 1994, Algerian terrorism took an interesting detour. While MIA was still concentrating on killing individual foreigners, a splinter calling itself the Armed Islamic Group came to the fore and quickly established a reputation as the most brutal of Algeria's Islamic terror groups.

The Armed Islamic Group, known by its French acronym, GIA, staged one especially significant class attack. In December 1994, GIA militants, dressed in security-service uniforms and wearing ID cards stolen from airport employees in an earlier robbery, boarded an Air France jet at Algiers's Houari Boumedienne Airport on the pretext of conducting a security check. Once onboard, they took control of the aircraft and its 169 passengers and crew members and demanded to be flown to Paris. When government officials refused to allow the aircraft to depart, they began executing passengers, first an Algerian police officer, then a Vietnamese diplomat and a young French chef.

Fearful that similar fates awaited the forty other French citizens onboard, French authorities prevailed on the Algerians to allow the plane to depart, but the pilot managed to convince the hijackers that the aircraft lacked the fuel necessary to reach Paris and would have to refuel in Marseille. Once on the ground in Marseille, French commandos stormed the aircraft, killing the four terrorists and rescuing the remaining passengers.

French intelligence services were convinced that the hijackers planned to blow up the plane over Paris or crash it into the Eiffel Tower. Certainly, the assailants' behavior was consistent with such a plan. For one thing, they demanded twenty-seven tons of jet fuel in Marseille, three times the amount needed to fly to Paris. For another, they brought a large quantity of explosives onboard and distributed it throughout the aircraft.

The attack appears to have been a stunning precursor to 9/11—much more sophisticated in concept, if not in execution, than the more obvious antecedent, the February 1993 bombing at New York's World Trade Center. That incident, of course, involved an attempt by a ragtag group of Islamic fundamentalists inspired by

Abd-al-Rahman and managed by early al-Qaida operative Ramzi Yousef to bring down one of the towers with a truck bomb that had been left in an underground parking garage. The cell that staged the attack was rounded up within days, after law-enforcement authorities were able to link the rental truck used in the bombing to one of the conspirators.

Interestingly, al-Qaida learned from the failure of the Air France hijacking. No longer would it rely on professionals to pilot hijacked aircraft—the hijackers themselves would be trained to fly. Nor would hijackers depend on authorities to provide fuel; henceforth, they would commandeer aircraft adequately provisioned for long flights.

The United States, on the other hand, failed to take heed of both the intent to target the World Trade Center and the intent to use aircraft as weapons against ground targets, and we paid the price.

The Algerian military held firm against the Islamic militants and, by the end of the century, after intensive fighting through much of the country, had largely defeated them—to the point that by early 2000 foreigners began to trickle back into the country. Pockets of rebels remained, however, and in December 2006 they returned to action with a vengeance, demonstrating their continued interest in staging specific attacks against foreigners involved in commerce. More about that in the next chapter!

Chapter Seven

ATTACKS AGAINST SPECIFIC ECONOMIC TARGETS

Al-Qaida's first post-9/11 attack against a specific commercial target took place on May 8, 2002, in Karachi, Pakistan. A suicide-bomber detonated a car filled with explosives outside the city's Sheraton Hotel, killing eleven French technicians and wounding sixteen as they boarded a bus to a local shipyard. The attack was a double whammy, since it struck not only at the French but also at President Pervez Musharraf, who was one of the first Muslim rulers to sign on to the War on Terrorism. The technicians were in Karachi to upgrade Pakistan's submarine-warfare capabilities.

The assault against the French technicians came amid a flurry of attacks in Karachi, including the kidnap-murder of American journalist Daniel Pearl and a car bombing in front of the US Consulate. Since 9/11, we had warned repeatedly that Pakistan would be in al-Qaida's crosshairs, in part because of its proximity to Afghanistan, and we were especially concerned about Karachi, which had long been subject to high levels of political violence. We advised rigorous security precautions for Western personnel either visiting or residing in the city to include well-trained armed escorts. The two other countries about which we were especially preoccupied were Saudi Arabia and Yemen, and it would not be long before our concerns about those countries, too, would prove well-founded.

The Islamic terrorist complex's first attack against an oil-related target took place on October 6 of the same year. The French super-tanker *Limburg* was struck with an explosives-laden speedboat outside the Yemeni port of al-Shihr. The attack ignited a crude-oil fire that resulted in the death of a Bulgarian crewman.

The carefully planned operation, somewhat reminiscent of the October 2000 attack on the USS *Cole*, benefited from intimate knowledge of the workings of the al-Shihr port, a principal oil terminal that the tanker was waiting to enter when it was struck by the remote-control boat-bomb. The perpetrators also may have had inside information from sympathizers in Saudi Arabia's Ras Tanura oil terminal, where days earlier the *Limburg* had taken on a partial load of ninety thousand barrels of crude, for the blast was aimed specifically at the tanks aboard the ship that were full.

Most of that oil spilled out, polluting the coastline for miles and destroying the livelihood of local fishermen. The attack also triggered a tripling of insurance rates for shipping in Yemeni waters, a development that caused international maritime activity in ensuing months to fall by half. Rates subsequently stabilized, in part because the Yemeni government posted a $50 million indemnity bond with a global underwriter.

Yemeni authorities, who had already enlisted in Washington's War on Terrorism, made a score of arrests in connection with the *Limburg* attack, mostly of locals from the mountainous Hadramout region that lies inland from al-Shihr and is the ancestral home of the bin Ladin family.

Seven months later, on May 12, 2003, Islamic extremists staged their first large-scale, post-9/11 attacks in Saudi Arabia: suicide car bombings at three Riyadh housing compounds that killed twenty-six people, including nine Americans and seven Saudis.

Unlike Pakistan and Yemen, Saudi Arabia had tens of thousands of American residents, and our phones rang off the hook as companies contemplated evacuating their personnel.

Even before the Riyadh attacks, we had been advising that personnel based in Saudi Arabia reside in heavily fortified housing complexes and that they travel to stoutly protected worksites in armored vehicles with qualified, armed bodyguards. Now, we went a step further, advising that nonessential personnel and dependents depart the country. Essential personnel could stay, in our view, as long as their protection arrangements were brought up to the standards outlined above and they curtailed excursions to malls and other public venues to the extent possible. Our advice has remained constant to this day, despite the appreciable success of the Saudis' counterterrorism campaign.

Saudi authorities had been on the defensive since the 9/11 attacks, which were largely staged by their countrymen. Fifteen of the nineteen hijackers were, in fact, Saudis. They also were in denial, failing to grasp Global Jihad's *takfiri* mind-set and appearing to believe that if they left the extremists alone, the kingdom would not be victimized. Thus, they did not begin to pursue the militants until after the Riyadh attacks, and it took some time for them to get a handle on the problem. In the interim, Islamic extremists staged a series of attacks against oil-related installations and defense contractors.

On May 1, 2004, militants raided the offices of the Swiss-based engineering firm ABB Lummus at a refinery complex in the Red Sea port of Yanbu, shooting dead two Americans, two Britons, an Australian, and a Saudi. Two other ABB Lummus employees, an American and a Canadian, were wounded. The fatalities included three top officials of the firm, and the corpse of one of them was dragged through the streets of Yanbu by the assailants, who drove past two local schools and a residential area after departing the ABB Lummus offices, firing at a Holiday Inn and a McDonald's. The assailants eventually were gunned down by Saudi police. Some had been employed at the refinery complex and had used their access cards to gain entry to the ABB Lummus portion of the facility.

That same month, extremists assaulted two office buildings identified with the oil-service industry and a luxury residential compound across the Arabian Peninsula in the Persian Gulf town of al-Khobar, killing twenty-two people, including an American, a Briton, a Swede, an Italian, and three Saudi security guards. Four assailants in military garb swept through the office blocks, shooting at close range the handful of non-Muslims they encountered. As in the Yanbu attack, the body of the Briton killed in the raid was dragged through the streets by the assailants as they drove to the nearby Oasis residential compound.

After failing to detonate a car bomb at the gate to Oasis, they managed to break inside and round up forty-one foreigners, killing nine before apparently striking a deal with police negotiators for their own freedom in return for halting the slaughter. Three hostage-takers subsequently ran a police checkpoint in a pickup truck and escaped; the fourth was wounded and captured. The attack was the first claimed by al-Qaida in the Arabian Peninsula (QAP), al-Qaida's Saudi affiliate.

In the wake of the al-Khobar massacre, QAP also claimed several attacks against individual Westerners, including Robert Jacobs, an American employed by Vinnell Corporation, a Northrop Grumman unit that trains the Saudi National Guard. Jacobs was shot to death on June 8, 2004, in the garage of his Riyadh villa. Four days later, American Kenneth Scroggs, who was employed by Saudi-based Advanced Electronics, was shot to death in a similar attack, in the garage of his Riyadh villa. On the same day, American Paul Johnson, a Lockheed Martin employee, was kidnapped while driving near the capital's Imam University. Johnson, who was working on a project related to electronic-warfare systems in which Scroggs also was involved, was beheaded eight days later, after Saudi authorities refused a QAP demand to free extremists held in three prisons.

Shortly after beheading Johnson on June 18, Abd al-Aziz al-Muqrin, the military leader of QAP, was shot dead along with three of his lieutenants at a Riyadh police roadblock. One of the lieutenants is believed to have been one of the three al-Khobar hostage-takers who escaped. In the immediate aftermath of Muqrin's demise, twelve more QAP militants were arrested and stashes of weapons, including RPG-launchers and assault rifles, were confiscated, along with $38,000 in cash.

Muqrin's death slowed the pace of attacks on individual Westerners. But Irish civil engineer Anthony Higgins was shot dead on August 3,

2004, in Riyadh by a gunman who burst into his office at a Saudi-owned construction firm. And on September 15 in the Saudi capital, three suspected Muslim militants in a passing vehicle gunned down Briton Edward Muirhead-Smith, an employee of British telecommunications conglomerate Marconi, in a mall parking lot in eastern Riyadh.

French national Laurent Barbot, an engineer employed by Thales (formerly Thomson-CSF), was shot to death September 26, 2004, in the al-Zahra district of Jiddah. Gunmen in a passing vehicle opened fire at 1:00 a.m., just as Barbot was driving away from a Giant Stores supermarket located less than a mile from the Sierra Village residential compound, where he lived.

The Saudi counteroffensive took solid hold after the Barbot murder, with arrests of militants announced monthly. Indeed, it would be twenty-nine months until Western blood again was shed in the kingdom, and the next attack, on February 26, 2007, clearly was a crime of opportunity, undertaken on a sparsely traveled highway because the victims appeared European.

Four French nationals were gunned down as they took a rest stop along a road about ten miles north of the holy city of Medina and within range of the ruins of Madain Saleh, which recently had been opened to tourists. The victims all were male residents of Riyadh. Two were employees of Schneider Electric. The third was a teacher. The fourth was the seventeen-year-old son of one of the Schneider employees and his Moroccan wife. The boy was a Muslim, and his father was a recent convert to that faith. The Moroccan, two other women, and two children were spared.

A year earlier, on February 24, 2006, Saudi Arabia's critical oil industry barely escaped a terrorist spectacular. QAP operatives at the wheels of two explosives-laden pickup trucks breached the first security perimeter of the giant Aramco-operated Abqaiq refinery complex, forty-five miles southwest of Dammam, but failed to penetrate a second perimeter, possibly because of automatic-weapons fire from guards. Only one truck exploded, and damage was limited to a minor pipeline fire.

Three days later, police killed five QAP militants, four of them participants in the Abqaiq attempt, in a raid on a villa in eastern Riyadh in which weapons and explosives were also discovered. Among the four was Fahd al-Juweir, at the time the QAP leader. By some accounts, Juweir and another of those killed had paved the way for the suicide-bombers by shooting to death two guards posted at the refinery gate.

In late March 2006, police disrupted what appeared to have been another plot against Abqaiq, seizing two explosives-laden vehicles bearing the Aramco logo from the nearby home of an employee. The seizure led to forty additional arrests and to new discoveries of weapons and explosives.

The attempts against Abqaiq came as no surprise. Since late 2004, both bin Ladin and Zawahiri have repeatedly urged their followers to attack Arabian Peninsula oil installations as a means of undermining not only regimes traitorous to Islam (the Saudi monarchy is singled out as especially onerous) but also energy import–dependent America and Europe. Indeed, there is perhaps no more obvious means of striking at Western economies than crimping their oil lifeline. Even modest interruptions in supply cause prices to spiral upward; a major reduction would wreak even greater havoc.

QAP also has endorsed attacks against oil installations. After failing to post on the Internet for nearly two years, it came back online in early February 2007. The new entry, on its main propaganda Web site *Sawt al-Jihad* (Voice of Jihad), featured an article titled "Bin Ladin and the Oil Weapon" that outlined the al-Qaida leader's rationale for attacking oil production, stressing the harm that reduced oil production—and the consequent increase in oil prices—would do to the American economy. Included was an interview with one Badr bin Abdullah al-Hameedi, who was identified as one of the participants in the Abqaiq plot still at large.

Meanwhile, Yemeni supporters of al-Qaida on September 15, 2006, tried their hand at an Abqaiq-style attack, attempting to blow up two oil facilities in their country: the Canadian-operated al-Dhabba export terminal in Hadramout Governate and the Yemeni-operated Safir refinery in Marib Governate.

Security forces successfully repelled the assaults, both of which involved assailants driving vehicles packed with explosives. At 5:15 a.m., a driver dressed as a staff member followed by a driver dressed in a military uniform approached the al-Dhabba facility. Guards reportedly managed to blow up both vehicles before they reached their target. Both drivers and one guard were killed. Shrapnel from one of the exploding vehicles set an oil tank on fire, but the flames were quickly extinguished.

Thirty-five minutes later, two similar vehicles approached the Safir facility. Again, security guards confronted and blew up both vehicles, killing the two drivers. Both sets of attacks appear to have been timed to take place during shift changes.

A month after the attacks, Yemeni authorities announced that they had broken up the cell responsible for them. Four Yemeni nationals were arrested after a seven-hour siege at their Sanaa safe house, during the course of which the suspects hurled grenades at members of the security forces. Twelve bags, each containing about one hundred pounds of high explosives, were seized. In all, twenty-five defendants have been arrested and charged with participation in the plot.

Of course, not all commercially related attacks have taken place in Pakistan and on the Arabian Peninsula. On November 20, 2003, a suicide-bomber detonated a pickup truck outside the Turkish headquarters of the London-based HSBC bank in Istanbul, killing eighteen.

The attack came in the second set of twin bombings in Istanbul over a period of five days, raising eyebrows, since Global Jihad had never before (or since) managed to stage follow-on attacks so close to the originals. The first two keyed on synagogues, killing thirty people, most of them Muslim bystanders. The HSBC attack was paired with a suicide truck bombing at the British Consulate that killed fourteen.

Another economic attack bears mention, in that it may herald similar strikes. On December 28, 2005, operatives of LT, a Kashmiri jihadist group and one of al-Qaida's Pakistani affiliates, opened fire on scientists emerging from an international conference at the Indian Institute of Science in the southern city of Bangalore, the hub of India's information-technology industry, which largely has been the engine of the country's recent spectacular economic growth. The gunmen killed M. C. Puri, a senior professor at the prestigious Indian Institute of Technology (IIT) in New Delhi, and wounded four other scientists in what clearly was intended as an attack against India's soaring high-tech sector.

Also, after years on the defensive, jihadists have returned to action in Algeria, resuming attacks against both government targets and multinational corporations. They first struck against the latter at 4:45 p.m. on December 10, 2006, exploding a roadside bomb as a bus carrying oil workers from a US-linked firm exited a motorway en route to the Sheraton Hotel in the affluent Bouchaoui suburb of Algiers, six miles west of the capital's center. The Algerian driver of the bus was killed and nine passengers were injured, one seriously. The injured included four Britons, two Lebanese, an American, a Canadian, and an Algerian. The victims were employed by Brown & Root-Condor, a joint venture between a subsidiary of US-based Halliburton and Sonatrach, Algeria's state-owned oil company.

Two days later, the Salafist Group for Preaching and Combat, which was known by its French abbreviation, GSPC, a lineal descendent of GIA, claimed credit for the attack, describing it as a "gift to all Muslims who are suffering from the new Crusader campaign targeting Islam and its holy places." The statement, on an Islamist Web site, also warned Muslims to stay away from infidels, suggesting that there would be further attacks. A month later, the GSPC swore fealty to Usama bin Ladin and al-Qaida, renaming itself the al-Qaida Organization for the Islamic Mahgreb (QIM).

Another shoe dropped on March 3, 2007. Three Algerians and a Russian were killed, and several Russians and Ukrainians were wounded in a roadside-bomb attack against their minibuses near Kaadat Souane, eighty miles southwest of Algiers. The victims were employed by Russia's Stroitransgas, which was building a natural-gas pipeline in the area. QIM claimed credit.

The first strike in particular demonstrated a relatively high degree of sophistication. A video released after the attack—and featuring footage of the assault itself—demonstrated that it had been preceded by a thorough surveillance. Also, the bomb had been made more lethal by the addition of shrapnel, in the form of bolts and pieces of steel. Furthermore, the device had been placed exactly at the point at which the bus had to slow down as it turned off the motorway.

On April 11, 2007, QIM displayed its operational muscle in specific attacks on government targets. **(Note the date: Global Jihad has a penchant for striking on the eleventh of the month in homage to the 9/11 attacks.)** Three simultaneous suicide car bombings struck the offices of Prime Minister Abdelaziz Belkhadem in the center of Algiers and a police installation in an eastern suburb of the capital, killing thirty-three and injuring more than two hundred.

QIM's renewed interest in targeting foreigners and the operational clout it displayed in the April car bombings were a matter of grave concern to multinationals operating in Algeria. For the next several months, QIM appeared to concentrate on attacks against the security forces, but on September 21 French media reported that two French nationals employed by Aeroports de Paris, which operates Houari Boumedienne Airport, had been withdrawn from Algiers after intelligence reports suggested that QIM was planning to kidnap them.

Later the very same day, a suicide-bomber rammed a car laden with explosives into a convoy carrying several foreigners employed by the French construction firm Razel. The attack took place near Lakhdaria, about fifty miles southeast of Algiers in the Kabylie region, where QIM is especially active. Two Frenchmen and an Italian were wounded, along with an Algerian driver and five police escorts.

The attack against Razel came a day after a call by Zawahiri to strike at Frenchmen and Spaniards across North Africa, and, in an audiotape claiming credit, a QIM spokesman boasted of having hit "crusader Frenchmen."

On December 11 (there's that date again), QIM struck once again in Algiers, staging simultaneous suicide car bombings against the Constitutional Court building and at UN offices in the Hydra district, which is home to many multinationals. At least thirty-seven people were killed, including several foreigners employed by the United Nations, with dozens more injured in the attacks, which confirmed, if indeed any confirmation were needed, that foreign entities, along with instrumentalities of the despised secular government, were in the terrorists' sights.

On June 8, 2008, QIM murdered a French engineer and his driver with a roadside bomb in the Kabylie town of Beni Amrane.

The string of developments triggered a spate of evacuations of dependents of expatriate employees of French multinationals, and Razel withdrew all foreign employees. A new rush for the exits had begun.

Chapter Eight

CLASS ATTACKS:
COMMERCIAL AVIATION

Al-Qaida did not originate the tactic of attacking commercial aviation. Criminally authored midair bombings of commercial aircraft date from the 1930s, and secular-left Palestinian groups began attacking planes linked to Israel, the United States, and other perceived enemies in the late 1960s. They continued to do so through the late 1980s, when the collapse of the Soviet Union, their principal sponsor, caused them to wither away. The Palestinians even dabbled in simultaneous attacks, heralding what would become an al-Qaida hallmark. But al-Qaida took commercial aviation–related terrorism to a new level with the 9/11 attacks, effectively turning aircraft into guided missiles.

Al-Qaida and the Sunni extremists it has inspired continue to be fixated on attacking commercial aviation. On several occasions since 9/11 they have tried to hijack, bomb, or shoot down commercial aircraft, in all cases unsuccessfully. Some of the misses were near misses, however, and, with aviation security still relatively porous, especially in some developing countries, it is only a matter of time until they are again successful.

Terrorists attack commercial aviation in part because aircraft flying at thirty thousand feet or higher can be brought down by even modest amounts of explosives and because of the sheer horror involved in striking at human beings when they are at their most vulnerable. But they also target aviation because of the crucial role it plays in commerce, and this is especially true of Global Jihad. A

75

strike against aviation not only harms the targeted airline and, indirectly, its competitors, it also reverberates throughout the economy, causing commercial flights to be suspended, as was the case in the United States after 9/11, or prompting prospective travelers to cancel trips. To ground a large number of corporate managers in this day and age is to seriously impede the conduct of business.

At one time, terrorists hijacked airliners to obtain hostages who could be traded for imprisoned comrades, but in recent years hijackings for purposes other than turning aircraft into missiles have fallen out of fashion. Governments, even those that consider themselves to be revolutionary or avidly Islamic, have become reluctant to allow their territory to be used as a destination for commandeered aircraft.

The campaign by secular-left Palestinian groups against commercial aviation began on July 22, 1968, when the Popular Front for the Liberation of Palestine (PFLP) hijacked an El Al Israel Airlines plane en route from Rome to Tel Aviv. The aircraft, carrying thirty-two passengers and ten crew members, was diverted to Algiers. Most passengers were released relatively quickly, but seven crew members and five Israeli men were held hostage there for five weeks, until they were exchanged for sixteen prisoners held in Israeli jails. (The Israelis determined that the hijackers had departed Beirut fully armed and retaliated with a raid on that city's airport in which thirteen aircraft, most belonging to Middle East Airlines, were destroyed on the ground.)

The high watermark of Palestinian hijacking came on September 6, 1970, at the height of the Palestinians' Black September uprising against Jordan. Two aircraft bound for New York City, a TWA flight from Frankfurt and a Swissair flight from Zurich, were commandeered by PFLP operatives and diverted to Dawson's Field, a remote desert airstrip in the Jordanian town of Zarqa, later to be made infamous by one of its sons, Abu Musab al-Zarqawi, the founder of the al-Qaida Organization for Jihad in Iraq (QJI). Assailants also attempted to board an El Al flight from Amsterdam but were turned back by air marshals, whereupon they successfully commandeered a Pan Am 747, diverting it to Beirut and then Cairo, where it was emptied and blown up. (It was too large to land on the small Jordanian strip.) A fifth plane, a British Airways jet, was hijacked three days later from Bahrain and was also brought to Dawson's Field.

Five days after the initial hijackings, the Dawson's Field hijackers freed 310 hostages, while maintaining custody of 56 Jews and flight crew members. On the following day, they destroyed the four empty aircraft with explosives. Jordan's defeat of the uprising led to a deal on September 30, in which the remaining hostages were exchanged for four PFLP prisoners, one of them the infamous Leila Khalid, an early female terrorist operative who was captured during the failed El Al hijacking.

It was in fact Hizbollah, the Lebanese Shia terrorist movement, that scored the largest prisoner release from a hijacking. Two militants on June 14, 1985, commandeered TWA Flight 847 en route from Athens to Rome, forcing it to land in Beirut. One hundred fifty-four passengers and crew were taken hostage, of whom thirty-nine were held for the full seventeen days, during which time the hijackers killed an American sailor and obliged the aircraft to fly twice to Algiers and back to Beirut. The price exacted for the freedom of the hostages was the release of more than seven hundred Lebanese prisoners held by Israel.

Ground assaults against commercial aircraft also had their day, but it passed quickly, presumably because such attacks were simply difficult to pull off and not sufficiently terrifying. On December 26, 1969, two PFLP operatives sprayed submachine-gun fire and tossed grenades at an El Al airliner awaiting takeoff at Athens airport, killing a passenger and injuring a stewardess. Forty-five days later, on February 10, 1970, three terrorists from the Democratic Front for the Liberation of Palestine (DFLP), a PFLP derivative, attacked a bus at Munich's airport with automatic weapons and grenades. One passenger was killed and eleven were injured. In both instances, the assailants were captured by airport police.

This category of attack reached its zenith in December 1973, when another secular-left Palestinian terrorist group, the Libyan-sponsored Arab Nationalist Youth Organization (ANYO), an apparent predecessor of the Abu Nidal Organization (ANO), staged an attack against a Pan

Am 707 on the ground at Rome's Fiumicino Airport, destroying it with incendiary bombs and killing thirty passengers. The assailants then took five hostages and hijacked a Lufthansa 737, obliging it to fly to Athens, where they killed a hostage in support of their demand that two Arab terrorists be released from prison. Then they ordered the plane to Damascus and, finally, to Kuwait, where the assailants released the remaining hostages in a deal that gave them safe passage out of the sheikhdom. The ANO went on to stage both ground attacks and hijackings.

The PFLP-General Command, a PFLP derivative led by Ahmed Gibril, authored the first midair bombing of an Israel-linked aircraft. It took place on February 21, 1970. A device set off by a dual trigger— a timer working in tandem with a barometric trigger—exploded in the cargo hold of a Swissair Convair CV-990 bound from Zurich to Tel Aviv, killing forty-seven passengers and crew members. (The dual trigger was designed to ensure that the bombs exploded in the air and on the proper flight. Timing mechanisms alone are unreliable, since airlines cannot be depended upon to adhere to schedules. Barometric triggers alone, on the other hand, may cause the bomb to explode on an earlier leg of a targeted flight.)

The PFLP-GC actually attempted a second attack the same day, placing a similar dual-trigger device in a mailbag bound for Tel Aviv, but the triggers malfunctioned and the bomb exploded prematurely aboard an Austrian Airlines Caravelle flying from Frankfurt to Vienna. The explosion blew a hole in the fuselage but did not prevent the aircraft from landing safely.

The PFLP-GC subsequently perfected the dual trigger, the use of which initially was suspected in the December 21, 1988, explosion aboard a Pan Am 747 over Lockerbie, Scotland, that killed 270 people, including 11 residents of Lockerbie. Investigators, however, failed to find a barometric trigger, leading to the conclusion that the Pan Am bombing and a similar explosion the following year aboard a DC-10 operated by France's UTA over Chad that killed 171 people involved only timing devices and were the work of Libyan intelligence agents.

The first manifestations of the interest of the al-Qaida complex of Sunni Muslim extremist groups in attacking commercial aviation took place in 1994. On December 24, Algeria's GIA staged the Air France hijacking that was discussed in considerable detail in chapter 6.

An equally sinister plot was in process in the Far East. Thirteen days before the Algiers hijacking, on December 11, an Arab associate of al-Qaida operative Ramzi Yousef, the organizer of the 1993 bombing at New York's World Trade Center, staged a test run for what was intended to be an even more dramatic strike. The operative placed an explosive device aboard a Philippines Airlines 747 on the first leg of a Manila-Cebu-Tokyo run and then deplaned at Cebu. On the Tokyo leg of the flight, the bomb exploded, killing a Japanese passenger and injuring ten other people. The plane was crippled, but the pilots managed to land it in Okinawa.

The bombing, it turned out, was a test run for an intended January 21–22, 1995, spectacular, in which substantially more powerful bombs manufactured from a complex of liquid explosives were to explode aboard eleven US jetliners over the Pacific. But the plot unraveled two weeks earlier, when a fire in the Manila apartment in which the bombs were being prepared led to the arrest of several conspirators, as well as the eventual apprehension in Pakistan of Yousef himself.

The Ramzi Yousef plot was strikingly similar to one uncovered by British authorities in 2006 to bomb multiple commercial flights to the United States using liquid explosives concealed in beverage containers and detonators disguised as common electronic devices. Twenty-five British Muslims, most of them of Pakistani origin, were arrested in connection with the scheme, and seventeen were charged with offenses, including conspiracy to commit murder.

To date, al-Qaida has failed to reprise the 9/11 spectacular. Twice, however, Islamic extremists came close to bringing down individual aircraft.

On December 22, 2001, Richard Reid, the infamous shoe-bomber, a Jamaican-born, United Kingdom–reared convert to Islam, almost brought down an American Airlines 767 bound from Paris to Miami.

He was spotted by a flight attendant trying to ignite his explosives-laden shoes with a match and was overcome by passengers.

On February 13, 2003, Hazil Mohammed Rahaman, a thirty-seven-year-old Venezuelan Muslim, nearly succeeded in blowing up the British Airways aircraft that carried him from Caracas to London's Gatwick Airport. Security personnel at Caracas's Simon Bolivar Airport failed to detect the grenade in his backpack, his only item of luggage. (The grenade was wrapped in tinfoil and secreted inside an infrared massaging device, which in turn was concealed in a lead-lined wooden box.) Airline employees, however, did deny him permission to carry the backpack onboard because it was too large, obliging him to check it instead. The discovery of the grenade was made by customs officials at Gatwick.

On November 28, 2002, al-Qaida operatives tried a new tactic, firing two Soviet-made, shoulder-launched missiles at an Israeli charter jet taking off from the airport in Mombasa, Kenya, with 271 people aboard. The projectiles narrowly missed the aircraft. (Minutes later, a suicide-bomber blew himself up in the lobby of an Israeli-owned resort near Mombasa, killing eleven Kenyans and three Israelis.)

The only successful midair bombings of commercial aircraft since 9/11 were staged on August 24, 2004, in Russia by Chechen separatists seeking independence for their homeland. The Chechen extremists are second cousins to al-Qaida. They are Muslims but are not fanatically religious and they strike more out of fanatic nationalism than religious fervor.

A Volga-Avia Express Tu-134 and a Siberia Airlines Tu-154 both exploded while en route from Moscow to points in southern Russia, killing a total of eighty-seven innocents. In each case, a woman, after bribing her way past security guards, boarded the plane with sophisticated explosives secreted under her clothing.

The absence of al-Qaida attacks should not be taken to mean that commercial air travel is now entirely safe. If the plot uncovered in the United Kingdom in 2006 failed to provide ample testimony that Islamic extremists remain fixated on attacking airlines, corroborating evidence came in 2007 from two self-generated groups of Islamic extremists, one in the United Kingdom and the other in the United States.

Federal officials in June charged four Muslims from Guyana and Trinidad with organizing a plot to blow up a fuel pipeline at New York's John F. Kennedy International Airport. Authorities learned of the plot early on and were able to monitor it. The ringleader, an American citizen of Guyanese origin and a former JFK cargo worker, was placed under arrest in New York. The three other suspects were taken into custody in Trinidad. The plotters had links to Jamaat al-Muslimeen (Muslim Group), an Afro-Trinidadian Muslim group notorious in Trinidad for kidnapping, armed robbery, and narcotrafficking.

Later that same month came the attempt by the Indian doctor and the Iraqi engineer to ram an explosives-laden vehicle into Glasgow Airport (see chapter 3).

While significant strides have been made in screening passengers, especially in industrialized countries, concerns persist about screening procedures in developing countries and about other vulnerabilities. Authorities in many countries fail to sufficiently vet members of maintenance, food service, cleaning, and baggage-handling crews who have virtually unfettered access to aircraft. (One of the London plotters, in fact, had a pass allowing broad access to the Heathrow terminal.)

Europe may face a particular challenge in vetting workers from its large, indigenous Muslim population. The dimensions of this problem came to light in October 2006 when French authorities announced the suspension of aircraft access privileges of seventy-two Muslim workers at Paris's Charles de Gaulle Airport. Many of the seventy-two had traveled to Afghanistan or Pakistan, and several were suspected of having links to extremists or having trained in terrorist camps.

In the Western Hemisphere, the principal problem is corrupt airport workers who for years have been hiding narcotics and other contraband aboard aircraft. Terrorists potentially could bribe a worker to place a package aboard an aircraft that appears to contain narcotics but in fact is rigged as a bomb. The US Transportation Security Administration (TSA) initiated a hard look at airport workers in March 2007, after an airport worker was caught trying to load a stash of weapons and marijuana aboard a Delta flight bound for Puerto Rico. Policing the more than eight hundred thousand workers who enjoy flight-line access, however, is a monumental task.

Deficiencies in the policing effort were demonstrated vividly in November 2007, when federal and local authorities in Chicago arrested twenty-three illegal aliens who had fake security badges that gave them access to critical areas of O'Hare International Airport, including the tarmac. The twenty-three, including twenty from Mexico, two from Guatemala, and one from El Salvador, were employed by Ideal Staffing Solutions, Inc., to load freight and meals aboard aircraft belonging to United, KLM, and Qantas. Also arrested were Ideal Staffing's corporate secretary and an office manager who was herself an illegal alien.

Another cause for concern is the relative laxity, even in the United States and other industrialized countries, in the screening of air freight.

What can a passenger do to protect himself? The only real countermeasure is the use, in international travel, of carriers from countries perceived as relatively neutral in the War on Terrorism. It is worth noting, however, that even carriers from neutral countries may be hijacked by jihadists determined to turn them into missiles for attacks against American cities or those of its allies.

Moreover, given the absence of successful commercial aviation–related attacks since 9/11, it is difficult to argue that airlines associated with countries in the forefront of the struggle—such as the United States and the United Kingdom—be avoided, especially insofar as they probably pay the greatest heed to security.

Perhaps the most practical advice is to avoid higher-risk carriers when departing airports in developing countries and during periods in which international tensions are especially high.

Chapter Nine

CLASS ATTACKS: TRAINS AND SUBWAYS

B ombings aboard trains and subways, while they generally lack the dramatic impact of a midair explosion, can have a devastating effect on commerce in a major metropolitan area. The March 11, 2004, bombings of commuter trains in Madrid that killed 191 people paralyzed the Spanish capital for days, to say nothing of being a decisive factor in the parliamentary election held three days later. The July 7, 2005, suicide bombings aboard three subway trains and a bus in London, which killed fifty-two people, were equally disruptive to the economy of Britain's capital. Meanwhile, a string of seven bombings on July 11, 2006, aboard first-class coaches of commuter trains and on railway station platforms in Mumbai, India, that killed 186 people and injured some 700 was a shot across the bow of India's commercial class.

As in the case of assaults against commercial aviation, Islamic extremists cannot lay claim to originating the train attack. Other terrorist movements, most notably the Irish Republican Army (IRA), planted bombs in train stations and aboard trains in the 1970s and 1980s, often several at a time and generally with the objective of causing major inconvenience to commuters. Indeed, to emphasize that its objective was inconvenience and not slaughter, the IRA routinely announced its operations in warning phone calls.

Arab Armed Struggle, a designation used by Venezuela-born transnational terrorist Illich Ramirez Sanchez, better known as "Carlos," tried its hand at a lethal railroad attack in December 1983, planting a bomb aboard a high-speed train traveling from Marseille to Paris. The explosion killed three people and injured eight. Fortunately, the train had slowed to about eighty miles per hour to pass through a station when the bomb exploded. Had it been traveling faster and derailed, the loss of life would have been much, much greater. Twenty-five minutes after the explosion, a second bomb, also intended for a train, detonated in the baggage room of a Marseille station, killing two and injuring forty-one.

It was Islamic extremists, however, who took train attacks to new levels of brutality—and economic disruption. During the afternoon rush hour of July 25, 1995, a bomb exploded aboard an RER commuter train in Paris's St. Michel underground station, killing seven people and injuring one hundred. A similar attack took place during the morning rush hour on October 17 of that year aboard another train traveling the same line. Again, seven people were killed. Eighty-four were wounded. Yet another took place during the evening rush hour of December 3, 1996. Once again, the venue was a commuter train traveling underground through central Paris. Two people were killed and fifty injured.

The campaign was undertaken by the GIA, the same Algerian Islamist group that staged the 1994 Christmas Eve attempt to explode the Air France jet over Paris. Any doubts about authorship were dispelled when the GIA, on the heels of the third bombing, issued a communiqué announcing that it was at war with France. The spate of GIA attacks in France, which hit shopping centers, subway stations, and other targets in addition to trains, was brought to a halt by a string of arrests of operatives peppered among the roughly 1.5 million resident Algerians.

Al-Qaida's Chechen cousins have also staged subway and train bombings. The first took place on June 11, 1996, on a Moscow subway train, killing four people and wounding twelve. In ensuing months, Chechen terrorists repeatedly bombed trains in the Volgograd region of southern Russia and in the northern Caucasus, close to Chechnya. On February 5, 2001, they set off a bomb in Moscow's busy Belorusskaya subway station that injured nine. At the height of the morning rush hour on February 6, 2004, they staged their most lethal subway attack, blowing up a train traveling through central Moscow and killing forty innocents. More than one hundred passengers were injured.

On August 31 of that year, a female Chechen suicide-bomber blew herself up outside the entrance to the Rizhskaya metro station in northern Moscow, killing ten other people and injuring about fifty. The assailant had tried to enter the station but apparently abandoned that plan when she observed a pair of policemen at the entrance. The 2.2-pound bomb she was carrying would have inflicted far greater casualties in an enclosed area.

The first attack against a train system by the al-Qaida complex of Islamic terrorist groups—the March 11, 2004 (again, on the eleventh of the month and, indeed, eighteen months to the day after 9/11), bombings in Madrid—still stands as the movement's most successful, not only in terms of casualties but also in its political and economic impact. Indeed, the massacre, which remains the most lethal terrorist act in modern European history, may be said to have brought down, in a parliamentary election held just three days later, the center-right Popular Party (PP) government of Prime Minister José Maria Aznar. Aznar had offended militant Islam by contributing thirteen hundred troops to the US-led occupation of Iraq.

There can be little doubt that the terrorists' principal objective was to deliver the message to Spanish voters that they would be made to pay for the PP's support of Washington. They received an added bonus, however, when the government mishandled the initial investigation, ignoring indications of Muslim involvement because it rightly feared that it would be blamed for the tragedy, and pointing the finger instead at the indigenous separatist movement Basque Land and Liberty, known by its Basque acronym, ETA, which had attempted train bombings four months earlier. Aznar was succeeded by José Luis Rodriguez Zapatero of the left-leaning Socialist Party, who, upon taking office, made good on his preelection pledge to bring Spanish troops home from Iraq.

The attacks began at 7:37 a.m., when explosives in three gym bags detonated aboard a commuter train approaching Atocha station, the nerve center of Madrid's commuter rail system. The bombs exploded with such fury that human remains were sent hurtling through the shattered windows of adjacent buildings. Seconds later, less than six hundred yards away, another train was hit by four blasts. Had the devices on the first two trains exploded when the trains were inside Atocha station, as the terrorists presumably intended, the entire structure, including the rooftop parking garage, might have collapsed.

At 7:41 a.m., two bombs destroyed another train three miles away, at El Pozo del Tio Raimundo station. Finally, at 7:42 a.m., one more bomb detonated on a train at the outlying Santa Eugenia station.

Within a few hours, investigative leads began to point to Islamic extremists. By midmorning, a cassette tape of Koranic verses and a plastic bag containing seven detonators matching the type used in the bombings were found in a white Renault van abandoned near the Alcala de Henares train station, near Madrid. It is presumed that these materials were intentionally left behind to make sure that militant Islam received credit for the attacks. At the same time, wiretaps on ETA suspects revealed that they knew nothing of the attack plan.

That evening, investigators combing the wreckage hit the mother lode—a gym bag containing twenty-two pounds of Goma-2 high explosives surrounded by nails and screws and equipped with a detonator wired to a mobile telephone, the prospective trigger. (Two similar devices were eventually discovered unexploded.) They traced the phone's recent call records, which revealed a network of Muslim immigrants who already were known to Spanish intelligence officials.

One of the traced numbers led to Jamal Zougam, a Moroccan long suspected of having al-Qaida ties who owned a small cellular telephone and copy store near Atocha station. Zougam had been investigated by the security services after both the 9/11 attacks and a spate of suicide bombings in Casablanca, Morocco, in 2003. He was a known associate of Imad Eddin Barakat Yarkas, the suspected leader of a key al-Qaida support cell in Spain who was arrested shortly after 9/11 and was being held on charges of abetting terrorism.

When the new government took over, it continued to investigate the attacks aggressively. Seven prime suspects, including cell leader Serhane ben Abdelmajid Fakhet, known as "the Tunisian," blew themselves up rather than surrender when surrounded by police on April 3 in the Madrid suburb of Leganes. (The suicides were somewhat surprising, in that the operatives who had planted the bombs aboard the trains had shown no disposition to give their lives.) More than a dozen others were arrested in Spain and other European countries, the vast majority of them of Moroccan origin.

The self-generated cell that undertook the July 2005 London transit bombings, although more dedicated than the Madrid bombers (the four assailants surrendered their lives in the attacks), was decidedly less expert. Had the assailants been more competent, they certainly could have boosted the casualty toll far beyond the total of fifty-two innocents killed.

The suicide-bombers were young British Muslims, three of them of Pakistani origin and the fourth a Jamaican-born convert to Islam. Two are known to have visited Pakistan in the months before the bombing, though exactly how and when they came up with the attack scheme and assembled their homemade explosives, and who their contacts were in Britain and in Pakistan, are questions that investigators still are pursuing.

The three bombers of Pakistani origin, on the morning of the attack, drove in a rental car from their hometown of Leeds to Luton, on the outskirts of Greater London, where they rendezvoused with the Jamaican-born convert. At Luton, the four, carrying with them four large backpack-bombs containing acetone peroxide–based explosives, ball bearings, and nails, were seen by CCTV cameras boarding a Thameslink train to King's Cross, one of central London's main commuter hubs. Subsequently, a large amount of acetone peroxide–based explosives, concocted from readily available consumer products, was recovered by investigators from the rental car left in Luton.

At King's Cross, the assailants entered the Underground system, heading in different directions. Three bombs were detonated almost simultaneously at 8:50 a.m. One exploded on the Piccadilly line south, near Russell Square station, killing twenty-six innocents. The other two exploded aboard Circle Line trains, one killing seven and the other six.

The bus bombing occurred at Tavistock Square near King's Cross at 9:47 a.m. and killed thirteen innocents. It is presumed that the fourth assailant, too, intended to strike in the Underground system but was prevented from doing so by disruptions in train service brought about by the three initial attacks.

A second, apparently unrelated, cell made up of four Muslims of East African origin attempted to reprise the July 7 attacks fourteen days later. The explosives they used, however, were markedly different from those used in the earlier attack and failed to detonate. In each instance, passengers heard a bang and smelled smoke, and on the bus some windows were blown out, but there were no casualties. Each of the four managed to escape the bomb scene on foot, but their images were captured by London's expansive CCTV system, and they were quickly identified, tracked down, and arrested. One managed to make it to Italy before being apprehended.

The July 11, 2006, Mumbai train bombings (once again, note the fateful date) have been ascribed by Indian authorities to the Kashmir-based jihadist group LT. LT's reason for being is to win independence for the Himalayan territory of Kashmir, the richest part of which constitutes India's only Muslim-majority state. But the group also functions as an affiliate of al-Qaida and most likely would strike at India even if the fate of Kashmir were not in question. Fanatical Muslims abhor India for its Hinduism, which they equate with idolatry. They also fear and detest the country's growing economic prowess.

A total of seven bombs detonated in a span of eleven minutes beginning at 6:24 p.m.—the height of the evening rush hour. Six blasts occurred aboard first-class train coaches or on platforms at the Khar, Mahim, Matunga Road, Jugeshwari, Borivil, and Bhayander stations. The seventh took place aboard a train traveling between the Khar and Santa Cruz stations. The bombs aboard the trains were planted on luggage racks. All of the devices consisted of RDX, a military-grade explosive that is a staple of the LT arsenal, as well as ammonium nitrate and fuel oil.

Police took thirteen suspects into custody. Another was said to have been killed in the bombings, although there was no indication he intended to be a "martyr." Still another was slain in a shoot-out with police in central Mumbai on August 22, 2006.

The Mumbai train bombings had both a precursor and a sequel. At 1:43 a.m. on February 19, 2006, a bomb exploded in a train station in Ahmadabad, four hundred miles north of Mumbai in Gujarat State, which has a mixed Hindu-Muslim population. The powerful device, said by police to be sophisticated in its construction, was planted on a crate between a telephone booth and snack kiosk and brought down the roof of the platform. In all, twenty-five people were injured. The blast occurred just after two passenger trains left the station and immediately before another was due to arrive.

The sequel was a February 18, 2007, bombing aboard a train traveling from India to Pakistan, in which sixty-eight passengers, most of them Pakistani, were killed and twelve were wounded. Four explosions touched off a conflagration an hour after the train left New Delhi for Lahore.

The four bombs that exploded—and two others that did not due to timers that were set incorrectly—were secreted in suitcases. They appear to have been planted by two Hindi-speaking men who got on the train shortly before its departure from New Delhi and argued with a conductor after being told the destination was not Ahmadabad. The two had been allowed to jump off the train when it slowed down, about fifteen minutes before the blasts.

Over the years, terrorist groups of several different stripes have staged bombings aboard inter-city trains in India, and travel aboard such trains should be avoided. Clearly, there are safer alternatives—commercial air and automobile travel.

The avoidance of commuter trains and subways, however, is far more difficult. Indeed, many working people in both India and the

West are obliged to use them and thus are hard put to reduce their vulnerability to attack. Officials of cities such as London and New York in recent years have stepped up their monitoring of train and subway passengers in the hope of staving off bombings, but passenger volume is such that no effort of this sort can be entirely successful.

Our best advice to commuters in London, Paris, Madrid, Moscow, and Mumbai, and in other cities vulnerable to train and subway attacks, such as New York and Washington, DC, is to avoid the use of trains and subways, at least during rush hours, on the eleventh of the month, the day on which al-Qaida is most apt to strike.

Chapter Ten

CLASS ATTACKS: HOTELS AND HANGOUTS

As in the case of other class attacks, al-Qaida cannot take credit for originating the tactic of bombing business-class hotels. Peru's Maoist, outrageously xenophobic Shining Path organization struck hotels in Lima, Peru, several times in the early 1990s, and other insurgent movements have staged similar hits over the years. Islamic extremism, however, has refined the tactic, striking repeatedly at hotels in the Muslim world.

Are the strikes motivated by the desire to strike at infidels, or do they have an economic aspect to them? Most appear to have both components.

Al-Qaida's interest in attacking hotels actually predates 9/11. The Radisson SAS in Amman, Jordan, was among the targets of the so-called Millennium Plot directed at Jordan and the United States on or about January 1, 2000. Beginning in 1998, under the direction of Abu Zubaydah, a Palestinian lieutenant of Usama bin Ladin, plotters in Jordan accumulated bomb-making materials, including several tons of nitric and sulfuric acid acquired with false industrial licenses. They stored the acids in a large subterranean chamber tunneled under a house they rented in a poor suburb of Amman. Following instructions on a computer disk that contained a five-thousand-page guerrilla-warfare manual, one of the plotters, Raid Hijazi, an American citizen of Palestinian origin, experimented with samples of explosives on his family's farm, about an hour outside of town. He and three others then underwent training at an al-Qaida camp in Afghanistan in mid-

1999, with Hijazi focusing on bomb making and the others being tutored to become suicide-bombers.

The four did not make it back to Jordan as planned, however, for Jordanian security services, which had been monitoring the Amman cell's activities for months, were listening in on a phone call made by Abu Zubaydah to Khadar Abu Ghoshar, another Palestinian plotter, shortly after midnight on November 30, 1999. Abu Zubaydah advised that "the training is over" and ordered the staging of the attacks on "the day of the millennium." A police squad swooped down on Abu Ghoshar before he had even hung up, and within the hour, fifteen other members of the cell were taken into custody. Abu Zubaydah was arrested in Pakistan in March 2002 and, as this is written, is being held at the Guantánamo Bay detention camp.

The four targets selected for the millennium bombings in addition to the Radisson SAS, which was popular with both Israeli tourists and Christian pilgrims and fully booked for the New Year, were Mount Nebo, the spot from which Moses was permitted to view the Promised Land, the River Jordan camp of John the Baptist, and two border crossings into Israel.

The fact that the Radisson was grouped with several tourist sites suggests that the prospective strikes were motivated primarily by religious hatred, but surely it was not lost on the plotters that the attacks, had they been successful, would have had important economic consequences. Jordan's tourism industry, which is heavily dependent on Israelis and on Christian pilgrims, would have been in tatters.

A November 2002 suicide truck bombing at the Paradise Hotel in Mombasa, Kenya, also appears to have been motivated by anti-Zionism, as was an October 2004 car-bomb attack on the Hilton in Taba, on Egypt's Sinai Peninsula. The former was Israeli owned, and both catered mainly to Israeli tourists.

But other attacks at business-oriented hotels appeared to have the objective of driving off infidels—and even Muslims—who are economic players. Certainly this was the case in the August 5, 2003, suicide car bombing at the JW Marriott in Jakarta, Indonesia, that killed eleven locals and a Dutchman, all of whom were standing at the hotel entrance, and an October 28, 2004, bombing in the lobby of the Islamabad (Pakistan) Marriott that slightly injured an American and two Italians, and severed the leg of a hotel security guard.

Economics also appears to have figured in the al-Qaida Organization for Jihad in Iraq's (QJI) near-simultaneous suicide bombings at three Amman hotels, the Radisson SAS, Grand Hyatt, and Days Inn, on November 9, 2005, which killed fifty-nine innocents. The hotels are popular with Westerners, including businesspeople, tourists, and American contractors en route to Iraq, and QJI, led at the time by Jordanian-born Abu Musab al-Zarqawi, clearly had Westerners in its crosshairs. But the assailants' execution of the plot was incompetent, astoundingly so in view of the capabilities the movement had demonstrated in Iraq, and almost all the people they killed and injured were Arabs.

At the Radisson, the assailant inexplicably set off his bomb among attendees at a Sunni Muslim wedding, killing thirty-eight, among them the fathers of the bride and groom, and triggering a wave of revulsion, not only in Jordan but throughout the Arab world. The assailant at the Grand Hyatt did manage to detonate his explosives vest near the lobby bar, but, ironically, he killed two senior Palestinian intelligence officers and a prominent Palestinian banker who were enjoying an evening drink. The assailant at the Days Inn was shooed out of the hotel by a waiter and blew himself up just outside, killing three members of a Chinese military delegation.

Striking at captains of industry also appears to have been the objective of a suicide-bomber who blew himself up on January 26, 2007, at a side entrance to the Islamabad Marriott, also taking the life of an alert security guard who had denied him access to the facility. The bomber, it is assumed, was headed for a bar or restaurant in the hotel.

Clearly, the extremists' penchant for attacking hotels in Muslim countries imperils business travelers to those lands, mandating the employment of defensive strategies.

In my view, travelers to Muslim countries should seek out hotels in walled compounds with appreciable setbacks from public roads. Access points should be manned by armed personnel who rigorously inspect incoming vehicles and equipped with stout barriers to intrusion, such as delta barriers that permit guards to admit vehicles one at a time, after vetting and inspection. Ideally, the vehicular driveway to the hotel should have stout zigzag barriers, to prevent a high-speed approach.

The problem for travelers is that I have described the hotel of the future. Few hotels matching this profile are currently available. The next best options are boutique establishments and those with several low-rise outbuildings. In the latter, rooms should be selected away from entrance areas, the magnet for suicide-bombers. (Assailants wearing explosives vests, on the other hand, normally head for a bar, restaurant, or function.)

If high-rise hotels must be used, it is crucial to obtain rooms facing away from entrance/lobby areas, streets, and parking lots. Hotels with underground parking should be avoided.

Is it wise to avoid American-linked hotels? I don't believe so. While it is true that they probably bear somewhat greater risks than foreign chains, they generally offer better security. I, for one, would not hesitate to check into the Islamabad Marriott, one of the few facilities in the world that can lay claim to having stopped a suicide-bomber in his tracks.

The best strategy in choosing a hotel is to follow the advice of a reputable risk-analysis service. *Risknet*, for example, makes specific hotel recommendations.

Even more dangerous than hotels, for people visiting or residing in conservative Muslim countries, are Western hangouts, such as restaurants and clubs, which generally have even less protection. Some restaurants and clubs are especially offensive to Islamic radicals because they serve alcohol.

The quintessential restaurant attack took place on March 15, 2008, at the Luna Caprese, a notorious Western hangout in an affluent, heavily patrolled district of Islamabad. An assailant threw an explosive device over a wall into a garden dining area, killing a Turkish woman and wounding twelve other people, including five Americans, two Japanese, a Briton, and a Canadian. Four of the injured Americans were identified as FBI agents.

The Luna Caprese, popular with expatriates in part because it is one of the few restaurants in Islamabad that serves alcohol, had only one security guard at its main entrance. There is some thought that the assailant or assailants may have keyed on American Embassy personnel, who had telegraphed their presence by parking two large SUVs with diplomatic license plates outside the restaurant.

Chapter Eleven

CLASS ATTACKS: TOURISM

Once again, al-Qaida cannot claim credit for originating attacks against tourism. Numerous terrorist groups have targeted tourists and tourism as a means of generating publicity for their cause. Several times since 9/11, however, al-Qaida and its derivatives have taken attacks against tourism to a new level, striking repeatedly at targets in Muslim countries they deem unacceptably secular.

Attacks against tourism are a triple whammy for the zealots. First, they victimize Westerners, thus satisfying their basic hatred of infidels. Second, they hit Western tourists, who, by definition, engage in activities offensive to Islam, such as drinking alcohol, dancing, and sunbathing. Third, they strike at the economic underpinnings of fundamentally secular states.

Global Jihad's first successful attack after 9/11 was aimed at tourism in Tunisia. An April 11, 2002—there's that date again—suicide truck bombing killed fourteen German tourists, a Frenchman, and six Tunisian bystanders outside the historic el-Ghriba synagogue on the resort island of Jerba. (This attack may be described as a quadruple whammy, since it also involved a synagogue.) Although sponsored by al-Qaida, the attack was planned and executed by a local man who had escaped detection by Tunisia's pervasive security services because he acted virtually alone.

Nizar bin Muhammad Nawar, the twenty-four-year-old suicide-bomber, was a drifter with no history of political activism or religious extremism. In mid-2000, however, he left Tunisia and eventually landed in Afghanistan, where he received training at an al-Qaida camp.

He returned home in late 2001, suddenly possessed of enough money to buy a satellite phone and a refrigerator truck and have a large tank fitted inside the vehicle, purportedly for transporting olive oil. On the morning designated for the attack, he filled the tank with liquid propane and drove to the synagogue, stopping outside its entrance and detonating his charge as a busload of tourists milled about.

Subsequently, it was learned that Nawar received his final instructions on the satellite phone from a Pakistan-based associate of Khalid Sheikh Mohammed, a senior lieutenant to Usama bin Ladin and a key planner of many al-Qaida operations, including the 9/11 attacks. Mohammed was apprehended in Pakistan in March 2003.

Four days after the Jerba attack, the Islamabad offices of two London-based Arab newspapers received a faxed statement of responsibility from the so-called Islamic Army for the Liberation of Holy Sites, which claimed that it had acted to avenge "Israeli crimes" and punish Arab governments for "refusing to allow their people to launch jihad against the Jews." The statement also included Nawar's handwritten statement of "martyrdom."

Still, for an entire week, Tunisian authorities, anxious to protect a tourism industry that hosts five million visitors a year, improbably asserted that the Jerba explosion had been an accident. Indeed, it took an emergency visit by Germany's interior minister to get them to admit that it had been an act of terrorism.

Five months later, on October 12, 2002 (again, there may have been a last-minute glitch that caused the attack to be postponed a day), Jemaah Islamiyah (JI), or the Islamic Group, the South Asian affiliate of al-Qaida, struck on the resort island of Bali, a largely Hindu enclave in predominantly Muslim Indonesia, staging Islamic extremism's most lethal tourism-related attack to date. A small bomb exploded inside a pub on popular Kuta Beach, forcing people onto the street. Then, a van packed with explosives blew up across the street, directly in front of a crowded dance club. The majority of the 202 people killed were Australian and European tourists.

On October 1, 2005, JI reprised the Bali attack, but on a much smaller scale, suggesting that an offensive mounted by the Indonesian security forces in the wake of the first strike had taken its toll on JI's operating capabilities. The suicide bombings took place on a Saturday evening at crowded restaurants in Kuta Beach and the more up-market tourist hub of Jimbaran. In each case, a single assailant set off a back-pack loaded with explosives and ball bearings. In all, twenty innocents were killed—five of them foreigners—and about one hundred and fifty were wounded. Thirty-eight of the wounded were from abroad.

The three bombings occurred within a few minutes of each other at about 8:00 p.m. One target was Raja, a three-story steak and noodle restaurant in Kuta Beach that is wedged between a McDonald's and a KFC in a crowded outdoor shopping area. Not far away is the Hard Rock Beach Club.

The other two blasts occurred about five miles away in Jimbaran at the Nyoman and Menaga seafood cafes, which are about fifty yards apart. About five hundred yards away is the Four Seasons, one of several luxury hotels in the resort town.

The other focal point for Islamic extremist attacks against tourism, not surprisingly, has been Egypt, which, you will recall, suffered severe economic repercussions from the Gama'a campaign of the 1990s. Two groups have been heard from. One was an organization of Sinai Bedouin who had embraced militant Islam and may have received instruction from Palestinian terrorists. The other, much smaller, was the Islamic Brigades of Pride in Egypt, a self-generated cell of Cairo zealots who learned terrorist tactics from Internet sources.

The Sinai militants, calling themselves al-Tawhid wal-Jihad (TJ), or Monotheism and Holy War, burst onto the scene on October 7, 2004, bombing the Hilton Hotel in Taba, near the Israeli resort of Eilat, and two campgrounds at nearby Ras Shitan, killing thirty-four people, many of them Israelis. Those attacks, which took place on a Jewish holiday, appeared to be aimed more at Israelis than at tourism in general.

On July 23, 2005, however, in the deadliest terror attack ever on Egyptian soil and one clearly aimed at European tourism, TJ suicide-bombers struck the Ghazala Gardens Hotel and two other sites in the southern Sinai resort town of Sharm al-Sheikh, killing sixty-four people, twenty of them foreigners and many of them Europeans.

On April 24, 2006, TJ suicide-bombers struck yet again, bombing two restaurants and a market popular with European tourists in the Red Sea resort of Dahab, halfway between Taba and Sharm al-Sheikh, killing twenty-one innocents, including three foreigners, and injuring eighty. Each assailant detonated his explosives belt at precisely 7:15 p.m. local time.

Following each attack, Egyptian security forces swarmed the Sinai Peninsula in an attempt to quash the terrorist movement, arresting hundreds of Bedouins. The first two campaigns failed to neutralize TJ. The third and most onerous sweep appears to have been more successful, but only time will tell if that is truly the case.

The Cairo cell gave notice of its existence on April 7, 2005, when an eighteen-year-old assailant blew himself up along with three foreign tourists, two French citizens, and an American, in Cairo's popular Khan al-Khalili Bazaar. Police quickly made three arrests. Among those picked up was Akram Mohamed Fawzi, the cell's alleged ringleader, but other operatives remained at large.

Twenty-three days later, on April 30, 2005, another member of the same cell jumped from a bridge into a central Cairo square, setting off a similar device, consisting of explosives packed with nails. He killed himself and wounded four foreign tourists—two Israelis, an Italian, and a Swede—and three Egyptians. The square houses the Egyptian Museum, a popular tourist attraction containing treasures from the tomb of Pharaoh Tutankhamun.

In a second incident on that same day, two veiled women, said to be the sister and the girlfriend of the man who had killed himself at the Egyptian Museum, fired at a bus carrying Austrian tourists near the Citadel in southern Cairo. None of the tourists was injured, but the sister shot to death her accomplice and then killed herself. Two other members of the cell were apprehended on the very day of the second attack, and the cell has not been heard from since.

On July 2, 2007, jihadists once again struck at tourism, this time in Yemen. A suicide car-bomber struck a group of Spanish tourists visiting the ancient Queen of Sheba Temple in northeastern Yemen's Marib Governate, killing seven Spanish tourists and two Yemenis.

The attack was staged by a twenty-one-year-old from Sana'a who was said to have been recruited and taught to drive by a taxi driver, who in turn reported to an Egyptian, the purported chief of the cell. The Egyptian was killed in a shoot-out with police in Sana'a, and forged passports and identification documents were found in his apartment. Four members of the cell were also killed in clashes with police, and nine alleged participants in the plot were arrested.

On January 18, 2008, Yemeni extremists struck again against tourists, killing two Belgians and two Yemeni and wounding four other Belgians in a shooting attack on a five-vehicle tourist convoy in south-central Hadramout Governate. The tourists, it seems, had been headed to Shibam, a historic town of mud-brick houses, some as high as nine stories.

Both attacks were claimed by the Yemen Soldiers Brigades (YSB), a self-described al-Qaida affiliate.

The fact that there is still tourism in Yemen, let alone in Hadramout, the ancestral home of Usama bin Ladin, where Islamic fundamentalist sentiment runs especially high, is testimony to the greed of travel agencies and ignorance of their clients.

Indeed, the countermeasure to the campaign against tourism is relatively painless for multinational corporations and their personnel: the avoidance, for the time being, of resorts in Muslim countries. Muslim countries dependent on tourism will take great issue with this advice, but the fact is that the attack in Tunisia, a virtual police state, and the two in Bali, considered safe because of its nature as a Hindu enclave, proved their vulnerability.

It is rare indeed for corporate personnel to be obliged to visit a resort. Repeatedly, in recent years, I have advised corporations to forego regional meetings in Cairo or Casablanca, and hold them instead in Cyprus or Malta. It is not advice I dispense with relish, but it does reflect current realities. There is simply no reason to place personnel at risk unnecessarily.

SECTION 3

■

DEALING WITH KIDNAPPINGS, EXTORTIONS, THREATS

■

Chapter Twelve

CHAOS BREEDS KIDNAPPING

Kidnapping is bred by chaos. Ransom kidnappings overwhelmingly take place in areas in which law enforcement is weak. Where law enforcement is ineffectual, kidnapping, for terrorists or criminals, is a low-risk, high-reward undertaking.

Conversely, where law enforcement is strong, as in the United States, Canada, the United Kingdom, France, other parts of Western Europe, Japan, and Australia, ransom kidnappings are a relative rarity. When they do occur, perpetrators almost invariably are arrested, making kidnapping a high-risk activity for criminals. In general, more-sophisticated criminals seek opportunities elsewhere, leaving the field to amateurs.

Professional law-enforcement services generally have little trouble solving kidnappings. Indeed, in no other crime (with the possible exception of extortion) is there a protracted dialogue with the criminals (the negotiation), leading to close contact between the criminals and the victim's sponsors (the ransom delivery), followed, ideally, by the release of the victim, who has lived for a period of time among the kidnappers. This chain of events gives police, especially agencies with first-rate technical capabilities, unique opportunities to develop investigative leads.

Weakness in police services generally has two principal roots, which often go hand in hand: an absence of professionalism and a culture of corruption. These two factors have enabled Nigerian kidnap gangs to run rampant in the country's oil-rich Niger Delta.

They also have been major factors in the development of the kidnapping problem in Mexico, where police services, especially state agencies, are notorious for protecting kidnap gangs or even staging abductions themselves.

A shortfall in police professionalism also has been a major factor in the recent ballooning of kidnappings in Venezuela. President Hugo Chavez, the country's leftist strongman, has de-professionalized police services, replacing officers experienced in handling kidnappings with novices considered more reliable politically.

There are exceptions to this rule, but relatively few. Colombian police services generally are quite professional. Still, kidnappings spiked there in the 1980s and '90s simply because they were overwhelmed by the FARC insurgency. At its peak in the 1990s, FARC had operating cells in all parts of the country, including the major cities, and controlled vast swaths of rural territory, making it easy for guerrillas to hold hostages for long periods of time with little risk of a rescue. In recent years, President Alvaro Uribe's successful counterinsurgency campaign has placed the guerrilla movement on the defensive, pinning down its forces for the most part in remote rural areas. Kidnappings have gone down appreciably.

Not all countries with weak law enforcement develop kidnapping problems. Indeed, it is not unusual for one country to develop a serious problem, while a neighboring state, with comparable law-enforcement capabilities, experiences few cases. For example, kidnapping is an enormous problem in Honduras but not so in neighboring Nicaragua. The explanation, to a degree, may lie in cultural differences, but in many cases the cultures of the two countries are reasonably similar.

What accounts for this phenomenon? **To a large degree, kidnapping is contagious, particularly within a given country.** (Media coverage sometimes helps the contagion spread beyond a country's borders, but this phenomenon is less clear-cut.) A criminal gang stages a kidnapping and collects a ransom. Gang members boast of their success to criminal acquaintances, who then decide to attempt an abduction of their own. Sooner or later, a particular case garners media attention, alerting still other criminals to opportunities for easy money.

Over time, ransoms escalate, as kidnappers become more adept at negotiation and obtain a better appreciation of payment possibilities. Over the past three years, ransom payments have risen dramatically in Nigeria's Niger Delta, as relatively unsophisticated kidnapping gangs have gained an appreciation of just how much multinational oil and oil-service companies are willing to pay to secure the release of kidnapped employees.

Kidnap gangs do not necessarily key on foreigners employed by multinational corporations. Indeed, the belief, widely held among corporate decision makers, that American and European managers are more likely to be kidnapped than their local peers, is mistaken. Indeed, the Nigerian case is something of an exception.

There have been other instances in which kidnappers have feasted on foreign managers and technicians: Argentina, where leftist guerrillas collected huge ransoms for foreign executives in the early 1970s; El Salvador and Guatemala, where guerrilla groups abducted foreign managers in the late 1970s and early '80s; Colombia, where FARC and its sister leftist guerrilla movement, the National Liberation Army (known by the Spanish abbreviation ELN), became quite adept at dealing with multinationals.

As a general rule, however, kidnapping gangs, especially those that are purely criminal in nature, prefer to victimize fellow nationals. Why? Probably because they believe that abductions of foreigners bring them too much heat. Local authorities become agitated. The victim's embassy gets into the act, and perhaps law-enforcement agencies from his home country respond. Also, there are the problems of entering unknown territory—and dealing with a far-away corporate entity, rather than a family.

The preference of many kidnapping gangs for targeting locals, of course, does not get multinational corporations off the hook. Gangs targeting affluent locals cannot be counted upon to differentiate between entrepreneurs and senior managers employed by

multinational corporations. **Indeed, it is not unusual for them to assume that the general manager of a given factory in fact owns the facility, especially if the name on the door is not readily identifiable as a major multinational.**

Kidnapping gangs vary in the way they target entrepreneurial or managerial families. Some key on the breadwinner, while others prefer to leave him (or her) free to raise the ransom and focus on his (or her) children. Wives also are taken on occasion, but not as often as children. Modern divorce statistics may have something to do with this phenomenon. Papa, some gangs appear to believe, will be more disposed to pay a large ransom for his offspring than for his mate.

Most kidnap gangs carefully study prospective targets. After all, they don't want to waste their efforts on victims whose families or sponsors cannot raise sizable ransoms and they certainly do not want to take unnecessary risks in staging their assaults. (The exception to this rule is countries in which law enforcement has broken down to the point that the kidnappers' risks are negligible. Colombia was in that state a few years back, and Nigeria's Niger Delta recently has been in this condition. In these countries, gangs have run rampant, taking any corporate-linked foreigner— indeed, any foreigner they can get their hands on. In Colombia, guerrillas were notorious for "fishing" at roadblocks, while in Nigeria, kidnappers, in addition to ambushing foreigners along the roads, have raided bars and even residential compounds.)

In countries in which law enforcement is sufficiently robust to present would-be kidnappers with appreciable risks, they are much more deliberate in preparing abductions. As part of their homework, they may read the newspapers, especially the business and society pages, in search of viable targets. Or they may stake out expensive schools or golf courses. Finally, they normally follow prospective victims for a time as part of their assault planning, to minimize risks of being caught.

Prospective victims can reduce their risks by lowering their profiles, by being as unpredictable as possible, and by learning to read surveillances and other indictors of an attack.

Not all executives, however, can lower their profiles and still perform effectively. And not all can make themselves unpredictable by varying the times at which they arrive at and depart the office. Higher-profile managers and those who must be predictable may be obliged to hire bodyguards. Their children also may require protection. It is almost impossible to impose unpredictability on children, who, perforce, must arrive and depart schools at a fixed hour. This enforced predictability may help to explain their attraction to kidnappers.

More will be said in later chapters about unpredictability, surveillance recognition, and the use of bodyguards and armored cars.

It is important to point out that this discussion has centered on ransom kidnapping. There are several other categories of abduction. Al-Qaida has been known to kidnap Westerners with the objective of beheading them, to sow terror among their peers. Sexual predators kidnap children to abuse them. Parents sometimes stage kidnappings in connection with custody disputes.

Even among those who kidnap for ransom, there are wide differences in the treatment of hostages. Here, cultural differences seem to be decisive. Kidnapping gangs in Chechnya, in the Russian Federation's northern Caucasus region, are among the cruelest and are prone to cutting off hostages' fingers and sending them to their families as a negotiating ploy. Some (though certainly not all) Mexican and Guatemalan gangs also mutilate, and there have been instances in which they have sent parents videos of their daughters being raped.

Colombian kidnappers generally do not mutilate, which has earned them the reputation of being somewhat more civilized than their counterparts elsewhere. FARC and the ELN, however, because they control territory, are wont to hold hostages interminably, which can take an enormous psychological toll.

Still, in my experience, hostages who enjoyed good mental health at the time of their seizure and were treated relatively humanely have emerged from the ordeal with their stability intact. I confess to being in awe of Fernando Araujo, who escaped from his FARC kidnappers on the last day of 2006 after an astounding six years in captivity and was named Colombia's foreign minister just six weeks later. On the other hand, hostages who had psychological problems before they were abducted emerge from their ordeal often with far greater problems.

The Araujo case, unfortunately, is not the only example of an interminable kidnapping in Colombia. Three Americans, whose light aircraft made an emergency landing in rebel territory in February 2003, were held by FARC until July 2008, when they were rescued in dramatic fashion by the Colombian army. The Americans, employed by a Northrop Grumman subsidiary, had been searching for cocaine labs on a US government contract. FARC had been trying to trade them for guerrilla prisoners.

Economic hostages generally receive better treatment than their political counterparts. I worked one case in the early 1990s in which three American oil-service technicians were held for thirteen months by the ELN in northern Colombia before their release could be obtained. The three reported relatively civilized behavior on the part of their abductors. They had been kept together, which helped maintain their morale, were given books, were fed fairly well (generally the same rice-based dishes their abductors ate), and had gotten a lot of exercise, as their captors marched them periodically from one camp to another.

When they came out, we immediately put them through the usual battery of medical and psychological tests. To my surprise and delight, all passed with flying colors.

Early in the kidnapping, we had been worried about the health of one of the hostages, who took daily medication for hypertension, and we tried through the good offices of the local bishop to communicate to the kidnappers his need for the medicine. We were never successful in getting this message across, but it turned out that our efforts were unnecessary. The hostage, it seems, had lost thirty-five pounds during his captivity and, when he came out, no longer required his pressure pills.

I want to make it clear that, in recounting this case, I am in no way endorsing "the ELN Diet." Indeed, thirty years in the business of recovering hostages has left me with nothing but contempt for kidnappers. **Kidnapping, whether it is undertaken purely for economic reasons or for political motives—to sustain an insurgency or simply make a point—can never be justified. It is among the most despicable of the activities in which the depraved, felonious fringe of our species engages.**

Chapter Thirteen

KIDNAPPING: THE ULTIMATE CORPORATE NIGHTMARE

I have given countless presentations to corporate crisis management teams to prepare them for the decisions they will face in securing the release of a kidnapped employee. It is not an especially upbeat presentation, for an effort to secure the release of a kidnap victim is fraught with pitfalls, with decision makers in many instances obliged to pick the "least bad option."

The leave-taking of the participants, at the end of the presentation, is always the same: "We love you, Mike, but we hope we never have to use your services." Indeed, the overwhelming majority of those who undergo crisis management training never do call me in an emergency, suggesting that corporations that prepare themselves for the eventuality of a kidnapping and take sensible precautions by and large are not victimized.

The Crisis Management Team (CMT) normally consists of a decision maker, usually the CEO or his designee; a coordinator, often the head of international operations or the corporate security director; the general counsel or his designee; a finance officer; a human resources officer; and a media-relations specialist. The coordinator, as his title implies, is the most active member of the CMT. It is he who devotes the greatest amount of time to the recovery effort. The other team members, meanwhile, go about their other duties, though they may confer frequently about the case.

The three key members of the team are the decision maker, coordinator, and general counsel, and we sometimes refer to them as the triad. The roles of the first two are obvious. The general counsel plays a key role because the recovery effort often involves legal questions, both in the country in which the kidnapping has taken place and in the victim's home country. More about those later in the chapter!

The first critical decision facing the Crisis Management Team is the selection of a responder, the specialist retained by most corporations to help them navigate the crisis, and, ideally, this should be done in advance of an emergency. Many corporations that purchase KR&E insurance find that the decision is taken out of their hands: they are obliged to use the responder retained by their insurance carrier if they wish to be reimbursed for the responder's fees, which can be considerable. (Some major multinationals, at the time the insurance is bound, insist that their contracts be modified to allow them to use a responder of their choice, but this is relatively unusual.)

I have often wondered why savvy risk managers purchase policies that tie the hands of their corporation in this manner. Why be obliged to use a particular responder, and why use a responder so closely tied to the insurance carrier? Doesn't the tie-in at a minimum raise the possibility that the responder will act in the best interests of the carrier that retains him rather than in the interests of the insured?

We have been retained for thirty years by Chubb Corporation, a major US insurance carrier but under an arrangement that is, to my knowledge, unique, at least among the majors. Although Chubb recommends that its insured utilize our services, it is prepared to pay the fee of any reputable responder the insured chooses to use.

If the insured selects us, we stipulate in a brief contract that decision making is entirely its domain. That is the way it should be. It is our job to put recommendations before our client; decisions are his. Certainly, the carrier should have no role whatsoever in decision making.

In addition to independence, there are several qualities to look for in a responder.

First among them is operating philosophy. Does the responder aim to secure the release of the hostage through negotiation, or by kicking down a door? We are pure negotiators and have never attempted a rescue. Indeed, I could envision recommending this course of action to a client only as the absolute last resort—if there were no hope of resolving the kidnapping through negotiation and we believed the hostage to be in imminent danger of execution. I suspect that some of my former SEALs would relish an opportunity to conduct such an operation, and certainly they would be eminently qualified to do so, but I for one hope the situation never presents itself.

Second is experience. Perhaps the most important attribute of a responder—the main reason for retaining him in the first place—is the fact that he has been through this before, ideally with a strong track record of success. The recovery process is not for the uninitiated. If you think otherwise, please read on.

The third thing to look at is the responder's conception of his role in the negotiation. Some cast themselves as advisers. I don't know about you, but when I am hiring a lawyer, a surgeon, or a plumber for that matter, I am not looking for an adviser. I want someone who will roll up his sleeves and accomplish the task at hand, while deferring to me for critical decision making, for example, whether to bring suit, whether to have surgery, whether to install a $100 faucet or a more expensive one. Even in the decision-making process, I expect to be guided by strong recommendations, not cover-your-ass pronouncements about the potential pitfalls of various options that put the burden of decision making squarely on *my* shoulders.

Our firm prides itself on being full service and hands-on. We conduct the negotiation, deal with the police, protect the ransom money, even deliver it, if it is appropriate to do so. Our recommendations are always straightforward, though it is the client corporation's prerogative to accept or reject them.

We are also very conscientious about providing reports to the client. Indeed, they receive a transcript of every contact with the kidnappers no later than the following morning, along with a proposed script for the next contact, on which they are asked to sign off.

The fourth quality to look for in a responder is language competence. The responder ought to be able to operate in the language of the kidnappers, even if it is not intended that he speak directly with them. Sometimes, as in the case of some esoteric dialect, one has to depend on an intermediary. Indeed, in most instances, responders use locals to talk with kidnappers, since it is inadvisable to introduce a communicator who obviously comes from abroad. But ideally, the responder should understand what is being said. It is inexcusable for him not to be able to follow the dialogue if it is in a major international language, such as Spanish, Portuguese, or French.

The final critical attribute of a responder is availability. You must be confident that you can reach him immediately in the event of an emergency call to the CMT. I am accustomed to taking emergency calls in the middle of the night and am always a little taken aback by the fact that callers are pleasantly surprised to have reached me. It has to be that way. This is one situation that will not wait until the next morning or next business day. The responder has to be available twenty-four hours a day, seven days a week, and he has to have staff members pre-positioned in regions in which emergencies are likely to occur.

Even if the corporation retains a full-service responder, it is in for a rough ride. Decision making in a kidnapping can be—and usually is—onerous.

The challenge of a kidnapping quickly distinguishes the strong occupants of the executive suite from the weak. Strong executives reluctantly rise to the challenge that has been thrust upon them but with full appreciation that the life of an employee—to say nothing of the reputation of their corporation—is at stake. Weaker individuals, on the other hand, run for cover, sensing that they are ill-prepared for the life-and-death decision making and that failure of the enterprise could scuttle their careers; they delegate the responsibility for securing the safe release of the hostage to someone down the line, often far down the line.

In one case relatively early in my career, the chief operating officer (COO) of a major US multinational managed to place the decision making on my shoulders. The kidnappers, Colombians, had levied upon the company a sizeable demand and threatened, as they usually do, to kill the hostage if it were not satisfied in full. We had developed information to the effect that they, indeed, had killed a hostage in a previous case, but we also had learned that that negotiation had been horribly mishandled.

With the COO's blessing, we had made an offer that was substantially less than the demand, and, though the kidnappers still were holding to their figure, they gave us every indication that we were getting close to a settlement. We were encouraged, but the COO was growing impatient and was terrified by the death threat. He sent me a message through his corporate security director, an FBI veteran who was on the scene with me, that I was authorized—though not directed—to offer the full amount being sought by the kidnappers, an action that would have completely undercut our negotiating stance.

The security director was shocked by the gambit, as was I, and let me know that he would not blame me in the least if I met the full demand, which was the only way I could take the monkey off my back. I could not do so in good conscience, however, and held fast to the strategy that had previously been approved. The case was settled, on my terms, within forty-eight hours.

Months later, I was surprised to read that the COO had been promoted to chief executive officer, but his tenure was exceptionally brief. Presumably, his lack of intestinal fortitude had played out in other aspects of his job as well and had become obvious to his board.

Allow me a word on the preparation of executives for life-and-death decision making. Aside from crisis management presentations specifically aimed at this subject, there is none. Any sergeant in the army or the Marine Corps is better equipped to make life-and-death decisions than most senior executives. This should surprise no one. The subject is not taught in business schools, and certainly no one would expect that it would be. Most business schools, however, do not give their students even a basic appreciation of the impact that terrorism may have on their companies-to-be. On the contrary, the emphasis at business schools on financial decision making may be counterproductive to the task at hand: Throwing money at kidnappers is about the worst thing a decision maker can do.

In a considerable number of cases, incidentally, the role of decision maker or coordinator in a recovery operation is assigned to a military or law-enforcement veteran. In general, such an individual performs admirably, provided that he or she is sufficiently senior in the corporate structure to be confident there won't be second-guessing.

Ideally, corporations, immediately after selecting their responder, should prepare for an emergency by installing a certain amount of infrastructure in areas with high kidnapping risks. First and foremost is the dissemination of instructions to local personnel to immediately contact a member of the CMT—and, secondarily, the responder—in the event of a kidnapping or suspicious disappearance. (Disappearances sometimes prove embarrassing to all concerned. More than once in my experience, individuals who were reported to CMTs as missing in action have turned up a day or two later, having gone off on a short jaunt with a paramour. Still, disappearances in areas in which kidnapping is a problem have to be investigated.)

The CMT member receiving the emergency call immediately summons other key members of the team to a meeting, often using a code word such as "condition red" to convey urgency. He then calls the responder, who normally participates in the initial meeting of the CMT via speakerphone.

Early notification of the CMT, and the responder, is critical because important decisions made in the early hours of a kidnapping cannot be undone. One of the most important early decisions involves the notification of the police. In the United States, notification of the FBI is a no-brainer. We can count on the Bureau to conduct itself professionally and with due regard for the safety of the hostage.

Kidnappings abroad, especially in developing countries, are a different story—for two reasons. First, police in some countries are notoriously corrupt and either stage kidnappings or protect those who do. Mexico and Argentina in particular have had problems with corrupt policemen. Moreover, even if the police are above reproach, their agenda is different from that of the victim corporation. Our first priority is the safe, early return of the hostage. Police agencies, on the other hand, while concerned about the safety of the hostage, consider the arrest of the kidnappers to be their first priority.

Their position is entirely understandable. As representatives of the community, their objective is to stem the kidnapping problem. Certainly, they do not want to see kidnappers get a big payday. (Good police officers hate the idea of passing money to criminals. Indeed, this attitude is so strong and so universal among good policemen that it often helps us to separate the good from the bad. I will never forget a case I worked in Mexico, into which a state police agency had been brought in even before we were. Its representative sat in on strategy sessions and kept insisting that we were doomed to failure because we simply were not offering the kidnappers enough.)

Our interests are not those of the community. Seen from the police perspective, we are being selfish. Indeed, I have heard many people, in the abstract, decry the payment of ransoms, but I've never seen a parent, sibling, spouse, or employer of a hostage place community above proprietary interests.

Police almost invariably want to follow our man when he delivers the ransom. Again, this makes sense from their point of view. The delivery is the only point in most kidnappings in which we have close contact with the bad guys. The police want to apprehend the kidnapper on the spot and interrogate him, forcing him to reveal where the hostage is being held. The interrogation, of course, is a prelude to a raid on that location. This course of action makes perfect sense to many policemen. It is certainly not in the best interests of the hostage. In the environments in which we usually work, even under the best of circumstances with the most professional SWAT (Special Weapons and Tactics) teams, the chances of his surviving a raid are no better than 50 percent.

In developing countries, we always object to police intervention in the delivery in the most strenuous terms possible. I have spent many an hour trying to convince senior police officials that

it is possible to pay a ransom to secure the release of a hostage and then arrest the kidnappers, often through leads obtained in the course of the negotiation.

I'll never forget a case that I worked in the 1980s in the Dominican Republic. The victim was the seven-year-old son of a Dominican corporate manager, and cases involving kids are always the most heartrending, the most difficult to work. As in the Mexican case referred to above, the police had been notified early on, even before we were, and they were more than suspicious of the gringo who, they soon learned, presumably through a tap of the victim family's home phone, had been summoned to lead the negotiation.

I set up a meeting with the victim's parents at their home at 6:00 a.m. on the morning after my arrival, hoping the police would not be on the job as yet. I was wrong. They were waiting for me in the lobby of my hotel (all peering at me from behind newspapers in classic Hollywood fashion), then following my taxi to the meeting, making no attempt whatsoever at discretion. I felt as if I were leading a parade.

After talking with the family, I was summoned to a meeting with the police general. As I rode to the meeting, I rehearsed over and over my arguments against police intervention. I would point out the overwhelming importance to all parties of preserving the life of a seven-year-old. He would counter by assuring me that his men were fully capable of staging a rescue.

I entered the chief's office, only to encounter a bit of serendipity. Twenty years earlier, during a leftist insurrection, I had gone to the Dominican Republic as a CIA operative and had briefly crossed paths with the general, then a young captain. We recognized each other and traded a couple of war stories. Then we got down to business, with the discussion going much along the lines I had envisioned.

I begged him to let me do it my way, assuring him that I would go all-out after the boy's recovery to secure the arrest of the kidnappers. He finally agreed but wagged his finger at me, warning that I had better get the negotiation right—and help him get the arrest.

The negotiation was relatively quick, and the ransom payment was effected soon after sundown on the third day. Nervously, we waited for the release of the young hostage—always the most angst-ridden part of any recovery effort. Perhaps it would come during the evening. Possibly, the youngster would be dropped off at a clinic, something kidnappers often do. No such luck!

I slept very little that night, and the next morning, when I went down to breakfast, I found that I had little appetite. Then the call came from the general. He was sending a car for me. So much for the old days! I was in for a major dressing down, if not worse.

The general was about twenty minutes into his harangue, berating me not only for impeding his investigation (for which he repeatedly threatened prosecution) but also for getting the victim killed, when the news came. The youngster had been discovered, alive and well, in a "hot-pillow" motel, the kind that rents its rooms by the hour. What had happened?

Well, the boy in fact had been dropped off the previous night, with a small supply of food and water. The kidnappers apparently chose that particular motel because each room had its own garage—to protect the identities of the "guests." The kidnappers apparently felt that the garage would afford them the opportunity to drop off the young victim without being observed. Why did it take so long to discover the boy? Business, it seems, was slow, and the maid had not entered the room to clean it until the next morning.

The news of the boy's discovery was followed shortly by another positive development. The kidnappers apparently did not know that Dominican motels of a certain reputation were required by the police to note the license plates of all customers. The clerk had complied with this directive, and the plate had checked out as legitimate. The kidnappers were arrested within the hour. No one, with the possible exception of the police chief, was happier than I was.

In many instances, as in the Dominican case, the abduction itself is witnessed by several people who immediately call the police, so the victim corporation has no alternative but to cooperate with them. In most other instances, the CMT makes the decision to notify the police, which is perfectly fine with us as responders. We want to have input, however, into the choice of the police agency, and in some cases the specific officer, to be notified. In many countries there are several police services, and there may be vast differences in professionalism among them. Ideally, we want to work with a well-reputed senior officer of the country's most professional police service. In many instances, we will have cooperated with him previously, and perhaps succeeded in obtaining arrests, which may make it easier to convince him to give us some latitude.

The process of communicating with the kidnappers merits some discussion. The most important point to bear in mind in this regard is the fact that the kidnappers dictate the means and the pace of negotiations. There is little that we can do to change this. I don't have their numbers in my Rolodex. There is really nothing we can do but wait for them to contact us. Some kidnappers, well aware that we are desperate for news of the hostage, are in no rush to make the initial contact. They routinely use time as a weapon.

The means of communications has evolved over the years. In the past, incoming communications usually took the form of written messages or telephone calls. Today, we are just as likely to receive e-mails, which may be traceable but almost always originate in anonymous locations, such as Internet cafés.

We may be obliged to respond by telephone or by placing an ad in a local newspaper. In some cases, kidnappers deliver written messages or send e-mails directing us to place ads with specific wording, specifying a telephone number that they can call.

I'll never forget one case in Cochabamba, Bolivia, in which the kidnappers of a corporate executive directed us to place an ad specifying that we had lost a brown female Doberman and were offering a reward for her recovery. We supplied a telephone number and, agonizingly, took eleven calls from people claiming to have found the Doberman before the one we were waiting for finally came through. Cochabamba is not a huge city, and I was astounded that there were so many lost brown Dobermans at large in its confines.

I have very little to say here about the negotiating process, as it is not my intention to share our strategies or methods with prospective kidnappers. **I will say, however, that it is almost always necessary to negotiate, rather than merely agree to the kidnappers' ransom demand.**

The reason is simple. Apart from cop shows on television, there is no such thing as a simultaneous exchange of ransom for hostage. The kidnappers insist on picking up the money, counting it, and preparing their escape before releasing the hostage.

Because there are no simultaneous exchanges of ransom for hostage, there is nothing to prevent the kidnappers from accepting delivery of an agreed-upon amount and then demanding a second payment, a process we call double-dipping. Indeed, the likelihood of a double-dip increases exponentially if negotiators accept the kidnappers' initial demand. They can only draw the conclusion that they had not asked for enough.

Ultimately, most kidnapping gangs do release their hostages. What is their incentive for doing so? The answer is simple. They are in the business of selling hostages for ransoms and, to preserve their "reputation" in the marketplace, they are obliged to deliver the goods.

The closest I ever came to a simultaneous exchange was in the early 1980s in Guatemala. When I demanded proof of survival prior to payment of the agreed-upon ransom (a prerequisite for any ransom delivery), the kidnappers of an American oil-service technician—an unusually unsophisticated lot—invited me to helicopter to a specific point in the Petén jungle, where they would display the hostage. Upon confirming that the hostage was okay, we were to drop the ransom and then leave the area for no less than twenty minutes, during which time they would make good their escape.

The oil-service company's Guatemalan pilot and I set out in the helicopter and followed the agreed-upon script, observing the hostage, dropping the ransom and then departing the area for the requisite twenty minutes. Then we choppered back in and picked up the hostage, who had been held at gunpoint during his captivity and, needless to say, was delighted to see another American. Once the hostage was in hand, we notified the Guatemalan authorities of what had gone down, and they had no trouble intercepting the kidnappers. Indeed, there was only one road out of the area.

While the rationale for negotiating makes sense to the detached reader, it does not necessarily register with the hostage's loved ones, whose deep emotional investment in the outcome understandably clouds their objectivity. I have spent many an hour painstakingly explaining to them that I share their objective of getting the hostage back as quickly as possible, but that the failure to conduct a serious negotiation could actually lengthen his or her time in captivity.

It is critically important to keep family members informed of developments in the recovery process and onboard with the general strategy. There have been instances, albeit never in a case that I have worked, in which relatives of the hostage, convinced that the company was not doing enough to secure his release, made their case in the media. Such criticism not only tarnishes the firm's image, it also can impede the negotiation by conveying to kidnappers the impression that pressure is building on the victim company to settle the matter on their terms.

While open communications with the hostage's family in most cases can stave off a family initiative to take the case to the media, little can be done to prevent the threat of a lawsuit, especially when the hostage is an American. It usually does not take long for the family attorney to recognize the potential in a kidnapping for a payday. Most threatened suits hinge upon the company's alleged failure to have properly warned the victim that he was putting himself at risk and to have properly protected him. The recovery effort may also figure in the suit, though less often. In most instances, settlements are made before the lawsuits come to trial: companies that have just been through a kidnapping have little taste for reliving the nightmare in court.

Often, we are obliged to negotiate matters other than the size of the ransom. As suggested in the Guatemalan case discussed above, there must be agreement on the ground rules for the ransom delivery, and negotiations sometimes stall over this issue.

The classic example of this was the 1991 kidnapping of Mauricio Macri, then president of the Boca Juniors soccer club and now the mayor of Buenos Aires. (The Macri family has given me license to discuss the case, which has been chronicled in-depth in Argentina.) There was relatively quick agreement on the ransom amount, but the negotiation bogged down over delivery arrangements. The kidnappers insisted that the delivery be made by Franco Macri, Mauricio's dad and one of the most prominent businessmen in the country. Franco was inclined to agree to the demand. "It is something that a father has to do for a son," he told me. But I was equally determined not to place this powerful industrialist in the sights of the kidnappers. It was bad enough that they had his adult son in hand.

The atmospherics of this case were unusual. It had become public, and, since Franco's profile in Argentina was akin to that of Donald Trump in the United States, the media was camped out en masse outside his Buenos Aires mansion. I was holed up inside, arguing with Franco good-naturedly about whether or not he would make the delivery, when it occurred to me that we might use the media presence to our advantage. Franco was well known to have a heart condition and was being visited every day by his personal physician. I suggested that we conspire with the physician to stage a "cardiac episode" that would confine Franco to bed and thus exclude him from a role in the ransom delivery.

Franco liked the idea, and the physician agreed to take part in the ruse. He left the mansion after his regular morning visit, only to return minutes later on the run. Then an ambulance showed up, and finally an oxygen tank was delivered—all grist for the media mill. At that point, the doctor stepped outside the mansion and announced that Franco had suffered a cardiac episode. Since he wanted to continue to participate in the negotiation, he had rejected the doctor's advice to go to the hospital, but he had agreed to confine himself to bed.

The kidnappers called within a couple of hours and agreed to accept a ransom delivery by Mauricio's chauffeur. Franco and I did not learn until Mauricio was released later that evening that our plot had received an important assist from the hostage. When the kidnappers told him that his father had suffered a heart problem, Mauricio had the presence of mind to advise them to seal the deal quickly. If his father died, he warned, his brothers wouldn't pay a cent for him.

One of the most difficult aspects of a recovery operation is protecting a large ransom. Perhaps my most harrowing experience in this regard was a case early in this decade in which eight oil-service technicians, seven Canadians and an American, were taken hostage by a mixed Ecuadorian-Colombian criminal gang, some members of which may have been former Colombian guerrillas, in Ecuador's oil patch, along that country's border with Colombia. Negotiations were long and difficult, but after several months a ransom of $3.5 million was agreed upon. It was further agreed that the ransom would be in US currency and that the delivery would be staged from the border town of Lago Agrio, a lawless area along the Colombia frontier.

That amount of dollars was not readily available at the time in Ecuador, and, with a wink from the Ecuadorian government, which had been involved in the negotiation from the outset and, along with its US and Canadian counterparts, had been looking over our shoulder, we decided to fly the ransom in by chartered jet. I flew to Quito with three former SEALs, who ostensibly were my bodyguards but were really focused on my carry-on luggage. Another former SEAL was already on the ground in the Ecuadorian capital, where he had arranged weapons for our party, again with a wink from Ecuadorian authorities. (Securing the appropriate weapons for a ransom detail is always a challenge. There is no Hertz Rent-a-Gun.)

At Quito airport, our party transferred to a propeller aircraft for the short flight to Lago Agrio. Soon after landing, we learned that we had paid a price for taking the Ecuadorian government into our confidence. For political reasons I still fail to grasp, the interior minister had held a press conference and announced that the case of the eight oil-service technicians would be resolved soon and that a ransom of $3.5 million had been agreed upon.

Well, everyone in the country could surmise that the staging point for payment of the ransom would be Lago Agrio, which is the kind of place where a person could be killed for far less than $3.5 million. Our stout party could do nothing but try to make us look invincible, something that appears to come naturally to SEALs. No one, not even local criminal gangs that undoubtedly had superior numbers and firepower, wanted to take them on. I can't tell you how many times during my sojourn in Lago Agrio and in subsequent years I have congratulated myself for having had the foresight to bring them along.

The kidnappers did not make matters easy for us. We had arranged to have a local priest make the delivery. Priests are excellent for this sort of thing. They are in the business of saving souls and thus often willing to undertake deliveries. Also, they are usually well known locally and are considered trustworthy by the bad guys. (Following a successful delivery, I am always happy to make a contribution to the priest's parish. Indeed, I am probably one of the larger Jewish contributors to Catholic parishes in Latin America.)

We thought we had a bit of good luck, because the kidnappers radioed us the very night that we arrived in Lago Agrio and told us to stand by for an imminent delivery. The priest departed with the loot about thirty minutes later, and we settled back to await his return, relieved that the money was no longer in our direct possession. Three hours later, however, the priest returned with the cash in hand. Apparently, it had been a trial run.

We were obliged to sit on the ransom for another forty-eight hours. Finally, on the third night, the kidnappers arranged another delivery run, and this time they took the money. It took several days for the hostages, who were deep in the jungle, to be released, but all came back safe and sound.

The negotiating process is never easy. Kidnappers are the worst vermin, traders in human life. While some are reasonably straightforward in their dealings and take good care of their hostages, others are brutal, threatening to kill, rape, or mutilate. To deal with them is akin to undertaking the most delicate surgery.

For reasons I have never entirely understood, corporate decision makers have an even tougher time with mutilation threats than with death threats. Perhaps it is because death threats are levied, at least implicitly, by most kidnapping gangs. They are part of the package. Mutilation threats, on the other hand, are usually rendered very specifically.

A Mexican case comes to mind in this regard. The kidnappers, in this particular case, did not render a specific mutilation threat, but we were able to confirm by studying other cases in which they had been involved that they, indeed, had cut off the finger of one of their victims, apparently because an inexpert negotiator had managed to infuriate them by asking once too often for proof of survival.

(While a request for proof of survival is a legitimate part of the recovery process, and, indeed, a ransom should never be paid until kidnappers furnish proof that the victim is alive and well, repeated demands on the part of negotiators can be counterproductive. Proof of survival, incidentally, can come in a variety of ways: a photo of the victim holding up a current newspaper; a tape of him referring to a recent baseball score; a written message in his own hand; the answer to a question on some matter to which only the victim and a few loved ones are privy, such as the name of the hotel in which he spent his honeymoon.)

In any event, as you can imagine, we took more than the usual pains in this case not to offend the kidnappers in any way, and, as I said, there was never a threat of mutilation. Still, the prospect hung over the negotiation, and you can imagine our consternation when the victim's son received a phone call from the manager of a local service station, saying that he had "something" for him. We steeled ourselves for the transfer of a package containing an amputated finger—and you can imagine our delight when the son called and reported that he had dropped his wallet at the station and that the manager had called to return it to him. Under normal circumstances, he would have been delighted to have had his wallet returned, but he suggested to us that in this case the recovery of the lost article had not been worth the stress he suffered in the ten-minute drive to the station.

No client of mine has ever suffered a mutilation. I like to think that this record is attributable at least in part to the care we take in our negotiations, but I am exquisitely aware that good fortune has been a major contributor to this successful record. Sometimes, no matter how careful you are, you cannot control the sociopaths with whom you are obliged to deal.

Every recovery takes an immense toll, not only on the victim and his loved ones but also on corporate decision makers, who never want to reprise their role. Indeed, even hardened responders are wont to ask themselves why they got into this business to begin with and whether there isn't some better way to make a living.

Chapter Fourteen

CASES FROM HELL

C lients sometimes ask, rather sheepishly, about our success ratio. It is certainly a legitimate question. Ten years ago, I myself asked that question of a surgeon who was about to perform delicate surgery on my cervical spine. A bone spur was pressing on my spinal cord and impeding my mobility. It had to be removed. Removal involved tricky decompression of the spine, and there was a possibility of paralysis. When I asked the surgeon about the chances that I would wind up a quadriplegic, he answered this way: "For a surgeon with my qualifications, the chances are less than 5 percent." The key words, of course, were *with my qualifications.* In the hands of a less-qualified, less-experienced surgeon, the odds against a successful outcome clearly would increase. Fortunately for me, the surgeon performed brilliantly, and I awoke from anesthesia in full control of my extremities.

I've been personally involved in well over one hundred and fifty cases, and we have had three unsuccessful outcomes. In one case in Mexico, the victim was injured in the course of being abducted and, apparently, bled out. After finding blood in his automobile, we tried to accelerate the negotiation and quickly reached an agreement with the kidnappers, but they failed to provide proof of survival, and the case ended there. Paying money without proof of survival is a fool's game.

In another case, the victim had a heart attack and died during his lengthy incarceration in Colombia. The autopsy showed that the forty-two-year-old man had been suffering from advanced coronary artery disease. We had no idea that he even had a heart condition. Indeed, he had been kidnapped while jogging in the countryside (proving the folly of jogging in a high-risk area).

The third unsuccessful outcome involved a case in Guatemala in the early 1980s. A leftist insurgent group kidnapped an American executive and held him for several months, refusing to budge from its sky-high ransom demand. The police, meanwhile, were working against the insurgents and began to roll up their safe houses. This instilled a sense of terror in us, because we feared that it was only a matter of time until they came upon the house in which our hostage was being held. Our only recourse was to try to obtain a meeting with the police chief and beg him to proceed with caution. We didn't really believe that he would curb his successful campaign, but it was our only shot, and my representative was actually in the chief's office making our case when the bad news came in: The police in fact had entered a safe house, sparking a firefight, and the body of the American hostage had been found inside. The victim, it appeared, had been murdered by his captors as soon as the shooting began.

Unfortunately, we tend to learn more from cases that turned out badly than we do from cases that turned out well. What I learned from the three cases previously cited is that, no matter how great our sense of urgency about resolving a case, it is never sufficient. Always mindful of the toll that captivity takes on a hostage, both physically and mentally, we have made it our mission to resolve cases as quickly as possible. But rarely are we satisfied with the speed of resolution, for it is the kidnappers who control the tempo of the negotiation, and often they are determined to use time as a weapon against us.

It is in the spirit of learning from mistakes that I will offer some comments on a case in which we were not involved but that was documented in considerable detail in a June 30, 2001, *New York Times* article written by Joseph B. Treaster. It teaches several important lessons.

It was apparent from the start that the case would be a difficult one. In the wee hours of October 12, 2000, eight oil-service technicians, five Americans, a New Zealander, an Argentine, and a Chilean, were kidnapped from a camp in northern Ecuador's oil patch, not far from the Colombian border. Also taken were two French helicopter pilots. The assailants commandeered a helicopter and ordered the pilots to fly north, to a point just shy of the Colombian frontier. The hostages were separated into two groups, and the helicopter was abandoned. The French pilots managed to escape soon after the abduction, but not the technicians.

They were employed by three different companies, Helmerich & Payne Inc. of Tulsa, Erickson Air-Crane Inc. of Central Point, Oregon, and Schlumberger Ltd., with headquarters in New York. Each brought in its own response firm. Also around the strategizing table were officials of the Ecuadorian police and representatives of the FBI and the other interested governments.

Eighteen days after the abduction, the kidnappers levied their demand: $80 million. It was several times higher than the initial demand in the case in the very same region that we had resolved the previous year by paying $3.5 million, though it was suspected, on the basis of the kidnappers' communications MO, that they were linked to the previous case. For two weeks, the parties participating in the strategy sessions debated their first offer.

Some backed a hard line, while others proposed to be more generous, so a negotiation ensued among the responders, their sponsors, and the government officials as to the appropriate offer. Finally, more than a month after the hostages were seized, a consensus offer of $500,000 was put forward. (Our initial offer in the previous case had been $1 million against a $20 million demand.)

The kidnappers responded that the offer "had nothing to do with reality" and threatened consequences—a body thrown out onto a road.

The responders decided against raising their offer until the kidnappers reduced their $80 million demand, or at least provided answers to proof-of-survival questions.

On January 4, nearly three months after the kidnapping, the bad guys broke radio contact.

By the time they reinitiated communications eleven days later, the responders had changed communicators, and the new man assured the kidnappers that he was working to obtain permission to make a higher offer. He was given fifteen days to put serious money on the table.

On January 30, the companies offered $1 million. The next day, one of the American hostages, an employee of Helmerich & Payne, was found dead—wrapped in a sheet that bore the message: "I am a gringo. For nonpayment of ransom."

Understandably, the families of the remaining hostages, who until then had kept silent, became frantic. A vigil was mounted outside Erickson's Oregon headquarters. The father of one of the surviving Helmerich & Payne hostages went on CBS's *Early Show*, demanding that a ransom be paid for his son's release. An executive of the company was interviewed on the same show and was asked to respond. There was little he could say.

On the day the body was found, the kidnappers threatened to kill another hostage in fifteen days. The companies immediately raised their offer to $7.7 million. The kidnappers came down from their $80 million demand, and agreement was reached on a payment of $13 million.

What lessons can we glean from this case?

First, in my opinion, it is unwise to enlist three different response groups in a recovery effort, even if the victims come from different companies. If confronted with a similar situation, I would resist to the fullest participating in a joint effort, and would urge the companies to settle on a single response group, even if that firm were not my own.

We have never been faced with exactly that situation, but I do remember one case in which the hostage served on two different corporate boards and each dispatched a responder. The coordinator was inclined to employ us in tandem, but we both advised against it.

Some things, though precious few in my experience, are best done by committee. Recovering hostages is not one of them. There has to be one steady hand on the tiller.

If a client of mine were to insist that I participate in a joint effort with other responders, and I found myself faced with a situation in which I thought that a consensus offer would put our hostages at risk, I would recommend that we withdraw from the common negotiation and open a separate dialogue with the kidnappers. Undoubtedly, this would make us very unpopular with the other parties, but in the end it would protect our hostages. I have never been one for popularity contests.

The second lesson is that it is extremely difficult to get kidnappers to agree to a ransom substantially lower than has been paid to them in a preceding case involving hostages of a similar profile. In the case I just described, there were eight foreign hostages, the same number as in the case we had worked the previous year. The victims in both cases were technicians. The responders suspected, on the basis of communications MO and other indicators, that they were in fact dealing with the same band. They appeared to have believed that we paid too much for our hostages—in fact, I don't think we did. Whatever their feelings may have been, however, they were stuck with our precedent.

In ransom kidnapping, as in all other economic activity, there is a market price. We had set it. Had they garnered a 10 or 15 percent discount, the achievement would have been remarkable. Indeed, keeping the price in range of what we had paid would have been an accomplishment, because, as everyone knows, there is no gravitational pull to pricing. On the contrary, prices tend to rise.

Though knocking down the market price would have been difficult under any circumstances, it was an especially risky course in a case involving multiple hostages. Kidnappers holding several hostages have the opportunity to make an example of one of them. We were scrupulously aware of this possibility in our case, in which the kidnappers also threatened repeatedly "to throw a body onto a road."

The risk exists in any kidnapping that the bad guys will decide to make an example of a hostage. They can kill even a lone hostage, with the objective of intimidating future negotiating partners, although most do not think in these strategic terms. With multiple hostages, as the case under scrutiny clearly demonstrated, the effect of murdering a hostage is immediate—and devastating.

Chapter Fifteen

DEALING WITH EXTORTION

Multinational corporations are much more apt to be confronted with extortions than with kidnappings, and in many ways they can be equally insidious. Indeed, some types of extortions threaten the "brand," the company's reputation, even more directly and more severely than kidnappings do. Furthermore, the problem is much more widespread than kidnapping, which in general is confined to a relatively small number of countries. Extortions pop up everywhere and they take many forms:

- Guerrilla groups that engage in kidnapping and attack corporate properties sometimes demand the payment of "war taxes" to ensure against abduction or assault. Among the movements that levy war taxes are Colombia's FARC, Spain's Basque Land and Liberty (Basque acronym: ETA), and the Philippines' New People's Army (NPA). All have been relatively successful in raising revenues in this manner from companies operating on their turf. All three target both local and foreign companies.

- Organized-crime gangs also demand payments to "protect" personnel and property. The practice is especially common in the former Soviet Union, but it has also spread to Brazil and Central America. The gangs mainly victimize local firms, though approaches to multinationals certainly are not unknown.

- Singletons and smaller gangs, which I will group together under the heading "singletons," sometimes pose as guerrillas or large, organized-crime gangs to demand war taxes or protection payments. Again, both local and foreign firms are victimized.

- Other singletons that target corporate assets specialize in:

    —Threats to contaminate products, known as product-contamination extortions

    —Threats involving Web sites and databases, which are usually grouped under the heading of cyber extortion

While the nature of the extortion dictates the specific nature of the response, we generally are able to take a harder line in responding to extortionists than in negotiating with kidnappers. After all, to one degree or another, we still control—and can take steps to protect—the person or asset being threatened.

The protection of the person or asset being threatened is only half of the equation. The other half usually involves pursuit of the extortionists, an effort we invariably undertake in tandem with law-enforcement agencies. In my thirty years in the business, I have never been involved in a case in which we merely acceded to an extortionist's demand.

In some cases, we work only the defensive side of the equation. When confronted with demands from guerrilla movements, including FARC, ETA, and the NPA, for example, we recommend simply ignoring them and concentrating on bolstering defenses. In some instances, we may try to enlist the cooperation of local law-enforcement and military authorities in strengthening defenses.

The defensive effort, I must point out, should not encompass the formation of paramilitary groups, as wealthy landowners and rural-based businesses did in Colombia in the 1990s. Affluent Colombians, you will recall, encouraged the development of the AUC (United Self-Defense Forces of Colombia) in the hope that it would protect them from FARC. It was not long, however, before the AUC turned on its sponsors and began demanding regular protection payments. It was payments of this sort that got Chiquita Brands into so much hot water with the US government.

In my experience, even before the United States in 2001 passed the Patriot Act, making payments to terrorist groups illegal, multinationals generally had been reluctant to pay war taxes. In part, they acted out of principle, and in part, they adopted the stance because such payments are a sure way to infuriate the host governments that sanction their right to do business in their countries. The Colombian, Spanish, and Philippine governments, among others, have lobbied insistently against payoffs.

Extortions by organized-crime gangs, be they Russian or Eastern European mafias, or Brazilian or Central American gangs, bear a lot of similarities to extortions by guerrilla movements. In both cases, the threat is against personnel and/or property, and in both cases, the threatening entity undoubtedly has the capability to make good on it. Multinational corporations, however, appear to get something of a pass from the Russian mafias, and the Latin American gangs also key on local businesses, especially bus lines and small stores operating in working-class neighborhoods, and bars, restaurants, and nightclubs. In general, they have not worked their way up to threatening multinationals, at least not yet.

Our recommended response to extortion attempts by organized-crime gangs is much the same as it is for those originating with guerrilla groups: Ignore the demand and concentrate on bolstering defenses.

Singletons or members of small groups are another matter entirely. Often, they "fish" for victims, sending computer-generated letters or e-mails to a hundred or more companies, in the hope that one will bite. In many cases, they pose as guerrillas or representatives of larger organized-crime gangs, but their incoming messages are readily distinguishable from the genuine article. In any case, these fishing expeditions are easily distinguishable by their lack of specificity: other than the name in the salutation, there is no real reference to the individual or the company being threatened.

When our clients sustain approaches that are not company specific, our advice generally is to ignore them. The risks from fishermen are slight, and, usually, there is someone else out there willing to waste time and money chasing them down.

In a variation on the "fishing" theme, extortionists in Mexico, Brazil, and a few other Latin American countries phone potential victims, provide sketchy information about their families, and threaten dire consequences if a sum of money is not sent immediately to a particular bank account. Again, we look for specificity about victims' routines, not just information that might have been gleaned from a newspaper or elicited from a servant or coworker. If specificity is lacking, our advice generally is to ignore the approach and decline further calls from the perpetrator. Many of these calls originate from convicts with time on their hands. Indeed, payment is often demanded in the form of telephone charge cards, a sure tip-off that the call originates from prison.

Company-specific extortions from singletons or small gangs are treated differently. While they entail significant risks and need to be taken seriously, they also afford the greatest opportunity for us to work both sides of the equation—that is, to shore up defenses and pursue the offenders.

Threats can take a number of different forms. Extortionists may threaten to kidnap, kill, or harm personnel. Or, they may target a corporate property, Web site, or database, or threaten to contaminate a food product or pharmaceutical.

Product-contamination extortions peaked in the 1980s, while cyber extortions, as far as can be determined, reached their zenith in the early years of the current century.

Food and pharmaceutical manufacturers have improved the packaging of their products to discourage contamination, though from time to time a master counterfeiter will duplicate packaging and have a go at an extortion attempt.

Similarly, companies have become much more adept at protecting their IT assets from cyber-criminals threatening to cripple their Web sites via Distributive Denial of Service (DDoS) attacks or to steal customer lists or other sensitive information from their databases. The extortionists are still out there and still surface from time to time, but they are not nearly the problem they were just a few years ago.

Generally, we negotiate with singleton extortionists and small gangs and, in concert with the appropriate police agencies, attempt to lure him (them) to a payoff. The problem often lies in getting them to accept payment.

Extortionists, as a rule, lack courage. I suppose that if they *had* courage they would be out robbing banks. Sending out an extortion letter is easy, but coming forward to accept payment is a different story. They get to thinking about the risks and often back off at the last minute, leaving the case unresolved. That, incidentally, frustrates the hell out of responders like me, who like to tie up their cases with red ribbons.

On the other hand, some extortionists can be very sly. Germany suffered a spate of product-contamination extortions in the 1980s, in large part because perpetrators spotted a chink in law enforcement's armor. In Germany, the various states have jurisdiction over extortions, and at the time, the cooperation among them left a lot to be desired. Perpetrators typically would order the person making the payoff onto a train, wait until the train crossed one or more state borders, and then signal in some manner to toss the ransom. Meanwhile, state law-enforcement agencies would scramble, unsuccessfully, to follow the action. When coordination among state agencies improved, the problem faded away.

Generally, extortionists are not strategic thinkers. I have gone up against numerous perpetrators over the years, some with relatively ingenious collection scenarios, but never have I found a scenario that could not be defeated.

In one case, in Canada, the perpetrator, rightly concerned that the police had laid a trap for him, hired a male prostitute to pick up the ransom, while he himself hung back in a video game parlor. It didn't take the police long to pick up and flip the prostitute. By the time they got to the parlor, the extortionist had fled, but, based on identifying material provided by the prostitute and some denizens of the parlor, they arrested him within a few days.

While we normally work extortions in tandem with police agencies, the decision to take the matter to the authorities is never automatic. Client corporations are often reluctant to turn the matter over to police, either because they doubt their competence or because they believe that bringing in the police will add to their problems.

For example, not long ago I worked a case in Eastern Europe in which a banker had been contacted by a private detective who said that he had obtained a sensitive list of customer accounts and offered his services to uncover the source of the leak. Scams of this sort by shady private detectives are common in Eastern Europe, and when the gumshoe presented his exorbitant retainer proposal, bank officials quickly realized that they were being extorted.

The officials quickly discovered that an employee was the source of the leak and were able to link him, circumstantially at least, to the private detective. The case, gift-wrapped, was ready to be presented to the police. Bank officials, however, had understandable reservations about this course of action on several grounds. First, police agencies in the country in question were notoriously porous, and they feared that the press might quickly discover details of the embarrassing leak. Another concern was that the details would become public at trial. Some members of the CMT wanted simply to fire the errant employee, reject the private detective's proposal, and keep their fingers crossed that the matter would go away. (Corporate decision makers often express similar sentiments in dealing with frauds perpetrated by their employees. They are reluctant to take the case to the police for fear that media coverage of the matter will put the company in a bad light.)

We had to argue long and hard for notification of the police. While accepting the validity of the CMT's concerns, we pointed out that it was unlikely that the gumshoe would not find a way to release the embarrassing data if his proposal were turned down, especially since his confederate inside the bank was going to be fired. Thus, the more prudent course of action was to work with the police and hope that they would not only maintain confidences but also pressure the perpetrators to avoid bringing further problems upon themselves by releasing the data. Moreover, if the confidential information were to come out, the bank could assure the public that it had sealed the leak and was working with police to prosecute the perpetrators. In the end, our proposed course of action was accepted.

Dealings with foreign police agencies can be difficult on other grounds. Indeed, there is never complete agreement over how exactly to proceed.

In one case several years ago, in Colombia, we were faced with an extortionist who was threatening to poison a pharmaceutical product. We enlisted the cooperation of the police, and I immediately found myself in a confrontation with a police colonel about which of us was going to provide the communicator. The colonel insisted that it be a policeman, while I was intent on using the company's lawyer, whom I already had spent hours training. I wanted the communicator to identify himself as a corporate lawyer and was dubious that a cop, even one trained in the law, could pull off the ruse. Most cops use jargon that readily identifies them as such. Also, by accepting a police communicator, I would concede any shred of control over the conduct of the case.

We went back and forth with the colonel, who was understandably territorial and at one point threatened to throw me in jail. Ultimately, I prevailed, and the lawyer, who turned out to be very, very good, kept the perpetrator on the phone long enough for the police to identify the public phone he was using (again, this was before the throwaway cell phone) and arrest him. All's well that ends well! The colonel retired soon after the case ended and has long been associated with The Ackerman Group. Now that he is on our side of the fence, he sees the validity of using civilian communicators.

Not all apprehensions take place exactly as we, or the police, envision. In another Canadian case (Canada is not especially prone to extortions, but some of the more interesting cases in which I have been involved seem to have taken place there), an extortionist was threatening to contaminate a popular brand of milk. The authorities in Quebec Province, where the extortion took place, were particularly agitated, since children are the largest consumers of milk, and were determined to catch the perpetrator. The Surete Quebecois set up a massive operation to snag the culprit during a call to a company representative (again, these were the days before the throwaway cell phone) and, indeed, narrowly missed him when he called from a public phone booth outside Quebec City.

At that point, we had no option but to go to Plan B. The authorities put out on the airways a recording of the perpetrator's voice, which was somewhat distinctive. Tips flooded in from a public outraged by the threat to poison milk, and he was apprehended in a matter of hours.

Chapter Sixteen

DEALING WITH THREATS

All too often today, large corporations are obliged to deal with threats against personnel or property. Indeed, threats are more common than extortions and far more common than kidnappings.

Like extortions, threats are levied worldwide, but a great many are made in countries with primitive judicial systems. In such countries, and they include Russia, China, and many third world states, there is no tradition of taking disputes to court. Disputants thus are programmed to play hardball—a prospect with which multinationals, most of which are based in countries with strong legal traditions, often are ill-prepared to deal. Even in countries with strong legal systems, some disputants may be inclined to play hardball—to settle matters "out of court," so to speak.

In many cases, threats are delivered anonymously. The source of the threat is often quite apparent, but it is delivered in a manner that allows the individual levying it to plausibly deny responsibility.

In other cases, threats, many of them implicit or vague in nature, are delivered quite openly by disgruntled employees or those undergoing dismissal. In a surprising number of workplace-violence incidents, perhaps the majority, the assailant has made known his disgruntlement and the fact that he is considering violent action, to coworkers or even supervisors, and it is essential that employees be made aware of the importance of reporting even the vaguest of threats and of the procedure for doing so.

Indeed, the effective collection of information on potential perpetrators is one of four pillars of an effective workplace-violence-prevention program, along with preemployment screening, including background checks, diligent exit interviews, and comprehensive access controls.

Permit me a word on preemployment screening. I can't stress enough the importance of thorough background investigations, not only on prospective employees but also on joint-venture partners, franchisees, vendors, and distributors. Time and time again, I have come across instances in which violence has been threatened or actually perpetrated by employees and other individuals who never should have been brought onboard in the first place. Clearly, background investigations are an expense, but, in the long run, they result in dramatic cost savings.

Most threats worldwide, both anonymous and open, are delivered by disgruntled employees or by those who have been dismissed. Others are leveled by competitors, unhappy joint-venture partners, vendors, distributors who have fallen out of favor, or trade union leaders.

Threats are a means of playing hardball. In most cases, the person or organization leveling the threat has no intention of following through. The threat is simply conveyed as a form of harassment.

Often, by studying the threat, we can conclude that the perpetrator does not intend to take action, and we advise the victim company to put in place only minimal defensive measures, or no measures at all. In analyzing a threat, we examine the level of organization the perpetrator demonstrates in conveying it and the degree to which he appears capable of making good on it.

I am reminded of a case a few years back in which a shipping company received a fax stating that the sender had placed explosives aboard one of its container ships and that the vessel would "blow up" at sea. I was struck immediately by the sender's failure to spell out with any specificity his grievances against the company, and I was even more impressed by the grandiosity of his threat. While it was conceivable that he had placed a small bomb aboard the huge vessel, it was hard to imagine that he could blow it up.

Still, the company executive with whom I was dealing was understandably concerned, all the more so because we both were struck by the impracticality of conducting an explosives search aboard the vessel, which already was at sea. Even if we had been able to place sniffer dogs aboard the ship, they would have been next to useless, since they would have been hard put to differentiate between containers holding explosives and those that currently were carrying or had carried fireworks and even nitrogen-based fertilizer.

My best advice to the shipping company executive—given with some trepidation, I have to admit—was to do nothing. The client asked me to put it in writing, which I did reluctantly. The vessel arrived at its destination without incident.

Sometimes, the decision about the threat's validity has to be made on the spur of the moment. In this connection, I am reminded of a call I received from a casino operator, who had just hung up on someone who said that he had placed a bomb on his premises. The caller hadn't said where he placed the bomb or when it would explode, which didn't make much sense, since his objective in warning the casino about the bomb presumably was to avoid injuring innocents.

The casino operator was desperate. An evacuation would have meant leaving substantial amounts of money on the table, and sorting out its ownership would have been a nightmare. Again, with some trepidation, I advised against an evacuation. Again, nothing happened.

I don't want to suggest by any means that all threats should be taken lightly. In some cases, the disgruntled party does take action. Indeed, in Russia, in the heyday of the mafias in the 1990s, it was not uncommon for the threat message to be delivered through the beating of a local manager.

In any case, as with extortion demands, threats should be evaluated carefully by competent security professionals.

Threats differ from extortions insofar as there is no direct demand for money. The party making the threat is in fact often seeking financial gain, for example, a settlement package, the favorable dissolution of a joint venture, reinstatement as a vendor or distributor or a new labor contract. There is, however, no direct cash payout, no demand for delivery of a ransom.

This makes our response a more difficult proposition. Extortionists, after all, are mostly arrested in the process of accepting payment.

Corporations should do their utmost to prevent disputes from ripening to the point that threats are forthcoming. This certainly does not mean that they should give in to every potential adversary. But they should be sensitive to potential problems and do their utmost to deflect anger. Ideally, potential problems should be identified early and sent up the line, to a member or committee of the Crisis Management Team.

In some cases, it may be cost-effective to go the extra mile to settle a joint-venture dispute, offer "constructive alimony" to an errant vendor or distributor, make a symbolic concession to a trade union, or sweeten the termination package of a dismissed employee.

In other cases, where it is unlikely that the dispute can be settled amicably, careful consideration should be given to the means of delivering the corporation's message to the potential adversary. One of the biggest mistakes corporations make in handling disputes is to relegate delivery of bad news, a dismissal, for example, to personnel on the scene—the very people most likely to be threatened. Over the years, I repeatedly have advised companies to send in an outside official to convey unpleasant news as a means of deflecting blame from local colleagues. This advice pertains to operations both within the United States and abroad.

In many cases, we recommend that the outside official be accompanied to the fateful meeting, often an exit interview, by a security professional. The security professional performs several functions. First, he provides protection to a company official caught up in an unpleasant and potentially dangerous situation. Second, he has the opportunity to assess the potential adversary's propensity for violence.

(In some cases, we link the security professional to a psychologist or psychiatrist experienced in judging propensity for violence. The good ones can make this judgment from afar, based on written or oral threats levied by the adversary and the observations of the security professional.) Third, he can make recommendations for the protection, short term or long term, of local personnel and assets.

In general, whether or not we are present at the interview, we follow a three-track approach in dealing with threats. We arrange to protect the person or property under threat, investigate the matter, and attempt to engage the perpetrator.

The investigation is often aimed at uncovering indications in the perpetrator's background that he may be prepared to employ violence. Does he have a criminal record, and does it include violent crime? Is he mentally unstable? Does he appear to be depressed? Is he known to be a drug user? Does he have weapons registered to him? Is he comfortable around weapons, as, for example, a hunter or a military veteran might be? Does he know how to use explosives, as, for example, a miner might? Has he made statements to coworkers indicating a propensity to violence? Does he have friends or acquaintances he could enlist in an assault?

The investigation may cause us to attempt to enlist a law-enforcement agency in responding to the threat. Companies, however, should not expect too much from law enforcement. Police in general are much better at responding to crimes than preventing them. In most cases, they are reluctant to pursue people leveling threats, especially vague threats and those that cannot be tied convincingly to a particular source, since prosecution can be very difficult. Also, they are aware that the overwhelming majority of threats do not lead to assaults and they are wont to consider other cases on their desk to be more pressing.

In the United States and other countries with well-developed legal systems, the investigation can lead to a restraining order, forbidding the person levying the threat from approaching the individual or property being threatened. A perpetrator committed to inflicting harm, however, will not be deterred by a restraining order. The best one can hope for is to catch him in violation of the order and press for his arrest.

Engagement of the suspected perpetrator of the threat may have several objectives. One is to assess his propensity to violence. Another is to explore potential means of resolving the dispute amicably. A third may be to deliver the message that competent security professionals are on the case and that recourse to violence will not be tolerated.

It is essential, in my view, when a particular employee has been threatened, that he or she be furnished protection and not be summarily withdrawn from the area in which the problem has taken place. Corporate decision makers often opt for withdrawal in the belief that leaving personnel who have been threatened in harm's way would be irresponsible. They are concerned about liability issues and, even more so, about living with themselves if an attack were to take place. Senior executives, as I pointed out previously, are distinctly uncomfortable with decisions involving physical risk to personnel and are apt to take the *prudent* approach.

Unfortunately, however, withdrawing personnel under threat can have serious consequences for the company. Invariably, it empowers the individual levying the threat. He deduces that his strategy has been effective and decides to press forward by levying additional threats, perhaps against the successors of those who have been withdrawn.

Admittedly, protecting an individual or workplace can be costly. Often it involves posting bodyguards round-the-clock at the office and residence and having them escort the individual or individuals under threat to and from work and other activities. In some cases, dependents may require similar protection, and it also may be necessary to mount a surveillance of the adversary as an additional precaution.

In potential workplace-violence cases, it is essential to focus on securing the workplace. Mainly this involves upgrading access controls. Armed guards should be posted at perimeter entry points. If they are already present, they need to be instructed *specifically* to bar the potential assailant from the facility. Otherwise, they may admit him on the basis of visual recognition, even if his corporate credential has been taken from him.

Protection costs, of course, must be weighed against the potential of a catastrophic event, and against the costs of an interruption of business. It is wise for corporations to protect against these costs by purchasing threat endorsements to their Kidnap, Ransom and Extortion insurance. The endorsements generally do not respond to the vague or indirect bluster common in workplace-violence situations, or most telephoned warnings of bombs, but they do cover a broad range of specific threats. Many overlook this aspect of the policy, but, given the frequency of threats, and their potential cost, it is crucially important.

SECTION 4

■

CONVENTIONAL CRIME PROBLEMS

■

Chapter Seventeen

EXPRESS KIDNAPPING

Express kidnappings differ from classical ransom cases in that there is virtually no prior planning. A victim is assaulted because he or she represents for the assailants a target of opportunity.

Express kidnappings sometimes are referred to as "random kidnappings," which is something of a misnomer. They are not quite random. Victims in most cases are selected because they exhibit some degree of affluence. They may be recognizable as Westerners or Japanese, nationalities that in themselves connote a certain level of wealth in underdeveloped countries. Or they may be locals who are sufficiently well dressed to suggest that they may have valuables on their person—expensive jewelry, credit cards, or ATM cards.

Many express kidnappings begin as carjackings (defined as stealing cars by force or intimidation). Some carjackers are merely interested in stealing the vehicle. Others also make it a practice of relieving a victim of his or her cash and valuables. A third class of carjackers decides, in the course of the assault, to take it a step further and force the victim to make ATM withdrawals or even hold him or her for a modest ransom. A fourth class of assailant is intent on express kidnapping from the outset.

The carjacking and express-kidnapping problems are most pronounced in Latin America, with Mexico and Venezuela being particular trouble spots, and in Africa. Some assailants use blocking maneuvers against vehicles in transit. Others confront victims stopped at red lights—to the point that in many high-risk countries it is accepted practice to roll through red lights at night. Many would-be kidnappers key on people approaching or leaving their vehicles, often in mall parking lots. Others lay in wait at residences, confronting victims when they exit their vehicles to open gates or garage doors, or waiting inside their cars for slow-moving automatic gate or garage-door openers to allow them entry. A fast, remote-control gate or garage-door opener is one of the best investments a homeowner can make in security hardware.

In Nairobi, Kenya, assailants tend to strike at intersections, traffic circles, and other choke points. In addition to brandishing firearms ranging from pistols to assault rifles, they use ruses of one form or another to get targeted drivers to stop. The crudest involves blocking the road with another vehicle or a pile of rocks, logs, or other debris. In other cases, they throw muck on windshields or bait Good Samaritans by staging roadside accidents. Kenyan assailants have also taken express kidnapping a step beyond most of their counterparts, occasionally obliging victims to drive them to their homes, which are then stripped of anything of value.

Kenyan criminals are notorious for their brutality. In one recent case, assailants armed with AK-47s shot to death in broad daylight two women traveling in a US Embassy vehicle twelve miles west of Nairobi, apparently because they failed to quickly heed a command to exit the vehicle, a Toyota Land Cruiser, a local favorite because of the rough terrain. The bodies of the victims were yanked into the street, and the assailants took off. An elderly man, a teenage boy, and a woman who were related to the victims exited the vehicle immediately and were not harmed.

In vehicle-linked express kidnappings, as in carjackings, the primary risk factor is the victim's car or SUV. Perpetrators on the lookout for indications of affluence naturally gravitate toward more expensive vehicles. A Mercedes-Benz spells affluence, as does a BMW or a Land Cruiser. Economy cars, on the other hand, tend to blend into the scene, although in some countries even they are carjacked for their parts. Also, I must admit that I have seen people driving compact cars who have dressed in a manner that conveyed affluence, so I would always advise motorists driving in high-risk countries to dress down and even remove their jackets and ties while driving.

In any event, it has been my unpleasant duty over the years to try to separate managers in countries with high risks of express kidnapping from their luxury automobiles. This has made me quite unpopular and certainly has not helped my stock with luxury car makers. I have tried to placate them by pointing out that they sell economy as well as luxury brands, but to no avail. The margins simply are not as good.

In some countries—Mexico, Argentina, and Indonesia come immediately to mind—express kidnappings often begin with a taxi ride. Hailing a green-and-white or yellow Volkswagen Beetle on a street in Mexico City is a recipe for disaster. Street taxis in the Mexican capital are largely unregulated, and a considerable number of drivers, though certainly not all of them, are career criminals. Mexicans of modest means for the most part get away with using the cabs (though there have been instances in which even they have been robbed or raped). For many of the drivers, however, picking up an obvious foreigner is a payday too good to be missed.

The foreigner will be driven a few blocks to an ambush set up with confederates, normally via coded cell phone conversation. At that point, the doors open and the assailants get in. The victim is robbed, often forced to make ATM withdrawals, and then dumped, sometimes sans clothing, on a lightly trafficked road.

The appropriate countermeasure in Mexico City, when corporate cars are not available, is the use of hotel or *sitio* taxis, which can be summoned by telephone from fixed stations. Airport cabs in Mexico City also are regulated and are considered safe.

In Buenos Aires, crooked cab drivers troll for victims near luxury hotels, restaurants, and nightclubs, on the lookout for Americans or Europeans who have not been forewarned and assume that, as in their home countries, they can enter a taxi with confidence.

Several months ago, three visiting British businessmen hailed a cab as they departed a nightclub in Buenos Aires's upscale Recoleta district. Not long after getting under way, the driver pulled over to the side of a dark street and two armed assailants jumped in. The three Britons then were driven to a series of ATMs and forced to make withdrawals until their card limits were reached. Next, they were driven to a remote area near the international airport, ordered to take off their clothing, and let go. (Why do express kidnappers order their victims to strip? Apparently, they believe that leaving them without clothing inhibits their ability to summon help. But it is also possible that they derive some pleasure from humiliating them.)

As in Mexico City, the use of street cabs cannot be sanctioned in Buenos Aires. Limos, known locally as *remises*, and radio-dispatched cabs are the safer alternatives. *Remises* also should be used to go to and from the airport.

In Venezuela, trouble begins at the airport. No airport taxi, ostensibly authorized or not, can be considered safe. In some cases, a bogus skycap leads the passenger to a taxi driven by confederates. Once under way, the driver stops and picks up armed accomplices who rob or express kidnap the unsuspecting traveler.

Even airport travel in corporate cars carries risks in Caracas, and this is also the case in Rio and Sao Paulo, as carjackers in all three cities troll roads looking for promising quarry. Corporate travelers should arrive and depart airports in those cities during daylight and be met by security drivers and armed escorts, preferably operating from two vehicles. More will be said later about the use of bodyguards.

A disturbing new trend in express kidnapping is the abduction of pedestrians. Again, assailants troll where the money is—outside business-class hotels and at banks and ATMs. Victims are forced into waiting vehicles, robbed, and driven to a series of ATMs.

Corporate Crisis Management Teams rarely learn of express kidnappings while they are in progress. Only in those relatively rare cases in which a victim is held for several days while ransom demands are made upon his loved ones do they become involved. In those instances, the recovery effort is handled similarly to a classical ransom kidnapping, albeit with the expectation that it will be settled quickly and at relatively low cost.

Carjackings and express kidnappings are not the only vehicle-related crimes that cause concern. Mexican and Venezuelan criminals, for example, while they also carjack and express kidnap, are notorious for staging armed robberies of motorists, which can be every bit as deadly. Victims often are robbed while caught up in Mexico City's and Caracas's constant gridlock, with many incidents taking place during the noon and early evening rush hours.

In Caracas, assailants working in pairs on motorcycles often approach the target vehicle from both sides, with the assailant on the driver's side displaying a weapon and forcing the driver to lower his window and hand over his valuables. If the driver refuses, the assailant uses his weapon to break the window.

Motorcyclists also are prepared to chase down their quarry and often fire into the vehicle to stop it. Not long ago, an Italian diplomat was shot in the leg during an attempted armed robbery on a main Caracas thoroughfare. A police patrol witnessed a Mercedes-Benz driven by the diplomat traveling at a high rate of speed, with two motorcyclists chasing close behind. A taxi driver then informed the patrol that the motorcycles had been following the Benz for some time and appeared to be trying to force the driver to stop. The police gave chase and, as they approached, saw the motorcyclists standing near the Mercedes with the passenger door open. When the assailants spotted the policemen, they opened fire, and in the ensuing gunfight one assailant was killed and the diplomat was wounded in the leg. The other assailant escaped.

An investigation revealed that the assailants, part of a gang known as the Roleros, because they specialized in stealing Rolex watches, had targeted the Italian because they had spotted one of the timepieces on his wrist. Caracas, these days, is not a place for either Mercedes-Benzes or Rolex watches.

Was the Italian wise to attempt to escape the attack? Without question, it is inadvisable to resist assaults—such as armed robberies and carjackings—that the victim can reasonably conclude are aimed principally at property. Admittedly, the victim is obliged to make a snap decision as to the motives of his assailants, but he can benefit from a solid understanding of local risks. In many countries, simple robberies or carjackings are far more common than ransom kidnappings or other violent assaults upon motorists and passengers, and so attacks may be presumed to be property directed. (The exception to this rule, and there always seems to be one, is Baja California State in northwestern Mexico, where women passengers have been sexually assaulted in recent carjackings.)

Some countries, Venezuela among them, have high levels of both kidnappings and carjackings, so the decision as to whether or not to attempt to escape becomes more complicated. The method of assault, however, may reveal the assailants' intention. The motorcycle-borne assailants chasing the Italian diplomat, for example, can be presumed to have been robbers, not kidnappers. Kidnappers almost certainly would have operated from automobiles and brought more firepower.

Resistance is more understandable in countries in which the risks of classical ransom kidnappings or other crimes against the person are high, and the motorist believes himself or his loved ones to be in imminent danger. But even in those countries, I would argue, heroics usually are ill-advised. This subject will be discussed in greater depth in chapter 21, "Modifying Behavior."

In instances in which there is a high expectation that the crime at hand is property related, instructions from assailants should be complied with immediately and without any sudden, unexpected movement, which may be interpreted by the assailants as reaching for a gun. Attempting to dissuade the assailants from continuing their assault and other forms of passive resistance also entail unacceptable risks.

From anecdotal evidence collected over the years, it seems to me that motorists are more prone to resist assaults than victims of other types of crimes, and they often pay the price. Perhaps motorists resist because they feel that their place at the wheel gives them the opportunity to do so. Also, protective-driving courses, about which more will be said later, may have given them confidence in their ability to use their vehicles to escape trouble. Still, they are wrong to put themselves and, in some cases, their loved ones, at risk over property. No possession, no matter how valuable, is worth it.

Chapter Eighteen

OTHER VIOLENT STREET CRIME

The streets hold many perils in addition to express kidnapping, and foreigners are especially vulnerable insofar as they are in unfamiliar territory and are often recognizable as being "from abroad." Indeed, in many poorer countries, Americans, Europeans, and Japanese—by definition more affluent than the locals—are seen as prime pickings for criminals, and no amount of dressing down can disguise who they are.

Violent street crime mainly consists of armed robberies (undertaken with either a gun or a knife—either can be deadly) and muggings, known in some places as choke-and-rob assaults, in which assailants rely on strong-arm tactics rather than weapons. In Colombia and a few other Latin American countries, assailants also attack victims with scopolamine, or *burundanga*, as it is known locally, a drug that renders victims docile. Although usually put into food or drinks, scopolamine can also be blown into the face of a pedestrian.

Even grab-and-run thefts, which normally are nonviolent, can turn deadly if the victim resists or because of some unfortunate circumstance. Many is the case in which women targeted by pillion riders on motorcycles have been dragged along with the cyclists because they held onto their bags or were carrying them in such a way that they were virtually attached to them.

Wisdom on the streets begins with knowledge of the local scene. In some countries—Singapore comes immediately to mind—the

161

streets are safe day and night, assuming the application of common sense, which is always in order. Indeed, the streets in some benign environments are markedly safer than those back home, especially if home is a US metropolitan area. In several other countries, walks can be undertaken well into evening, but only if the pedestrian remains in the more affluent parts of town.

It is impossible to overstress the importance, in most places—and my hometown of Miami comes immediately to mind—of knowing which districts are safe and which are unsafe and staying strictly within the safe ones. In some cities, affluent and downtrodden districts may abut each other, immensely complicating efforts to stay safe. (This advice pertains to drivers as well as pedestrians and is the basis for advising against visitors renting cars in cities—especially foreign cities—with which they are not entirely familiar.)

One rule of thumb is to inform oneself through risk-analysis services, such as _Risknet_, or ask resident colleagues or hotel concierges where it is safe to walk and to avoid becoming too adventurous. It is always astounding to me that people who would never cross to the "wrong side of the tracks" in their hometown do so without hesitation in a foreign country. Indeed, some do so intentionally, in search of "local color." Every year, it seems, there are reports of visitors being assaulted while taking photographs in the crime-ridden, drug-infested _favelas_ (slums) of Rio de Janeiro.

Another rule of thumb is to stay alert to your surroundings and trust your instincts. If you feel uneasy about walking down a particular street, don't do it. Do a smart about-face and return to the area in which you are more comfortable.

In some places, the streets are relatively safe during the day but dangerous after dark. In others, it is simply never safe to venture out on foot. Again, knowledge of the local terrain is all-important, and the rule of thumb is to err on the side of caution. When in doubt, it is wise to get around by car or taxi.

In many countries, care must be exercised in the selection of taxis. Consider, if you will, just how vulnerable you are in a vehicle

driven by a total stranger, especially in an unfamiliar land and one in which you do not speak the language.

As far as I am concerned, the degree to which a country regulates taxi service is an important indicator of its commitment to law and order. But, alas, many developing countries fail at regulation efforts, particularly insofar as street taxis are concerned, or they may make an honest effort at regulation but find their streets inundated with gypsy drivers, who make a determined effort to make their vehicles look like public taxis.

As a general rule, the safest taxis for travelers to use are those that regularly serve their hotels and that can be retained through the concierge or doorman. Next in the pecking order, and also normally safe, are radio-dispatched cabs.

In some parts of the world, women, especially Western women, occasionally experience problems in categories of taxis generally considered safe. In some instances, this is attributable to a belief on the part of taxi drivers, fed by Hollywood and network TV, that Western women are promiscuous. In other cases, the drivers appear to find Western women exotic. Whatever the case may be, there are far too many instances each year of sexual harassment, groping, and even rape.

Drivers often lay the groundwork for their advance by trying to guide a woman passenger into the front passenger seat. When picking up a woman at an airport, a driver may place her luggage in the back-seat, thus leaving her little alternative but to ride up front. **The cardinal rule for women is: "Never, never, never get into the front seat!" It is just too close to the driver. It makes you too vulnerable to flirting, groping, or worse.**

If a driver tries to guide you into the front seat, resist as firmly as you can. If he leers at you, turn away. Make a scene if you have to. But parry the approach while you are still outside the taxi, ideally with other people around. It is far better to be thought of as rude than to become a victim.

Indeed, do not enter any taxi in which you are the least bit uncomfortable. Men and women, follow your instincts on this one. Once inside the vehicle, you are at the driver's mercy.

Women also face special problems on the streets of some countries. Some Muslim countries are especially notorious in this regard, as is India. Problems for the most part are limited to catcalling and other verbal harassment, but instances of pinching and groping are not unknown, and there are occasional reports of sexual assaults.

Women often can forestall problems in developing countries by dressing conservatively. If confronted, they should refrain from addressing harassers directly. Instead, they should duck into a nearby shop or other safe haven until the offenders have gone. Solo evening forays are strongly discouraged, and even during the day, women should stick to beaten commercial paths.

Furthermore, it is wise for female travelers to appreciate that they have been stereotyped to a degree by the scandalous behavior of some American celebrities and by Hollywood's depiction of Western women as promiscuous. What seems to them to be an innocuous conversation with a local man may be interpreted by him as a sexual come-on.

Nonwhites also face special problems: mainly, violence perpetrated by skinheads, especially in central and eastern Europe, with Russia by far holding the highest perils. Hate crimes are common throughout the country, including Moscow and St. Petersburg, with Voronezh, three hundred miles south of Moscow, being a particular problem spot. While most attacks take place in marginal areas, skinheads can and do strike anywhere, including prominent venues, such as Moscow's Stary Arbat pedestrian street and St. Petersburg's Nevsky Prospect. Dozens of people are killed and many more seriously hurt in racial attacks every year.

There are at least twenty thousand members of skinhead or neo-Nazi groups and many more sympathizers and wannabes across Russia. Often identifiable by their buzz-cuts and jackboots, skinheads tend to hang out aboard and around public transportation, in parks and outdoor shopping venues, and in the environs of nightclubs. But they can and do strike everywhere.

Even hardened observers of the Russian scene were stunned by the emergence on the Internet in August 2007 of a video in which neo-Nazis savagely murdered two dark-skinned migrants. The clip, which experts declared to be authentic, showed the victims bound and kneeling before a Nazi flag, saying in accented Russian that they had been "arrested by Russian national socialists." Two masked men in camouflage uniforms stood behind them and gave Nazi salutes. Then one masked man beheaded one of the victims with a hunting knife, and the other shot the second migrant in the back of the head after shouting, "Glory to Russia!"

A caption on the video credited the murders to the previously unknown National Socialist Party of Russia. Other captions identified the terrified victims as being from Dagestan, a constituent republic of the Russian Federation, and Tajikistan, a former Soviet republic in Central Asia that is now independent.

Police also labeled as a racist attack the September 2007 stabbing death in an elite area of central Moscow of the son of an Iranian Embassy interpreter who was studying at the Moscow Energy Institute. There were no witnesses, but neither the money nor the laptop computer the victim carried was taken, leading police immediately to categorize the case as a hate crime.

While most victims are immigrants or students, businessmen have been assaulted in some instances, and there have even been a few incidents involving US Marine embassy guards. Some of the victims run afoul of the skinheads, who are insanely racist, by dating or marrying local women, while others are simply set upon because they are in the wrong place at the wrong time and are thus targets of opportunity.

The appropriate countermeasure for nonwhite corporate personnel in Russia and other parts of the former Soviet Union is to "dress up" in business attire, rather than dressing down, as we recommend in areas in which conventional crime is the main problem. It is also wise to stick to the beaten paths of the business community and move about in pairs or groups.

Nonviolent crime, such as pocket picking and grab-and-run theft, though it rarely involves bodily harm, can be very bothersome, especially if a reasonably large sum of money or a passport is taken. Pocket picking mostly takes place amid heavy crowds, and danger areas include tourist attractions and train stations. Ploys sometimes are used to distract the marks. These include planting a small sum of money on the sidewalk, asking for the time or a light, or staging an argument or fight.

The bottom line is that visitors should ignore attempts by strangers to engage them in conversation and should not stop to pick up fallen objects or to watch altercations or other spectacles. As a matter of routine, men should place wallets in front trouser pockets, or in concealment devices worn under clothing, usually around the waist or the ankle, but not in fanny packs.

Indeed, it should be understood that any accoutrement, be it a fanny pack, purse, or attaché or laptop case, is a magnet for thieves. To the extent possible, such items should be left in safekeeping back at the residence or hotel, as should conspicuous jewelry, credit cards, passports (unless the particular country requires that they be carried— authorities in most countries will be satisfied with a copy of the identification page or pages). Also to be left in safekeeping are large amounts of cash, although it is not a bad idea to carry about $50, with the idea that it would be surrendered in the event of an assault. Appeasing street assailants with a respectable amount of "throw-down money" is always a better idea than resisting.

It isn't macho, but, statistically, it is much wiser to appease muggers and armed robbers than to resist them. Not long ago, a seventy-year-old American enjoyed his fifteen minutes of fame for turning the tables on an assailant in the wild and woolly Costa Rican port of Limon. The American, a military veteran visiting the town from a cruise ship, was on a minibus that was boarded by three would-be robbers. He put a choke-hold on one of the attackers and killed him. The other two ran off.

The American demonstrated remarkable presence of mind and great courage, but I hate to think of what the outcome might have been if one of the assailants had had a gun.

Chapter Nineteen

ENTERTAINMENT VENUES

W hen I was a young man, all those decades ago, travel was fun. The streets were relatively safe, and so were most bars, restaurants, and nightclubs. That carefree era seems long gone. Today, one has to watch his—or her—step, very, very carefully.

Most better restaurants are reasonably safe venues, though in a few cities, such as Mexico City and Buenos Aires, there are occasional holdups of patrons. In these cities, it is wise to seek guidance from local colleagues or hotel concierges when planning to dine outside the hotel. Recommended establishments normally have armed guards at the entrance. In Muslim countries, because of terrorism concerns, it is best to eat in one's hotel, avoiding restaurants on the outside that may be regarded as Western hangouts but may not be as well protected.

Another problem related to restaurants in a growing number of countries is credit card fraud. In those countries, it is not a good idea when paying the bill to let waiters walk off with cards. In London and some other European cities, credit card scanners are routinely brought to the table.

It is the bars and nightclubs that are the real problem. Numerous bars and clubs throughout the world are nothing but clip joints, in which patrons can run up huge bills buying "drinks" for bar girls. When presented with the bills, they have little recourse but to pay. Bouncers are on hand to make sure they do.

Even worse, bar girls in some cities are notorious for spiking drinks with scopolamine or the local date-rape drug of choice, which renders the victim docile. The mark then is led off by the girl or her accomplices to his hotel room or another location, where he is stripped of all valuables and often just plain stripped. He wakes up hours later with no memory of the episode, no money, no passport, and a lot of explaining to do.

Bar girls and prostitutes also work extortion scams. In Rio and Sao Paulo, prostitutes have attempted to extort large sums from clients by threatening to say that they have been tricked into going to the client's hotel room, where they were raped. Some of the scammers work in tandem with corrupt police officers, who burst into the room and offer to settle the matter for a substantial cash payment. The client, embarrassed and at a distinct disadvantage in someone else's country, usually pays up.

Women travelers, too, can be victimized on a night out, though usually by Lotharios at higher-class establishments. They are, of course, vulnerable to rape as well as robbery.

Both sexes need to remember what their mothers told them about striking up conversations with strangers, no matter how attractive they may be, even in bars and restaurants of business-class hotels. Indeed, and I hate to break this news, but the more attractive the stranger, the more likely it is that she—or he—is up to no good. While it is flattering to be approached, the traveler needs to keep a tight grip on reality. If the approach seems too good to be true, it probably is.

Travelers also need to be wary of con artists of the same sex who work bars and restaurants of business-class hotels, attempting to provide introductions to locals or to lure them out to a party or night on the town. They often have excellent English and can be very polished, but the goal is the same—victimization of the mark.

As I said, trips abroad used to be a lot more fun. Travel was an opportunity to meet new people, really let one's hair down. There are still countries in which a traveler can enjoy the night life, assuming commonsense precautions of course—but the list is a short one. In most areas today, discretion is the wisest course.

Chapter Twenty

RESIDENTIAL CRIME

There are two basic categories of residential crime: burglary and home invasion. Burglary implies stealth, while home invasion is intended from the outset to be confrontational, making it much more dangerous to residents. Both are essentially property crimes, though in a small percentage of home invasions victims are gratuitously beaten or even raped. Beatings often result from the residents' refusal to furnish safe combinations or reveal where valuables are hidden. With armed assailants in control of the residence, resistance of this sort is foolish. Again, no material possession is worth risking injury to oneself or loved ones.

In burglaries, perpetrators generally attempt to enter and leave the home without being observed. Home invaders, on the other hand, often gain entry by placing under duress a resident or guest who is entering or leaving the house, or by trying to talk their way in through a ruse, such as posing as utility company employees.

In some Brazilian cities, especially Rio, home invaders have taken matters to a new level. There have been numerous instances in which they have used brute force to overcome guards or concierges and have taken control of entire apartment buildings (albeit usually smaller ones lacking redundant—meaning multilayered—security measures) and then gone door-to-door in an attempt to talk or force their way into individual units.

The differences between burglars and home invaders are by no means ironclad. Some burglars have no reservations about entering homes when occupants are asleep, and almost all arm themselves at least with knives to be used in the event the occupants awaken, they come upon someone who is unexpectedly at home, or they are interrupted by someone returning home. If interrupted, most use their weapons only to assure themselves a means of escape, but there have been instances in which burglars, sensing opportunity, have turned confrontational, placing residents under duress and obliging them to reveal where they keep their cash and jewelry or to open safes.

I want to offer a word of advice at this point to people who suspect that something is amiss upon returning to their homes. Instinctively, they often charge right in, which is exactly the wrong thing to do. It is most unwise to put yourself at personal risk by interrupting a burglary. It is far more sensible to summon assistance from police or private security sources.

As a general rule, the most effective defenses against burglars are physical security measures, such as solid-core doors, deadbolt locks, grilles, and alarm systems. While physical measures, including quick-opening driveway gates or garage-door openers, are also necessary to protect against home invaders, procedural security plays a greater role. Thus, residents of areas at high risk of home invasion should enter and depart detached homes as expeditiously as possible, keeping an eye out for loiterers, and both residents and domestic staff should be trained in the proper screening of persons seeking admission to the home.

Domestic staff can be critical in preventing burglaries and home invasions—or they can abet housebreakers. In many instances, the mere presence of someone in the home discourages burglars, and domestics trained to carefully screen people seeking admission can parry home invaders. On the other hand, in countless instances domestics who have not been properly vetted have aided both categories of housebreaker. It is impossible to overstate the importance of fully investigating people who are going to live or work in your home.

With the preliminaries out of the way, we can properly discuss principles of residential protection. In medieval times, occupants of castles surrounded themselves with berms or moats. The next line of defense was the castle wall itself. The idea was to develop as many concentric circles of security as possible. This principle has changed little over the centuries. Modern residential security programs continue to be based on the concept of concentric circles of security, or perimeters.

Areas in which risks of housebreaking are low to moderate may require but a single perimeter, the exterior of the house itself. Those in which crime rates are higher generally require additional concentric circles of security.

Indeed, the more perimeters that surround a home, the more likely it is that would-be burglars or home invaders will be dissuaded from attempting to gain entry. The stouter the defenses, the more likely it is that the criminal will move down the street or across town to a "softer" target.

A worldwide escalation in residential crime has caused people to band together to improve residential protection. Thus, there has been a dramatic rise in recent years in apartment living. Even more striking is the development of gated compounds, many of which are a good distance from city centers. In Buenos Aires, for example, more than four hundred gated communities have sprung up in recent years along the provincial shorefront, as members of the upper middle class reconciled themselves to long commutes in an attempt to replicate for their families the Argentina of old, with its negligible residential crime.

Apartment buildings and gated communities, however, are safer than detached homes only insofar as they provide effective, redundant security perimeters. Older apartment buildings lacking redundant security are generally no safer than detached homes and some may be inherently less safe.

I have never been a fan of controlling access through intercom/buzzer systems, for example. All it takes to defeat the system is one resident who is sloppy about identifying visitors before buzzing them in, or who allows an unknown person to slip inside the front door behind him. Indeed, in one recent case in Cairo's upscale

Zamalek district, a foreign woman, who was busy talking on her cell phone while unlocking the entrance door to her building, paid no heed to a man who followed her inside. The intruder then followed her into the elevator and tried to rape her. Luckily, her screams brought intervention from neighbors, who interrupted the attack.

The only really effective mechanism for screening visitors is a conscientious doorman, concierge, or security guard.

The ideal apartment complex, like the ideal gated community, should be surrounded by a wall at least ten feet high and be well illuminated. A gated entrance should be manned by a security guard who calls residents to verify the bona fides of any guests or callers.

In areas in which risks of housebreaking are moderate, this single barrier may suffice, provided, of course, that the security guard is well trained and conscientious and does not merely wave callers through his checkpoint. Also, even in moderate-risk areas, guests should be instructed to valet their cars or park in an outside area and walk past a concierge posted near the front entrance to the building. Use of the covered garage should be restricted to residents, who obtain access through a key card or remote transmitter. A key or key card also should be used to gain entry from the garage to the building proper, and the garage should be monitored by the concierge or gate guard through CCTV cameras.

In higher-risk areas and in apartment complexes with two or more buildings, a second perimeter should be established at the entrance or entrances to each building. In these instances, the lobby concierge should make a second call to the resident to confirm bona fides and then accompany the caller to the appropriate elevator, using a key or key card to grant access only to the floor being visited. Parking arrangements should be similar to those specified for lower-risk areas.

The next line of defense in higher-risk areas is the security cordon around the apartment itself. Even units in secure buildings require solid-core or metal-backed entrance doors equipped with stout deadbolt locks and 190-degree optical viewers. Sliding terrace doors should be grilled if even remotely accessible from adjoining units. Terrace doors or windows that are not easily accessible should be equipped with intrusion-detection alarm systems featuring both claxons and the instant notification of complex security guards.

Even in secure buildings, it is wise to stay away from apartments on the ground, second floors, and top floors (the latter may be susceptible to break-ins by "spiderman" burglars). It is also essential to ensure that the local fire department has the necessary equipment to reach the floor that has been selected.

Gated communities, like apartment complexes, should be surrounded by walls at least ten feet high. Again, a gated entrance should be manned by a security guard who calls residents to verify the bona fides of guests or callers. In a gated community, the entrance is the only barrier between the outside world and the residence or residential compound itself, so it is especially important that the security guard be well trained and conscientious, and, again, that he not merely wave callers through. Better gated communities bolster security with roving patrols. In the very best communities, residents can get away with equipping their homes with minimal physical defenses—generous lighting, solid-core, or metal-backed entrance doors equipped with stout deadbolt locks and 190-degree optical viewers, and intrusion-detection alarm systems featuring both claxons and instant notification of complex security guards.

In gated communities with less than effective access control, it may be necessary to secure the individual residence as if it were a detached home in an unsecured residential neighborhood.

In both unsecured residential neighborhoods and gated communities, it is worth noting, the presence of construction crews increases dramatically the risks of burglary, mandating special precautions, in some cases full-time guards. This phenomenon is near universal and appears to be predicated on the ease with which construction workers can case nearby homes and observe the patterns of both householders and household staff.

Detached homes are inherently more difficult to secure than units in apartment buildings with redundant access control systems simply because it is impossible to build much redundancy into them. Yes, they may have good perimeter fencing (fences seem to be getting higher, and topguards, which often consist of barbed wire or glass shards and may be electrified, are more difficult to overcome), generous lighting, and stout, quick-opening gates. Absent an armed guard or two, however, it is hard to adequately protect from potential home invaders the comings and goings of family members and guests. Also, detached homes generally require stouter—and more costly—physical security measures than apartments.

The element of aesthetics is always at play in planning defenses for a detached home. Aesthetics argue for subdued exterior lighting and a perimeter lined with attractive shrubbery and trees. Acceptable security, on the other hand, calls for bold lighting and a cleared buffer devoid of vegetation to deprive would-be intruders of climbing opportunities and concealment points. Usually, compromise solutions are achieved, but residents should realize that such compromises inherently weaken the home's defenses.

Once the outer circle of security has been established, the next line of defense is access points to the house—doors, windows, and skylights. Glass is probably the single weakest point of this perimeter. If aesthetics argue for the use of a lot of glass, it may be desirable to consider impact-resistant windows, which, although expensive, offer considerably more protection than more conventional counterparts. If conventional glass is to be used, it should be buttressed with grilles or at least stout locking devices and intrusion-detection alarms. If grilles are to be used, several, at critical egress points, should be hinged and padlocked, to permit residents to escape if a fire should break out. Many householders resist the installation of grilles for aesthetic reasons, but their value is well established.

Great care must be taken in the selection of locking devices. Any exterior entry door with glass panes in it or with glass panels alongside it must be secured with a double-cylinder deadbolt lock (which has keyways on both sides of the lock).

One of the most common mistakes we observe in examining executive residences is the use of a single-cylinder deadbolt lock with a thumb-turn knob on the interior. All the intruder has to do in these cases to gain entry is to cut or smash out the glass, reach in, and use the thumb-turn knob to open the door.

Of course, the same vulnerability presents itself if the resident leaves a key in the interior keyway of a double-cylinder deadbolt lock. Keys must be removed. They also must be easily accessible to family members, to permit them to exit the house quickly in the event of a fire.

Since it is difficult to provide foolproof locking devices for windows and sliding-glass doors, another circle of security must be established. This is most often accomplished through the installation of a redundant intrusion-detection alarm system featuring a full array of magnetic contacts on doors and windows, as well as glass-break sensors and motion detectors. The system, at a minimum, should employ a very loud siren or claxon to accomplish the desired deterrent effect, but the ideal system will also be linked to a central monitoring station that can dispatch a response team. Linkage should be via a cellular telephone to ensure against its being disabled by merely cutting the phone line.

One security mechanism that is often overlooked is a good-size, protective, barking dog. I have long kept German shepherds and regard them as indispensable to the security of my family. Yes, it is indeed possible for housebreakers to poison or shoot a dog, but dogs present one more security barrier, and a rather formidable one to overcome. Often, they cause burglars or housebreakers to look elsewhere, which is exactly what we want to accomplish. (In a vehicle, incidentally, they also serve as a deterrent to carjackers and express kidnappers.)

If an intruder does gain access to the home while residents are present, the dilemma is always whether to confront or retreat. In general, we discourage confrontation. Indeed, we recommend that only people thoroughly trained in the use of firearms keep them in their homes—and only in jurisdictions in which the possession of firearms is legal.

Training, in my definition, is not a case of a trip or two to the range. It is a painstaking affair, in which the trainee is prepared

both technically and psychologically to use his weapon. Also, as in all security training, an annual refresher is essential. An inexperienced person runs the risk of having his weapon used against him by an intruder.

Of course, any weapon kept in the home should be secured properly, but in such a manner that it is quickly accessible to the householder.

There are, of course, downsides to depending on firearms for residential protection. I vividly remember an incident recounted to me a few years ago by a friend who was a strong gun advocate and had made the decision to keep a 9-mm pistol in his home for protection. At 3:00 a.m. one morning, he was awakened out of a deep sleep by a noise at the rear of his home, got his pistol, went to the area from which the noise appeared to emanate, and saw a shadowy figure attempting to open a sliding-glass door to the patio from the outside. He challenged the intruder a couple of times but got no response. Then, just as my friend was about to open fire, he recognized the intruder as the teenage son of his neighbor, who was too drunk to know that he was at the wrong house. My friend was badly shaken by the incident.

Most of us do exactly the wrong thing when we hear a noise in our home. Dad usually sees it as his manly duty to investigate, with or without a weapon, thereby putting not only himself but his entire family at risk. After all, he is walking into a dangerous situation, often having just awakened from a deep sleep. He does not know how many intruders may be present, and how they are armed.

There is no more poignant example of the downside of confrontation than the recent murder in the Miami home of Washington Redskins star safety Sean Taylor. Taylor, sleeping in the master bedroom with his girlfriend and their young child, was awakened by a noise and left the bedroom to investigate. However, the star athlete, though at the height of his physical prowess and armed with a small machete, was no match for an intruder armed with a handgun.

Ideally, Taylor should have stayed put in the bedroom and called 911. After all, everyone he was trying to protect was in that bedroom. By leaving the room, he was putting himself at a disadvantage, and he would have been at a disadvantage even if he had had a gun. After all, there were five assailants in this case, and, although only one appears to have been armed, others well might have been.

The root of the Taylor tragedy was the fact that the home's alarm system had not been activated, reportedly because a relative of his girlfriend, who was staying at the home, was due to return later that night. There are dozens of reasons for not activating alarm systems— none of them good. In far too many burglary investigations, we find that householders simply failed to activate their alarms, thus neutralizing a critical line of defense.

The prudent alternative to confrontation is to retreat to a designated safe haven inside the home and call 911, or, in countries in which police response is not reliable, private responders.

Very few homes are built with a safe haven in mind. Thus, modifications such as replacing typical hollow-core interior doors with solid-core doors at least two inches thick or fire-rated metal doors most likely will be required to establish this line of defense. Doors should be equipped with single-cylinder deadbolts, with the keyway on the outside and a thumb-turn on the inside. (The keyway is needed in case a child locks himself or herself in.)

Ideally, the layout permitting, the entire sleeping quarters of the residence should be converted to a safe haven. If this cannot be accomplished, it is common practice for one room, often the master bedroom or a walk-in closet or bathroom in the master suite, to be converted into the safe haven. Children should be instructed to head for that destination on a signal from the parents. An alternative, in the case of older children, is to convert their rooms into mini-safe havens.

Inside the safe haven, a cellular telephone should permanently be maintained on a trickle charger. It is always wise to keep flashlights and batteries, an all-purpose A-B-C fire extinguisher, and a supply of water on hand in the safe haven.

SECTION 5

■

PROTECTING EMPLOYEES FROM SPECIFIC ATTACKS

■

Chapter Twenty-One

MODIFYING BEHAVIOR

There are some places in this world, Baghdad and the Niger Delta, for example, where risks are so severe that no amount of behavior modification can ensure an individual's safety. In Baghdad, risks emanate from jihadists, Shia militias, and economically motivated kidnap gangs. In the delta, kidnap gangs are the principal problem. In areas in which risks are severe, heavy-duty protection, in the form of trained bodyguards and armored cars manned by qualified drivers, is needed to transport personnel between heavily fortified residential and office compounds. More will be said in later chapters about the use of armored cars and bodyguards.

In most medium-risk and even medium-high-risk areas, however, behavior modification is effective in discouraging kidnappings. There are three pillars to behavior modification: a low profile, unpredictability, and the ability to recognize surveillances.

These pillars are effective because both jihadists and conventional kidnap gangs do their homework. The latter, in particular, may read the newspapers, especially the business and society pages, in search of viable targets. Or they may stake out expensive schools or golf courses. Prospective victims thus can reduce their risks by lowering their profiles, though admittedly this often conflicts with the conduct of business. Executives in high-risk countries who must or choose to maintain a high profile may be obliged to hire bodyguards.

Furthermore, assailants seeking to murder or kidnap specific individuals generally seek out targets that are predictable. Predictability helps them plan their assaults so as to minimize risks of

intervention by police. Thus, potential targets need to make themselves as unpredictable as possible.

There are two aspects to unpredictability. One involves time variation and the other varying routes. By varying time patterns, managers force surveillants and/or assailants to spend a good deal of time on the street waiting for them—something they generally do not wish to do, because it increases the risks that they will be observed and reported to police. Route variation also complicates assault planning, since it makes it difficult for assailants to locate their quarry. A key aspect of route variation is the avoidance of choke points. **Generally, assault planners key on specific choke points—areas through which the potential victim must or is likely to pass and that lend themselves to an ambush.**

Maintaining unpredictability is not an easy task for managers, who usually need to arrive at the office within a reasonably narrow time frame, who often must work late, and who sometimes have a very limited choice of routes they must follow to and from work. Most of us can make ourselves less predictable during our leisure time—there is no need to have a standing tee time at 2:00 p.m. on Saturdays, for example. Business responsibilities, however, often do require set appointments or attendance at regular meetings. Again, managers at significant risk of kidnapping or other assault who cannot avoid predictability may require bodyguards.

Their children also may require protection. **Indeed, it is almost impossible to impose unpredictability on children, who, perforce, must arrive and depart schools at a fixed hour. This enforced predictability may help to explain their attraction to kidnappers.**

Training in surveillance recognition puts another arrow in the manager's defensive quiver. There is also a good deal more to grasping the essentials of recognizing surveillances than one might think. Most people, unless they are cheating on their spouses, are hard put to spot a tail. Indeed, most people are simply oblivious to what is going on around them. Their thoughts are elsewhere. Making them tail-wise is no easy task.

Surveillance-recognition training is also complicated by the fact that professional kidnapping gangs often utilize teams of surveillants who operate from at least two vehicles, keeping in touch by radio or cell phone and leapfrogging each other to reduce the chances that a prospective victim, even one who is unusually tail-wise, will "make" them.

We spent considerable time on this subject in CIA training, running what seemed like endless exercises, and I emerged from the process, and from years of needing to recognize surveillances by hostile intelligence services, with an ingrained sensitivity to what is taking place around me. (Some would say that I have taken this sensitivity to the point of paranoia.) Inculcating this kind of discipline in managers whose interests and responsibilities lie elsewhere is not easy, however.

Surveillance-recognition training normally is included in protective-driving courses, and may be the most valuable aspect of them. Protective-driving training in the main teaches motorists how to use their cars as weapons of a sort, crashing into attack vehicles if necessary to escape ambushes. They are fine in principle, but I have never been persuaded that the average manager can maintain his driving skills at a high enough level to escape an attack.

This prompts a discussion of an age-old question: When is it wise to resist an assault? There are so many variables that a pat answer is impossible. How many assailants are there? What kind of arms are they exhibiting? How are they attacking? What special skills does the intended victim have that might help him to escape? Is there, indeed, an avenue of escape?

My stock answer to the question is that, just as in crimes against property, it is unwise under most circumstances to resist. Statistically speaking, the victim's best chance of surviving an assault lies in compliance. Even in a kidnapping, the key to survival is allowing oneself to be taken hostage and, eventually, ransomed. But there is another side to this argument. While writing this very chapter, I learned that a friend and valued colleague who had been confronted while jogging along a road in an upscale district of Caracas escaped would-be kidnappers by scaling a guardrail and tumbling forty yards down a hill.

Clearly, my friend was foolish for jogging in Caracas. It is not clear whether the kidnappers were targeting him specifically or just out for a target of opportunity—any jogger who appeared affluent.

Jogging in high-crime areas, in any case, is a high-risk activity. Ransom kidnappers key on joggers because they usually run at a predictable hour and because they are extremely vulnerable when running alone. Express kidnappers also are attracted to their vulnerability. In any case, joggers have been abducted time and again.

On the other hand, kudos go to my friend for escaping what surely would have been an unpleasant time in captivity. You have to applaud his courage—to say nothing of his cool, for he even had the presence of mind to note the license plate of the attack vehicle during the assault.

Still, my friend is a former police officer and veteran security professional, and, as such, was much better prepared for the course of action he chose than the average corporate manager would have been. The course of action he decided upon is not for everybody.

Another question put to me frequently is whether a hostage should attempt to escape. Again, there are many variables. Is he being held in a remote area, or do there appear to be neighbors nearby? How many people are guarding him? How alert are they? What is the hostage's physical condition? What is his prospective path to freedom?

I can say with certainty that a hostage who does attempt to escape had better be successful. If he is caught, he surely will get a beating, or much worse.

Again, I would err on the side of prudence. In my view, the hostage's mission, first and foremost, is to survive. He should enhance his chances of survival by following his captors' instructions and doing his best to come across to them as a decent human being. (Several companies offer two- or three-day courses in hostage behavior. Such lengthy sessions are probably superfluous, except for people assigned to the very highest-risk areas. What works for hostages is to maintain their hope and come across as decent.)

That may be difficult in some cases. Executives are used to being in charge and have a hard time following orders. Some have a harder time than others. I will never forget one instance, in which a CEO took me aside shortly after a kidnapping and urged me to get the hostage back as quickly as possible, no matter what the cost. "The kidnappers are not going to like him," he said. "Frankly, *we* don't like him either."

The recovery effort took longer than the CEO had hoped, but the hostage survived. Indeed, he quickly took stock of his circumstances and managed not to antagonize his kidnappers. I never did follow up and determine whether his attitude toward his colleagues changed after his release.

People traveling to or residing in areas in which conventional crime—not kidnapping—is the major concern do not have to pre-occupy themselves with unpredictability and with "making" surveillances. But they still should practice good procedural security. They do need to be alert to loiterers and people displaying an interest in them for some nefarious purpose.

Criminals, at least the competent ones, instinctively seek out the easy mark, or soft target. They learn to distinguish between people who are distracted and oblivious and those who are alert and observant. They see the former as a pool of ready victims and normally pass on the latter.

While much of this section will discuss security enhancements, in the form of bodyguards and armored cars, it can be argued that there is no substitute for a trained, alert, observant individual. Indeed, even an executive who has been furnished an armored car and/or bodyguards should participate to the fullest in his protection, first by understanding the role that armoring technology and competent security personnel can play in ensuring his safety, and second by disciplining himself to be alert, observant—and suspicious.

One of the most important things that a man or woman can do to ensure his or her security is to study people—to become a serious people watcher. Most men are people watchers only insofar as attractive women are concerned, while many women mainly notice "hunks." There is nothing wrong with girl- or boy-watching as long as it is not carried to the point of distraction, but it is my strong recommendation that you become accustomed to observing *all* those around you, attractive or not, and especially people who appear to be displaying an unusual interest in you.

My first rule of thumb is to focus like a laser on anyone who is focusing on you. In some cases, an individual's interest in you is understandable. Let's say that you are exiting a hotel. The valet may offer to get your car. The doorman may ask if you need a cab, or, if there is no doorman, the taxi driver may scrutinize you as a potential fare. A beggar may see you as a potential benefactor, a prostitute as a potential customer.

You can pretty much dismiss all of these people as potential assailants (pretty much, but not entirely, because in fact any of them can be using their professed activity as a cover and working with criminal cohorts).

The guy you need to be most concerned about is the one eyeing you without a readily apparent reason for doing so—the guy who stares at you from across the street or who inexplicably follows you after you take off down the block, the guy who quickly looks away when you catch him looking at you.

Recognizing potential assailants takes discipline and patience. You can't be in a hurry when you leave the hotel. You have to stop and look around. A whole generation of my CIA case officer peers took up pipe smoking because lighting a pipe when leaving a hotel or other venue provided an excuse to stop and take a good look around without attracting the attention of hostile surveillance teams. Well, I have long since done away with the pipe, and these days I rarely worry about surveillances, but the habit of being super-alert to the people around me has become part of my core being.

If you depart a hotel or office and suspect that you are being followed, blatantly show that you are tail-wise. Stop to look in a shop window and see if the potential assailant also stops. If he is up to no good and sees you watching him, he will probably cut away and go on to another potential victim. If he persists, enter the shop. If he still does not back off, summon help.

Likewise, if you are about to park in a parking space and observe one or more loiterers in the area, pull away and look for a space around the corner. Do not risk an unpleasant encounter. Always follow your instincts.

Be especially certain to follow your instincts when getting into a taxi or other vehicle driven by a stranger. Know that once you are in that vehicle you are for all practical purposes at the mercy of the driver, especially if you are in a foreign country. Never hesitate to reject a taxi if anything about the driver makes you uncomfortable, even if it is going to earn you cross looks from the driver and the dispatcher.

While maintaining an alert, purposeful demeanor and obeying your instincts can help to insulate you from criminality, these are only two aspects of a solid defense. It is also wise to (1) lower your profile, (2) offer as little information as possible about yourself to the world at large, and (3) be inherently suspicious of strangers.

You can lower your profile in higher-risk areas by dressing down to the degree consistent with the conduct of business and by traveling in inconspicuous vehicles. Certainly, you should do without eye-catching jewelry. Many, if not most, experienced travelers have inexpensive watches that they use for trips, with Rolexes left at home.

It is also wise to zealously guard personal information. We Americans are too ready to offer information about ourselves. Put any official-looking form in front of us, and we'll spill our guts. I'm a believer, however, in providing as little personal information as possible, since we can never be certain whom the end recipient of the information may be.

Immigration forms should be filled out in generic terms: It is best to describe your occupation as businessperson, lawyer, or consultant. It is not necessary to identify yourself as vice president, marketing, XYZ Corporation. Save the title to impress your mother-in-law. Nor is it necessary to supply detailed identifying data on hotel registration forms. Again, I would say as little as possible.

Certainly, it is never wise to offer information about yourself to people calling on the telephone, no matter what their pretext. Indeed, dependents, domestic servants, receptionists, and administrative assistants in both high-risk countries and those with only moderate perils should be reminded periodically to refrain from providing information of any sort to callers not personally known to them.

It is also best to withhold personal information from acquaintances made in public conveyances, such as trains or airplanes, or in hotel bars.

It is not my mission here to make you paranoid, but I am suggesting that you be alert, observant, and suspicious as you go about your business, both at home or abroad. In particular, I recommend:

- that you develop sound defensive instincts and follow those instincts;
- that you not feel pressured to get into a taxi if the driver makes you uncomfortable;
- that you not feel obliged to continue down a side street that makes you uneasy;
- that you not feel obliged to go off with a group of strangers that you meet in a bar, no matter what assurances they offer that they mean no harm and that you will have the time of your life;
- that you value prudence above machismo.

I wouldn't have chosen my line of work if I were not inherently a risk taker. But I have learned to take only risks that are truly obligatory. When I am presented with opportunities to reduce my exposure to perils, both mundane and exceptional, I take full advantage of them, and I do so without either hesitation or embarrassment. The process is called survival.

Chapter Twenty-Two

ARMORED CARS

I n my opinion, the protective properties of the armored car have been vastly oversold. The appeal of the armored car, or hard car, as it is known in the trade, rests largely on its image as a quick technological fix to the problems of kidnapping and violent crime. Also, it has become something of a status symbol and a "standard perk" for senior executives living in high-risk countries. My peers have them. Why shouldn't I?

Some corporate security directors find such vehicles to be a convenient box that can be checked off: Mr. Jones faces risks, but we addressed them by getting him an armored car. The finance people like them because they are a one-time investment and not a monthly expense item, like bodyguards. In many cases, armored cars, indeed, are less costly than bodyguards, but whether they really are cost-effective in terms of the security they provide is another question.

Clearly, the armored car does have protective properties, but they are limited, and purchasers often do not always fully grasp these limitations.

Let's start by considering the advantages of the well-armored car, and for purposes of this discussion I will assume that the vehicle is armored up to level three on the National Institute of Justice (NIJ) scale, which is what most business executives have. Let's also assume that it has sufficient horsepower to travel at the rate of an unarmored peer. (Armoring, of course, adds substantial weight to the vehicle and must be compensated for with additional power.)

An armored car is at its best in protecting against a roadside

bomb. Indeed, it forces assailants to be extremely precise in detonating their devices. Most properly armored vehicles can withstand a near-miss roadside bomb, meaning that the assailants have to hit the vehicle square-on as it is passing through their "kill zone." If they are off by more than a fraction of a second, they may do some damage to the vehicle, but in most cases the occupants escape without injury.

That is exactly what happened in an October 2005 FARC attack against Senator German Vargas Lleras, a strong supporter of President Alvaro Uribe, who had launched a very successful counteroffensive against the leftist guerrilla group. A roadside bomb exploded as Vargas's motorcade drove through an affluent neighborhood of northern Bogotá. The senator's armored car saved him from injury, but three of his bodyguards, in an unshielded trailing car, were injured, along with six bystanders. (Vargas had just completed a radio interview and was assaulted within blocks of the station. Clearly, the fact that he participated in a live interview at a specific, well-known location facilitated the assault.)

To obtain the precision needed to overcome armored vehicles, Iraqi insurgents have used a dual-triggering mechanism. The first trigger arms the device when a spotter confirms that the target vehicle will be next to pass through the kill zone. Then, the second, usually some form of movement sensor, actually detonates the bomb when the target vehicle breaks its plane.

To my knowledge, a sophisticated dual-trigger has been used only once against an executive traveling in an armored car, and that was some years ago in Germany. The Red Army Faction (RAF), a leftist urban guerrilla organization that in fact was a creature of the STASI, the old East German intelligence service, in November 1989 killed Alfred Herrhausen, the CEO of Deutsche Bank and West Germany's most prominent banker.

Assailants had armed the bomb—had activated the first of the two triggers—after visually confirming that an advance car carrying some of Herrhausen's bodyguards had cleared the kill zone. (The first trigger was activated by means of a wire that had been secreted beneath the sidewalk. RAF operatives had actually cut a groove in the sidewalk and then covered it with asphalt.) The second trigger was activated when the banker's car broke an infrared beam.

The fact is that roadside bombs, while they are often used against political figures, rarely are employed against business executives. That may happen someday. But there is no sign that "someday" is approaching. Business executives at present run the risk of being kidnapped, carjacked, robbed, or fired upon, but it is the rare instance in which they are assaulted with a roadside bomb.

Let's move on to kidnapping attempts and violent assaults in general. Precisely what level of protection does a hard car provide?

First of all, let me make it very clear that the protection afforded by an armored car is only as good as its driver. The driver must be trained, retrained, and trained again in protective driving.

An armored car in the hands of a trained driver affords the occupants of the vehicle a few precious seconds that may be crucial to escaping a shooting attack. There are numerous examples of such escapes, among them one that took place near Beit Hanun, Gaza, in March 2007.

Reportedly, three masked gunmen leapt from a car that had cut off an armored vehicle (flying a UN flag) that was carrying Irish national John Ging, the director of the United Nations Relief and Works Agency (UNRWA) for Gaza. The masked gunmen initially fired into the air and then tried to force open a door to the vehicle, in an apparent attempt to kidnap Ging.

At this point, the driver pulled away, and the gunmen began firing at the moving vehicle. They pumped fourteen rounds into it, but only one penetrated the armored shell. The UN car made good its escape. It reportedly had been in a convoy of three vehicles, the other two of which were manned by Palestinian Authority security personnel, but there is no indication that the security men played any role in thwarting the attack.

The bottom line on armored cars is that, to be effective, they

must be moving. Even the best-trained driver cannot hope to escape an attack in which traffic is gridlocked, as is the case these days in many of the world's cities. Chances of escape also hinge on the driver's capacity to react coolly under fire. No matter how well the driver is trained, we can never be entirely certain that he will respond effectively in a crisis, with adrenalin rushing and split-second decisions imperative. Even combat experience is not an absolute guarantor of an appropriate response.

When moving at a good clip the armored car is a very useful piece of security technology. But the widespread conception that it is some kind of protective cocoon is simply mistaken. If the driver freezes or is stuck in traffic, with no means of escape, the car will not render its occupants invulnerable to attack, at least not for very long.

Assailants armed with 9-mm pistols, if able to put their rounds into a tight circle from fifteen to twenty feet, can breach the window of a level-three armored car in about six seconds. Assailants armed with AK-47s, if equally accurate, could take even less time to break through, and it is wise to bear in mind that the polylaminate security glass used in armored vehicles deteriorates over time, especially in warm, sunny climates. Thus, the glass of an older vehicle that has not been reconditioned could probably be breached in even less time.

I remember being chilled by photographs of the February 1984 murder in Rome by a faction of Italy's Red Brigades of American Leamon Hunt, the director-general of the Multinational Observer Force in the Sinai.

Hunt was assaulted as he sat in his armored Alfa Romeo, waiting for the front gate of his villa to be opened by a remote transmitter. Two assailants sprang from a Fiat 128 and opened fire with AK-47s, with one of them mounting the rear bumper of Hunt's vehicle and pumping armor-piercing ammunition into the rear window until he blew a hole through it. Then, he killed the victim with a single shot to the head. Hunt's Italian driver froze during the attack, making no attempt to

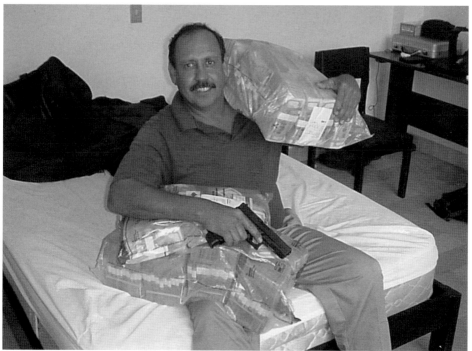

José Trevino, a retired US Navy SEAL master chief petty officer, with the $3.5 million ransom in Lago Agrio.

Working through a kidnapping in The Ackerman Group "war room."

The classic proof of survival: a hostage shown with a current newspaper.

Former hostage and current mayor of Buenos Aires, Mariano Macri (*standing*), with his father, Franco, who told Ackerman, "There are some things a father has to do for his son."

The Ackerman Group's Eamonn O'Brien (*right*), leading a protection detail in Algiers in 2007 for Admiral James Loy (*left center*), the former assistant secretary of Homeland Security. Note the low-profile vehicle, and the fact that Admiral Loy is being directed to the backseat.

Director Richard M. Helms
I have never met anyone with a stronger sense
of honor or with less pretentiousness.

Richard S. Welch
His passion was intelligence and he pursued it
with matchless vigor and enthusiasm.

David Atlee Phillips
"The ideal case officer is an intellectual marine."

Jim Flannery
"Perfect security means doing nothing in a vacuum."

Mike Ackerman as a young lieutenant in a Strategic
Air Command security command center.

Director Helms with the Ackerman family, minus Joshua, who was and remains camera shy. *Left to right,* Lauren, John, Director Helms, Mike (holding Arielle), and Jenna (January 1994).

throw his vehicle into reverse and try to move the Fiat out of its path. He was rewarded for his inaction by surviving.

There have also been instances in which assailants have used sledgehammers to breach the armor, and Brazilian criminals of late have taken to countering refusals by drivers to open the doors of their armored cars by pouring gasoline on the vehicles and setting them afire.

Armored cars or bodyguards? The ideal, if budgeting allows, is to have both, but I strongly believe that, dollar for dollar, you buy greater protection with well-trained bodyguards.

Chapter Twenty-Three

BODYGUARDS

Security practitioners differ on the value of bodyguards. Advocates argue that they are the best means of protecting key personnel in high-risk areas, better even than armored cars, albeit even more effective when used in tandem with hard cars. Critics argue that bodyguards are an unnecessary indulgence and that they bring unwelcome attention to the individual or family being protected. They generally regard armored cars as an acceptable alternative.

The decision as to whether to use bodyguards or armored cars depends in part on the nature of the risks in a particular area. In Nairobi, for example, where risks mainly emanate from carjackers—and where traffic is relatively manageable, affording a well-trained driver the opportunity to escape an assault—an armored car may be acceptable, assuming that most trips begin and end in protected office and residential compounds. In Caracas, however, where there are pronounced risks of kidnapping, as well as armed robbery, and where traffic gridlock is the rule—making escape a virtual impossibility for even the best trained driver—bodyguards are a far better solution.

In general, I have to admit to advocating the use of bodyguards, especially for very senior executives traveling to high-risk areas, resident colleagues prominent in those areas, and any personnel dispatched to ultra-high-risk environments. Asked to choose between bodyguards and armored cars for protecting people in these circumstances, I would go with bodyguards every time.

Still, I recognize that bodyguards are often employed for the wrong reasons or are misused. And just as often, they are poorly

trained and/or deployed improperly. Indeed, just as with armored cars, there is a great deal of misunderstanding about what bodyguards can and cannot accomplish and how they can be employed to the greatest effect.

For some people, bodyguards are a mere status symbol. Indeed, more than one American CEO has chosen his director of corporate security from the ranks of the Secret Service because he wants presidential-style protection, even though he resides in the United States and faces fairly modest risks. (I would not suggest, however, that all appointments of former Secret Service agents are made for reasons of vanity, and even those that are based on vanity often turn out well. After all, Secret Service agents are superbly schooled in protecting both personnel and property, and most also have broad investigative experience, an attribute often overlooked by the general public.)

Others—Hollywood celebrities being an excellent example—tend to choose their bodyguards on the basis of appearance, which is not at all surprising for a segment of society that is fixated on image and tends to see the world through the prism of its own creative product. The more imposing the bodyguard, the better! Some are so imposing, so muscle-bound, that they can hardly move, which, of course, is a decided disadvantage.

Some of the best bodyguards I've known, in fact, do not look at all like protective personnel, and this often is an asset. Indeed, some of the most sophisticated bodyguards do their best to blend in with the principal's entourage, even going so far as to carry briefcases. Briefcases or encumbrances of any kind are anathema to most bodyguards, but, as a colleague with impeccable credentials once explained to me, a bag can be dropped very quickly. And blending in complicates planning for potential aggressors, who instinctively concentrate their initial fire on the bodyguard or bodyguards.

In fact, the bodyguard's brain is far more important than his brawn. It is especially important that the leader of the bodyguard detail be intelligent and experienced, but all members of the detail need to be smart, alert, and conscientious. The leader, incidentally,

must have "book smarts" as well as "street smarts." He must be capable of acquiring a thorough understanding of both the culture and the risk profile of every area in which he is called upon to work, and it certainly does not hurt if he is multilingual.

The detail leader must be capable of effectively "advancing" movement by his principal, be it an overseas trip or a short excursion within his city of residence. Laypeople often overlook the value of good advance work, but it is crucial to mission success. The detail leader must be familiar with all venues to be visited and all routes to be taken by the principal. He must be satisfied that local security contractors, if they are to be utilized, are well trained and professional. It is not enough for the detail leader to merely ride along, as portrayed in many movies featuring bodyguards. Like good house painting, good bodyguarding depends on thorough preparation.

A sharp mind is also required for the escort phase of the operation. The effective bodyguard recognizes that the best chance of avoiding an incident lies in being unpredictable—varying times and routes and, sometimes, vehicles. He must be surveillance aware and security conscious. He has to have "a good nose"—to be sensitive to the dangers lurking in the environment in which he has been called upon to work and have the confidence to act upon his instincts. If an assault takes place, he has failed in his mission. But if there is an incident, it is the ability to quickly and accurately identify the threat and then summon the courage to respond appropriately that defines the best of the breed.

In the United Kingdom and other parts of Europe, it is worth pointing out that bodyguards, who are often called close-protection specialists, almost always work without the benefit of weapons, meaning that all emphasis must be placed on prevention. For armed bodyguards, on the other hand, prevention is a mere 99 percent of the job.

Notwithstanding the public's image of bodyguards, which has been nurtured by movies too numerous to mention, protective personnel in most instances are not effective in responding to attacks in high-threat environments. The aggressors have the advantage of choosing the time and place of the assault, and, if they have done their surveillance, they will bring sufficient firepower to overcome protective personnel, who in many instances are armed with short-barreled weapons effective at a maximum of ten yards.

I'm a great believer in choosing bodyguards painstakingly and vetting them thoroughly. Not only do they require intellect, street smarts, and courage but also uncommon emotional stability. Their job is not an easy one. Long periods of relative inactivity are interspersed with (hopefully) infrequent potential emergencies. Few people, frankly, have the conscientiousness and the discipline to make the grade.

Next comes training. To be effective, bodyguards must be superbly instructed. Prior to their being "stood up," they should have mastered not only firearms and unarmed self-defense but also protective-driving techniques and medical response skills, and all of this training *must* be kept current. Most important, they should be thoroughly schooled in protective tactics, especially the recognition of surveillances and other indicators of danger.

It is certainly not enough to assume that because they served in the military or are ex-police officers they are prepared to perform effectively. Most soldiers and police officers, though they may be familiar with weapons and with self-defense techniques, lack tactical training, to say nothing of experience.

Identifying effective bodyguards can be particularly difficult in developing countries. Only a small percentage of the bodyguards my colleagues and I have assessed over the years in those lands are truly qualified for their positions. Many lack essential training, including crucial tactical, surveillance recognition, and protective-driving instruction. Relatively few have the requisite firearms training or sufficient time on the firing range. Indeed, when interviewing them, it is not unusual to find that they have not fired their weapons in months and were permitted only a few rounds of ammunition when they did fire. Most are underpaid.

Bodyguards of this caliber are little more than props. Indeed, they probably present more of a risk to their employers than the bad guys, in that they may promote an armed confrontation unnecessarily or fire their weapons accidentally.

At times, frustrated security managers try to make do with quantity instead of quality, which rarely works. Recently, I learned of a kidnapping that took place on the road to the regional airport in Nigeria's ultra-high-risk Niger Delta. The victim's SUV was being followed by a pickup truck filled with policemen who made no attempt whatsoever to stop the assailants as they emerged from their blocking vehicle—a response the assailants probably anticipated.

When asked to explain their failure to respond, they asserted that they did not want to risk harming the principal. More likely, they had little training and even less confidence and they had no incentive to put themselves at risk. (The cops, incidentally, in my view, were deployed improperly. They would have had more deterrent value, to say nothing of a better chance of responding successfully, if they had been in two pickups, one preceding and the other following the principal's vehicle.)

Other security managers, with an eye on budgeting, try to make do merely with an armed driver, or driver-bodyguard. I have a real problem with the concept of the driver-bodyguard, which strikes me as something of a contradiction in terms. In my view, driver-bodyguards should be used only in low-risk situations. For example, prominent American CEOs often are furnished driver-bodyguards, in many cases, retired police officers, to accompany them around their home cities. I see nothing wrong with this. It furnishes a key corporate asset with protection commensurate with reasonably modest risks.

It also may be appropriate to furnish a driver-bodyguard, armed or unarmed, to a senior executive visiting a country like Israel, where the risks of an attack directed specifically against the visitor are low but where he may be victimized incidentally, in the bombing of a café or market, for example. The role of the security escort in this case is to use his knowledge of the local terrain to keep the visitor from harm.

Driver-bodyguards should not be used, however, in areas in which there is potential for an attack directed specifically against the principal. The principal's driver simply cannot serve as a bodyguard. Nor should he necessarily be armed. The only time that his weapon is really available to him is when the principal is entering or leaving his vehicle. While on the road, the driver's weapon is essentially his vehicle. Except in a movie, I cannot imagine anyone driving and shooting at the same time.

Even if an armed driver were able to use his weapon, he would be wrong to do so, because he would, perforce, be drawing fire to the car in which the principal is sitting.

My own preference is to arm only one person in the principal's car, the detail leader, who usually sits in the front passenger seat. Firepower is generally concentrated in a second vehicle, which either follows the principal's car consistently or leapfrogs it. While the driver of the second vehicle may be armed, it is his partner who is the lead shooter.

A follow-car is used when the principal mission of the bodyguards is to deter attack, with the recognition of surveillances as a secondary objective. This is the norm in protection work and is quite sound. **A two-car convoy with apparent shooters in the second vehicle presents a much more formidable target to most assailants than a single vehicle.**

The leapfrog technique is used when the bodyguards' primary mission is not to deter but to detect surveillance. Sometimes the second car precedes the principal's vehicle and sometimes it lays back.

The ideal, of course, is to have two cars, one of which advances the principal's vehicle, while the other follows it. The use of a motorcyclist in lieu of a second car for advance work is acceptable under some circumstances, provided the motorcyclist's principal responsibility is reconnaissance. (He is too exposed to function as a classic bodyguard.)

Once identified, vetted, and fully trained, the bodyguard should be treated with the respect due a potential combatant who is prepared to risk his life to protect his principal. He is not a gofer. Many is the time that I have had to listen to members of protection teams complain about being sent out for coffee or on other errands, which, in addition to being degrading, renders them useless.

Seared into my memory is a conversation I had years ago with a Central American oligarch, a wealthy landowner and the patriarch of a large and well-respected family. A corporate client, his joint-venture partner, had asked me to take a look at his security, and, as he took me on a tour of his palatial home, he showed me the small room in which his team of bodyguards slept—on straw mats. When I suggested that he might inspire greater loyalty by getting them mattresses, he chided me for my lack of understanding of his culture. "I sleep on a mattress," he said. "They have to understand that they are on a different level."

When I interviewed the bodyguards, it came as no surprise that they had little understanding of their responsibilities and virtually no firearms training. They would not have dared to offer the patriarch security advice, even if they were qualified to dispense it. They were, in fact, scared stiff of him. I detected little loyalty and was left with the impression that, under assault, they might well join with the assailants.

When the patriarch asked me for an evaluation of his bodyguards, I told him that, essentially, they were useless props. He complained to my corporate client, and that was my last assignment for them. Truth telling is one of the hazards of the trade.

In societies in which the gulf between the principal and his bodyguards is as wide as it was in this case, it is almost impossible for a detail to perform effectively. The detail leader has to be able to communicate frankly and effectively with his principal, on a basis of mutual respect, and obtain the principal's agreement to cede to him the final say in security decision making, especially with regard to decisions that have to be made instantaneously.

There is little doubt that strained communications between the principal and his bodyguard contributed to the deaths of Dodi al-Fayed and Princess Diana. The Fayed family, father and son, were notorious in London close-protection circles for demeaning their bodyguards and tolerating no input from them on matters directly relating to their security responsibilities.

Trevor Rees-Jones, the bodyguard who accompanied Dodi and Princess Diana on their last ride through Paris, may reasonably be considered to have failed in his duty for permitting Henri Paul, a member of the Fayed-owned Ritz Hotel's security staff—but an untested and untrained driver—to take the wheel on the fateful night in 1997, allowing him to ignore the speed limit, and failing to ensure that the principals were wearing their seat belts. (Paul, it turns out, was drunk, but Rees-Jones, in his book, *The Bodyguard's Story*, writes that he was not aware that Paul had been drinking heavily. Yes, he had seen him drink something at the bar, but he could not imagine that a member of the security staff was drinking alcohol while on duty.)

Those criticisms might be valid if Rees-Jones had been the one in command of the vehicle. But he was not. Indeed, in his book he says that he had deep misgivings about Dodi's plan, on the night of the accident, to evade the paparazzi by leaving the Ritz through a back entrance and traveling in a single vehicle, but he saw no point in attempting to express his doubts. He fully understood not only that Dodi would not be dissuaded from his intended course, but also that he simply would not tolerate this kind of assertiveness from an employee.

One cannot read *The Bodyguard's Story* without appreciating that Rees-Jones, and his colleagues for that matter, had been thoroughly intimidated by Dodi and by his father, Mohammed. Working for the Fayeds, these staff members quickly came to understand that their job description encompassed whatever menial tasks their employers wanted them to perform, even if those tasks undercut their responsibilities. They were made to haul luggage, run errands, and take on other menial tasks.

Dodi, moreover, was in the habit of advising Rees-Jones of his intended movements at the last instant and had made it plain that any stated objection to his intentions, even on bona fide security grounds, would result in the immediate termination of his services. The path of least resistance was to shut up and go along with whatever course of action the principal decided upon.

Even in the relatively egalitarian United States, disparities in status between principal and bodyguard can undermine the effectiveness of the latter. The state trooper who was driving New Jersey governor John Corzine on the evening of his near-fatal accident in April 2007 can be faulted for not insisting that the governor buckle his seat belt, as required by state law. But was he really in a position to give directions to the governor, who sat atop his chain of command and had absolute discretion over the progress of his career?

Corzine may have been better served by having a more senior state police official present in his vehicle and, indeed, seated in the front passenger seat, where he himself had been sitting. The governor did in fact have a chase car, which in my view was entirely appropriate, given the seniority of his position and his level of risk.

SECTION 6

■

INTERACTING WITH
CORPORATE SECURITY

■

Chapter Twenty-Four

THE CORPORATE SECURITY FUNCTION

I feel obliged, at this point, to offer some comments on the corporate security function and on the interaction between protection consultants and corporate security directors. I fully realize that, as an outsider and a specialist, I have viewed the corporate security function mainly from a limited angle—terrorism and violent crime. Corporate security directors, of course, are obliged to deal with a multitude of other issues—due diligence investigations, fraud, technology theft, inventory theft, hijacking, counterfeiting, workplace violence, disaster recovery, bribery, and other compliance issues, to name but a few. Still, in today's world, terrorism is a principal concern for all corporate security directors, and I offer my comments in the hope they may help decision makers deal more effectively with their security directors and help security directors better utilize consultants.

In the course of my thirty-year career in the private sector, I have witnessed the dramatic evolution of the corporate security function. When I started, in the late 1970s, there indeed were corporations that had well-developed security programs, but they were in the minority. Many of them were oil or power-generation companies obliged to operate in hostile environments, pharmaceutical firms mandated by the Food and Drug Administration to keep careful track of their products, defense contractors called upon to protect sensitive information, and banks with obvious security needs.

In most corporations in the 1970s, however, security directors were marginal players. Some had acquired their positions after having been little more than guard-force supervisors. Others were safety engineers or property managers who were assigned security responsibilities.

Today, while there are still a few holdouts, large multinational corporations lacking full-time security directors are the exception rather than the rule. Indeed, in many companies today, the security director holds the title vice president, global security, with all the prestige and responsibility that a vice presidency entails.

I write these chapters with the assistance of three former security directors. One, Ernie Conrads, is widely regarded as one of the founding fathers of corporate security. His program at Westinghouse, then a major player in power generation, both nuclear and conventional, and in defense electronics, was already well developed when I began my career in the private sector. Indeed, it was Ernie who, having read my first risk assessment, on Puerto Rico, encouraged me to produce similar reporting on other countries. Ernie and I thus began a close collaboration that ended only with his retirement in 1994—amid the breakup of Westinghouse.

Ernie received a BS in Crime Control from the University of Maryland, spent two years in the army, and served four years in a civilian component of the office of the Chief of Naval Operations, first as an analyst and, ultimately, as the unit security officer.

In 1962, he joined the division of Westinghouse that was building nuclear-rocket engines as its security officer, and twelve years later he was appointed corporate security director. Shortly after this appointment, he was packed off to a three-month program in Advanced Business Management at Emory University to facilitate his interaction with senior management. As one top executive put it, "We are not necessarily going to understand what you are talking about, but you had better understand what we are talking about." He oversaw worldwide operations and budgets as high as $350 million per annum, including protection programs at nuclear weapons–related sites operated by Westinghouse under contract to the US government.

My interaction with the second of the three directors, Pat Keefe, was quite different. In 1985, I was summoned to meet with senior managers of Colgate-Palmolive and asked to help design a security program. The managers' initial concept was to outsource the security function to my company, but I dissuaded them from doing so, arguing that it was impractical for so large a corporation to operate without a full-time security director. They asked me for a recommendation, and, after obtaining the permission of Jim Atkinson, then corporate security director of Johnson & Johnson, I suggested Pat, who at the time was the security director for the Ortho Pharmaceutical Company, a J & J subsidiary.

Pat graduated from Norwich University, the nation's oldest private military college, and spent seven years in the US Army, first as an airborne ranger and then as a military police officer, achieving the rank of captain. He served in the United States, Europe, and Asia, acquiring experience in criminal investigations and the protection of high-value personnel and installations.

Pat had developed Ortho's security program from scratch and went on, with some small assistance from my firm, to accomplish the same feat at Colgate, building a program renowned for its excellence both inside and outside the company. He retired in 2007 as vice president, global security, having broken new ground in several fields of security, including, in the wake of the 9/11 tragedy in New York City, where Colgate is headquartered, disaster management.

The third of the security directors with whom I am collaborating is Jim Geer, who achieved notable success as director, corporate security (worldwide) of DuPont, from 1989 to 2001.

I have to admit that I have added Jim to the mix for balance. His path to corporate security was markedly different from those of Ernie and Pat. While both of them entered the field at a relatively young age, Jim was selected for the DuPont position at the age of fifty, after having served as assistant director in charge of the Intelligence Division, at the time, one of two operating divisions of the FBI. (The name has subsequently been changed to the National Security Division.) Prior to joining the FBI, Jim had earned a BS degree in Business Administration (Finance) from Tennessee Technological University and served three years as an officer in the US Army.

Also, Jim, unlike Ernie and Pat, was not a regular client of The Ackerman Group, although he did call upon us on occasion, as did Conoco, which at the time was a DuPont subsidiary. Since Jim's retirement from DuPont, however, I have come to know him well and to respect both his expertise and perspective on corporate security.

The four of us, in the two chapters that follow, are going to do our best to consider the selection of a security director and then explore the requirements for achieving success in the position.

Chapter Twenty-Five

WHAT TO LOOK FOR IN A CORPORATE SECURITY DIRECTOR

Executives tasked with selecting corporate security directors often ask whether it is wiser to go with a candidate who has proven himself or herself in a senior government position or one who may have served for a few years in the government or military but has spent most of his or her career in the private sector. The answer depends in part on the nature of the job and, to a much greater extent, on the quality of the individual.

Companies subject to a great deal of government scrutiny, such as defense contractors or pharmaceutical firms, may be inclined to go with a senior military officer or Drug Enforcement Administration (DEA) official, in the belief that he will be able to communicate more effectively with regulators and in effect lobby his old agency on the company's behalf. Ernie Conrads points out that his predecessors in the Westinghouse security directorship were an admiral and a general.

When government relationships are not the deciding factor, companies have a lot more latitude in their selection. Ideally, the candidate should have experience in both the government and the private sector. In most cases, however, I would favor an individual with substantial experience in the private sector over someone coming right out of the government, mainly because someone—anyone—coming directly out of the government is going to have to undergo a period of adjustment.

**On the other hand, a candidate who has had a successful gov-
ernment career is apt to be a quick study and may well perform
superbly in the private sector as well. The greatest advantage for
someone coming out of the government is his or her ability to call
peers still serving in senior positions.** The biggest potential pitfalls
with government retirees involve the possibility that they may have
been burned out by their previous positions or will not take their
responsibilities in the private sector as seriously as they did their government jobs.

**More important than background are the personal qualities of
the candidate. The corporate security director should be smart,
articulate, self-confident, and decisive. He or she should have
excellent people skills and be a team player. He should have the
capacity to stay cool in a crisis. He should be prepared to immerse
himself in his job. He should be capable of adapting to changed
circumstances and open to innovation. He should be sensitive to
corporate politics, yet not be an office politician. Above all, he or
she should possess absolute integrity.**

**If the company has significant overseas interests, it is impor-
tant that the prospective security director have international experience.** The new security director will have a great deal on his plate.
He can't be burdened by having to transfer experience acquired in the
United States to the international arena. It is extremely difficult for
people who have spent their entire careers domestically to make the
leap to operating abroad, in different cultures and different legal systems, where the methodologies of law-enforcement agencies and security providers may be vastly different from counterparts at home.
Although I have encountered some unusually capable individuals who
have managed the leap from domestic to international responsibilities
while managing corporate security departments, they are the exception
rather than the rule. International experience is best acquired in a
junior position, either corporate or governmental.

Ideally, the CEO should participate personally in the selection of
the corporate security director, especially if the candidate is coming

from outside the company, and the CEO's blessing is especially critical if the candidate is being called upon to establish a security department. Pat Keefe met with his CEO for two and one-half hours prior to his selection. A meeting of this duration is most unusual, but Pat believes that it was instrumental in getting him off on the right foot in establishing the security function at Colgate.

Jim Geer had a much shorter meeting at DuPont, but it was more than sufficient, especially insofar as Jim was taking over an established program from a predecessor who had held the same FBI assistant directorship as Jim did and who had been instrumental in Jim's selection.

Ernie Conrads does not recall specifically meeting his CEO prior to his selection, but in his case a meeting was not critical. Ernie, after all, was being promoted from deputy director of corporate security to director, and thus was well known to the CEO.

Chapter Twenty-Six

SUCCESS DEPENDS UPON: CREDIBILITY, AUTHORITY, BUSINESS ACUMEN

The success or failure of the security director will depend to a large extent on the degree to which his judgment is trusted by senior management.

Jim Geer recounts a story about DuPont CEO Ed Woolard, who in 1995 addressed a group of corporate security directors meeting under the auspices of the State Department–sponsored Overseas Security Advisory Council (OSAC). Woolard gave a short presentation and then entertained questions. One attendee rose to ask how he could best ensure access to his own CEO. The speaker answered with a single word: "Credibility."

The reply was as accurate as it was succinct.

Security directors acquire credibility by addressing issues head-on and by being prepared when called upon to meet with senior management, not only to outline in-depth the particular problem they are facing but also to suggest means for resolving it. Corporations are confronted with a broad spectrum of security problems, and no security director can be expected to have all the answers. He has to know where to find the answers, however. And in instances in which he is the one bringing the problem to the attention of management, which is usually the case, he had better survey those resources in advance of the meeting.

Many times I have been called by a corporate security director on the way into a meeting with senior management focusing on my field of expertise. Some have sought my input on an issue facing them, while others merely called to confirm their own action plan.

The good ones understand that their credibility is on the line every time they enter the executive suite. They anticipate the questions they will be asked and are prepared to defend their plan of action, frankly and honestly, acknowledging any potential pitfalls.

In addition to acquiring credibility with senior management, the corporate security director must be seen as having authority by his peers in middle-level management. Building this perception of authority is not always easy.

It is not possible for the corporate security director to acquire a reputation within the company for having turned around a money-losing operation or surpassed a profit goal. Indeed, many, if not most, of his successes will not be publicized at all. For example, it is often in the corporation's interest to keep under wraps the successful resolution of a threat or extortion, or even a kidnapping.

Unless peers in mid-level management have direct experience with the security director, which may not occur for years, their judgment of him will rest almost entirely on their perception of his standing with senior management, and to a large degree they will measure this by his access.

One of the common denominators in Ernie's, Pat's, and Jim's success was the immediacy of their access to senior management.

It is critical for the security director to report to a corporate officer one step down from the CEO. To have him report to someone two steps down is to undermine his authority. He will be perceived by others in the corporation as a minor, rather than a major, player.

Normally, the security director reports to the general counsel, senior vice president for human resources, or senior vice president for administration. If the director's responsibilities are mainly investigative, it is best that he report to the general counsel. If his responsibilities are mainly protective, it is perhaps more appropriate for him to report to the human resources or administrative chief.

Ernie reported to several different people during the course of his career: vice president, human resources; vice president, strategic planning; senior vice president, administration. In each case, his immediate supervisor reported directly to the CEO. Jim reported to the senior vice president-general counsel. Pat technically reported directly to the CEO, but in practice he dealt mainly with an executive vice president who was assistant to the CEO.

Pat's direct line to the CEO was important in establishing his authority. Jim, although he did not have that direct line, had something equally important: physical proximity. His was the only other office on the CEO's floor at the corporate headquarters.

There is such a thing as being too close to the CEO. Some corporate security directors travel constantly with their CEOs, and in the course of doing so come to be seen as bodyguards. This undermines their image as a trusted business resource. Certainly, there are times when it is appropriate for the security director to travel with the CEO, and occasional trips can help cement the relationship, but day-in, day-out travel distracts the security director from his other duties.

Some companies are highly centralized, while others, conglomerates, for example, are much more decentralized. No matter what the company's structure, however, the corporate security director should have direct authority over his counterparts in subsidiaries. The Colgate security function was perhaps the most centralized of the three companies we are considering. Westinghouse was much more decentralized, with large subsidiaries operating in fields as diverse as nuclear energy and defense electronics, and DuPont, in Conoco, had a major subsidiary with its own particular security problems. In all three cases, however, the corporate security director was seen as having authority over subsidiary counterparts, to include their selection, evaluation, and promotion.

Some companies place the safety function under the security director or the security department under the safety director. Except in smaller companies, this is a bad idea. Each of the two functions has grown increasingly technical, and these days there are few managers who are proficient in both areas. Invariably, one of the two winds up being the stepchild.

The initial impression made by the security director will go a long way in determining his ultimate success. While it is crucial for the incoming security director to approach his position with confidence, he also needs more than a dose of humility, especially if he is coming from outside the corporation and/or is organizing the security function. Pat, shortly after his appointment, met with each member of the Colgate management team, in each case asking, "What do you think I can do for you?" A few were dubious that he could bring anything to the table. Indeed, they did not believe that the company had significant security problems. That impression, however, was largely fed by the perception in the field, that, since the corporation had no security function, there was little value in reporting problems. After the word went out that the company, indeed, had established a security function, Pat was deluged with requirements.

All three of the former security directors I queried went to special pains to avoid the perception that they were the company cop. Many security directors and staff members, especially those coming directly from police agencies, have a hard time discarding their image as "heavies," which undermines their effectiveness in dealing with corporate peers. Some employees are just plain intimidated by security and go out of their way to avoid dealing with security personnel. Others view corporate security as mainly an enforcement function and see themselves potentially as the targets of enforcement operations. While corporate security does in fact have an enforcement aspect, it also has a protective side, shielding personnel from terrorism, crime, workplace violence, and other threats. It cannot be effective in this role without input from corporate employees, who must be at ease with the security staff and entirely confident in providing information.

I hope that I have made the case that, to succeed, the security director must have both credibility and authority. He also must be perceived as having business acumen. While not obliged to turn a profit, he is expected to run an efficient operation.

Above all, he must not be perceived to be an empire builder. A security director who thinks that he will be judged in the corporation by the size of his staff is in for a rude awakening. Most successful security directors run "lean and mean" operations, maintaining on staff a small core of effective subordinates, some generalists, and perhaps a few specialists, depending on the thrust of security operations, and complementing them, when necessary, with outside specialists.

The security director also needs to have a good understanding of the businesses his company is in and of their profitability. Ernie recalls visiting a Westinghouse plant that was building modular residential units. As sometimes happens in a conglomerate, the general manager had been transferred from an entirely different activity, in this case nuclear engineering. The nuclear engineer, who had known only one level of security, intensive, had gone about protecting his plant as if it were a nuclear facility. It was left to Ernie to point out to him that he was spending far more on security than could possibly be justified by the value of the lumber and other materials he was seeking to protect. He pared down the guard force and probably saved the operation from a steep loss.

I was handed another dramatic example of the value of a security director with business acumen while writing this book. We had been asked to do a background investigation on a potential franchisee in Russia and had rendered a report that, like many done on former Soviet countries, was decidedly gray. On the one hand, we had uncovered information to the effect that in the 1990s the subject had operated a business that was paying protection money to organized crime. Our report stipulated, however, that the subject appeared to have severed his connection to the organized-crime gang in recent years.

This pattern is not uncommon in Russia. In the 1990s most businesses paid protection money to mafias, but in this decade the gangs have lost a great deal of their power, and many entrepreneurs have managed to clean themselves up. Still, the business development manager was troubled by the allegation of past organized-crime connections. He requested a conference call on the matter, and I suggested that the corporate security director also participate. It turned out to be my best move that day—perhaps that month.

The director of business development opened the conversation by declaring that he understood that nothing in Russia was either black or white. He said that from his reading of our report, and his dealings with the individual in question, he would rate him about a 5 for probity on a scale of 1 to 10. I replied that I had been impressed by the indications from our Russian sources, who were well connected with law enforcement, that he had in fact attempted to clean himself up and was now thought to be free of organized-crime links. I might rate the individual even higher, perhaps 5.5 or 6.

The business development director continued to express unease. He was really looking for an 8 on his scale, a rarity in Russia, and it appeared that we had reached an impasse, when the corporate security director entered the conversation for the first time: "Why not offer him a contract with a buyback provision after two or three years—giving us a means of escape if new misgivings about his links to organized crime come to the surface?" The business development man immediately embraced the idea, and I silently congratulated myself for having brought the security director, a senior individual with outstanding business acumen, into the dialogue. Certainly, I didn't understand the business well enough to put forward his suggestion—and rescue a promising opportunity.

SECTION 7

■

EPILOGUE: A LOOK BACK AND A LOOK AHEAD

■

Chapter Twenty-Seven

A LOOK BACK AT MY CAREER

I could not possibly have imagined the adventures in store for me on the day in 1946 that I began elementary school at PS 28 in the Bronx. Like most of us, I have tried to be master of my fate, and in many cases I have succeeded in hunting down opportunities or seizing those that presented themselves. But I fully appreciate that, to an uncomfortable degree, my success or failure has been determined by forces far beyond my control.

Crisis responders are acutely aware of their dependence on outside forces. We do our best to build an experience base and a reputation, but ultimately we find ourselves waiting for the phone to ring. We cannot drum up business. To do so, even to approach a company known to have suffered a kidnapping or other emergency, is, in my judgment at least, highly unethical.

Even after we are invited into a case, we can hardly dictate its course. Indeed, any experienced responder will tell you that he expects to be buffeted between forces he cannot control, the perpetrators on the one hand and law enforcement on the other, and that he expends most of his effort trying to keep upright and headed in the direction of accomplishing his objective—the neutralization of the threat, the resolution of the extortion, the release of the hostage. Of all the qualities needed in an effective responder, perhaps none is as important as tenacity.

In hiring associates I have been obliged to reflect on the qualities required of a successful responder: after tenacity, there are street smarts, self-confidence, courage, the kind of perspective that fosters composure under fire. Dave Phillips, my first chief in the CIA, described the ideal operations officer as an intellectual marine. The same can be said for responders.

Where do we get our responders? Our principal sources have remained remarkably consistent over the years: the CIA, the FBI, the US Navy SEALs, the US Army Special Forces, the Foreign Legion (for French-language competence), and municipal police agencies.

For my response staff, incidentally, waiting for assignments has always been more difficult than accomplishing them. Responders, by definition, are type A personalities and, while they value some down-time, they do not handle well the inevitable droughts in emergency work. When at loose ends, they tend to scrap among themselves and argue with our analysts, most of whom are recovering journalists and with whom they rarely get along.

I trace my professional roots to my enrollment in 1957 at Dartmouth College, which itself resulted from a quirk of fate. I did not distinguish myself in my Long Island high school, and my application to Dartmouth clearly was a "reach." Somehow, I made the waiting list. I was also wait-listed at Tufts, but no other schools to which I applied saw fit even to place me in that category. It was not an easy time.

Then, an uncle of mine had an idea. He worked in my grandfather's demolition business and had done a favor for a gentleman named Amos Manser, who had a wrecking business in New Hampshire, Dartmouth's home state. Mr. Manser had contracted to take down a train station, but his crew was having trouble with it—too much steel. He called his New York counterpart for help, and my uncle sent a team experienced in heavy demolition.

My uncle thought that Mr. Manser might know someone on campus who could help get me elevated from the waiting list. New Yorkers always seem to think that in the provinces everyone knows everyone else.

A call was made, and, indeed, Mr. Manser confirmed that he did know a prominent Dartmouth alumnus. Both had been active in Republican politics. He'd see what he could do.

Within forty-eight hours I received a telegram inviting me to enroll. Mr. Manser's contact, it turned out, was none other than former New Hampshire governor Sherman Adams, who at the time was President Dwight D. Eisenhower's chief of staff.

I was launched into my college career by many people, Mr. Manser among them, wagging their fingers and admonishing me to work hard. I did and, chastened by the near fiasco in college admission, finished ninth out of a class of seven hundred—but I am getting ahead of my story.

The Soviets had launched *Sputnik* the year that I graduated from high school, and Americans had begun to take them seriously. There was a lot of talk about the need to study their language, and I enrolled in an elementary Russian course at the start of my freshman year.

In the summer between my sophomore and junior years, the Carnegie Corporation organized an experimental study program designed to immerse students in the Russian language for three months, with much of the time spent in Russia itself. Several Dartmouth students were nominated, but I was not among them. The reason for the omission, I learned when I approached the department chairman, was that I had not been enrolled in a Russian spring-term course. (Dartmouth had begun a trimester system that year, and I had decided to take a semester off from Russian. Indeed, no course offered that semester had really been appropriate for me.)

The chairman regretted the oversight and said that he would do all he could to see that I was included. There was another exchange of phone calls, and, again, I was last man on the bus.

My time in the Soviet Union was truly life altering. It was 1959. Stalin had been dead a mere six years. Nikita Khrushchev had emerged as the new dictator. An American Exhibition was under way in Moscow that summer, and inside one of the exhibits Khrushchev and then vice president Richard Nixon engaged in their famous Kitchen Debate.

We were a group of about twenty American students, with a few professorial chaperones, and we were encouraged to spend our time talking with the Russians we encountered. Striking up conversations was easy since the Russians were tremendously curious about us and about the outside world in general. But, except for a couple of instances in which people initiated frank exchanges (always on the street and thus out of earshot of the ubiquitous listening devices), conversations were always very guarded. Usually, the Russians said little about themselves, and even their questions were worded very carefully. Inquiries about the United States generally tracked with current propaganda themes. Repeatedly, for example, I had to answer questions about our unemployment rate, then 5 percent. Many subjects were taboo.

I will never forget an encounter with a Russian humanities professor, whom I happened upon in the Museum of the Revolution in Leningrad (now St. Petersburg). We found ourselves part of a group examining a photograph labeled "Council of Defense," which purported to show the Soviet Defense Council at the time of Russia's civil war. I remarked on the absence of Leon Trotsky, who in fact had been commissar for defense at the time. My statement was greeted with an awkward silence. Finally, the professor perked up, saying, "Trotsky played no significant role in the civil war."

"But you are mistaken," I insisted. "Trotsky was the military mastermind who, more than anyone else, was responsible for the communist victory." He refused to concede the point. I couldn't understand it. Trotsky's role in the civil war was historical fact. True, Stalin had done his best to downplay his arch-rival's role in Soviet history, but surely he had not obliterated it entirely. Moreover, there was talk of de-Stalinization. What was going on?

I didn't fully appreciate the significance of the exchange until the professor approached me again on the steps of the museum as I was leaving. "Do you have a moment, young man?"

"Yes," I said.

"Then tell me about Trotsky."

A mood of despondency had settled over the Russians. It was the despair of a good people of great intellect—a people that had given the world Tolstoy, Dostoevsky, and Tchaikovsky—now beaten into an obedient stupor. I returned to the United States and to my junior year at college, but I could not forget what I had seen. I had witnessed communism firsthand, seen how controlling, oppressive, dehumanizing it could be, and was ready to take it on.

Within a month of my return, I was presented with a means of doing so. Returning from classes, I found a brief note under my dorm room door. A college official was asking me to drop by for a talk. I did so, and, after carefully closing his door, he introduced himself as the CIA's campus spotter. A veteran of the OSS, our World War II–era intelligence service, he had been asked by then CIA director Allen Dulles to approach promising students. He was impressed by my language skills. At the time I was studying both Russian and Spanish at an advanced level.

Within a few weeks, I met with a CIA staff recruiter and began to consider seriously a career in the Agency. I didn't enter its headquarters, however, until three years later, in March 1963. In the interim, I finished college and also earned a master's degree in Government at Columbia. Even in 1963, I was not quite ready to begin my Agency career in earnest. We all had a military obligation back then, and I was packed off to the air force to complete Officer Training School. Then I spent about nine months as an air police officer on a Strategic Air Command (SAC) base in northern California.

Following my air force stint, I spent another nine months training for clandestine operations in a class of forty-five—all male. Some, about a third, were really first-rate—razor-sharp. They were intelligent and articulate. They knew who they were and where they were going. Others appeared to be along for the ride.

I had not been a standout in training—my instructors graded me down for failing to adjust to the role-playing that was required in their exercises, which I had considered somewhat Mickey Mouse. Also, I was reluctant to enter the Soviet Division, which had tapped me, because it was reputed to be a dead end for junior officers. It took years before they let you get close to a live source, and I was much too impatient for that. I expressed a preference for the more freewheeling Latin America Division, but it had already filled its quota. I was assigned to a staff instead of a geographic division, which was a decided setback. I detested the staff work and sought any opportunity to transfer.

Opportunity knocked in April 1965, when leftist insurgents took over the heart of Santo Domingo, the capital of the Dominican Republic. Fearful that another Cuba was in the offing, President Lyndon B. Johnson sent in the Marines, then the 82nd Airborne Division. He ordered the Agency to deploy fifty case officers. I hoped against hope that I would be one of them. No call came. They were looking for experienced officers, not raw trainees.

Latin America Division, however, had trouble finding fifty suitable officers and began to cast its nets. In the movies, intelligence officers are always given their assignments in the solemnity of the boss's office, but fate tapped me on the shoulder in the third-floor men's room. One of the senior officers of Latin America Division approached the urinal next to mine, looked over at me and said, "You speak Spanish, don't you?" My answer was, "Yes, sir," and I was on my way—Number 50.

On the day of my arrival in Santo Domingo, I was invited to lunch with the chief of station, the legendary Dave Phillips, a tall, ruggedly handsome former actor who had been shot down over Austria during World War II, escaped his POW camp, and made it back to American lines. After the war, he had found his way into the Agency and had established a crackerjack reputation by participating in a number of successful operations, among them the overthrow of Guatemala's leftist president, Jacobo Arbenz. Phillips was sometimes referred to as the Agency's John Wayne, a characterization that never made much sense to me. To my mind, it was the other way around: Dave was the prototype for the action heroes Wayne always seemed to play.

Also present at the lunch was Jim Flannery, the deputy chief of station, whose dictum "perfect security involves doing nothing in a vacuum" I quoted earlier. Like Dave, he was a Texan, and he had been Dave's deputy in a previous assignment. Another World War II veteran, he had landed at Utah Beach with the 79th Infantry Division and fought his way across Europe, rising to the rank of major while in his early twenties and earning the Silver Star in the process. They were quite a tandem. Jim, as rough-hewn as Dave was smooth, was a brilliant strategist and analyst. An incredible writer, I can see him still, sitting at his typewriter in his professorial mode, smoking his pipe and pouring out his thoughts a mile a minute.

It is widely believed that the founding generation of the CIA was straight out of the eastern establishment. Like most other generalizations about the Agency, it is pure nonsense. Yes, there was that element in the OSS and the Clandestine Services, but bluebloods were far outnumbered by guys like Dave and Jim, and by ethnics, who supplied the Agency with a good deal of its linguistic competence. In the course of my career I worked with officers from a range of ethnic and religious backgrounds: Cuban Americans, Italian Americans, Irish Americans, German Jews, Lebanese Christians, Mormons, even a Romanoff prince.

In any event, I could hardly believe my good fortune! Here I was, in a zone of conflict, answering what I was certain had been my calling.

While in the Dominican Republic, I worked in intelligence acquisition, covert political action, and special (paramilitary) operations. Our mission was to quash the leftist insurgency and support the development of democratic political institutions (no easy task, as our Dominican operation began only four years after the assassination of Rafael Leonidas Trujillo, who had governed the country—brutally— for thirty-one years). We were remarkably successful by any measure. For the past forty-two years, right-of-center and left-of-center parties have alternated in power, always accomplishing the transfer peacefully after elections deemed by international observers to have been fair.

I won Dave's confidence in a very improbable manner on what I remember as a very rainy night. I had acquired a nugget of intelligence from one of my sources that I recognized as both actionable and highly perishable. I drove immediately to Dave's house, which at the time did not have a working telephone, and was greeted at the door by his teenage son, who told me that Dave had gone to bed early. I asked the boy to wake him, and after a couple of minutes Dave came to the door, bleary-eyed. I told him what I had learned, and he told me to present the intelligence at the staff meeting the following morning.

I got back into my car and sat for a few moments, deciding what to do. They definitely had not covered this problem in training. On the one hand, I knew the value of the intelligence and knew it was highly perishable, but I was a rookie and had been told by my chief of station that the matter could wait until the morning. On the other hand, I knew that Dave, who had been working eighteen-hour days, had not been fully awake when I talked with him. Should I take the matter "down the chain of command," thereby violating a major taboo in both the military and the Agency?

I had always been self-confident, but now I crossed the line into real hutzpah. I stopped at a public phone and called Jim, who did have a working telephone. Talking around the matter at hand, I managed to draw him to a meeting at a gas station that was about halfway between his home and my current location. We were both standing ankle-deep in water when I briefed him on the evening's developments.

He put his hand on my shoulder and said, "I'm glad you called me. Go back to Dave's house, tell him that you talked to me and that I said he needs to drink as much coffee as he can tolerate and be at the office in forty-five minutes." Jim would round up the other case officers whose presence was required.

I didn't really relish the trip back to Dave's, but I did manage to convince his son, who I'm sure by this time saw me as a crazed rookie, to awaken him again. Dave came to the door, now looking really annoyed. I invoked Jim's name and relayed his instructions. He assured me that he would be at the office at the appointed time.

Dave began the meeting by saying that he had learned a very important lesson that night: "No matter how tired you are, and no matter how much you need a night's sleep, never take a sleeping pill in the Dominican Republic." I was bowled over by the unprompted admission, and from that night saw him as ten feet tall. (Previously he had been more than eight feet.) I was delighted a few weeks later when he invited me to return as a member of his station.

By the time I left Santo Domingo in 1968, I was fast-tracked for promotion and stayed on that track for the rest of my career. Never again would I be the last man in. Indeed, much to my astonishment, only seven years after leaving Santo Domingo, I would be the first man out of the Agency.

After Santo Domingo, I was paired with another legendary officer, Dick Welch, as the junior member of a two-man team given a sensitive assignment in South America. Dick was a Harvard classics scholar (magna cum laude) and one of the best strategic thinkers I encountered in my Agency career. He would have gone to the top in any field he chose, but his passion was intelligence, and he pursued it with matchless vigor and enthusiasm, and with a wonderfully urbane sense of humor. Dick was a tough adversary but a gentle friend. There is no question in my mind that, had he lived, he would have risen to the Agency directorship.

After completing the assignment in 1970, I spent four years trying to recruit so-called hard targets—Soviets and Castro Cubans—to provide intelligence information. I worked in Latin America, Europe, and Africa under several different guises. I was still single and acquired a reputation as something of a risk taker. It was not all that difficult to stand out among my peers. The ratio of effective to ineffective case officers proved to be about the same as the one I had observed in training. A third or less of the operators carried the others on their backs.

I was in Miami when the Watergate scandal broke and could not have imagined that it would trigger a chain of developments that would put an end to my career.

The Agency had no role in Watergate, but it was close enough to its margins to be affected by the stench. Two of the participants in the burglary plot were former Agency officers. A third, Eugenio Martinez, was still on the payroll of the Miami station, mainly, as I understood it, for "old time's sake." He met periodically with an ineffective case officer (a more competent operator would not have been wasted on a contact as marginal as Martinez). Had the case officer been more able, he probably could have smoked out the cabal, and Agency higher-ups might have put a stop to it, or at least to Martinez's involvement.

Watergate led directly to the resignation of Dick Helms, who had been the director for most of my tenure at the CIA and had been widely respected, even revered. He was pressured by President Nixon to have the Agency take the rap for the scandal, or at least block the investigation into it on national security grounds. When he refused to do so, he was obliged to resign. As a consolation prize, he was given the ambassadorship to Iran. To my mind, Helms was one of the heroes of Watergate, unsung because his act of political courage took place at a time when various Agency misdeeds became public.

I was as surprised as anyone else by those missteps, especially the monumentally ill-advised effort to enlist the Mafia in an effort to assassinate Fidel Castro. I knew that the Agency had its cowboys, mainly leftovers from the wild and woolly days of the OSS, but I had assumed that they had been made to toe the line. Indeed, it was my hope and expectation that my own generation, among the first to receive extensive training, would take the Agency to new heights of professionalism. It never got the chance.

The misdeeds I cannot deny, though I ascribe them in large part to the fact that the Agency always saw itself as the president's instrument and, until Helms drew the line at accepting responsibility for Watergate, had been far too quick to heed presidential directives, no matter how questionable. Helms himself depicted quite frankly some of the agonizing exchanges he had with both Presidents Johnson and Nixon in his excellent, posthumously published autobiography, *A Look over My Shoulder*.

The CIA director, unlike his counterpart at the FBI, serves at the pleasure of the president, but this does not explain entirely the Agency's willingness to comply. The president was the president, and we were his men. More than once during my career I heard the words, "This comes from the White House."

I began to feel the shockwaves from the congressional investigation of the Agency in late 1974 while posted to Europe—ironically, the first cushy assignment I had had in my career. Repeatedly, my proposals for initiatives against hard targets were turned down. Again and again, I was told that this was not the time to take chances. No longer, it seemed, were risk takers in demand. On the contrary, we came to be viewed as potential liabilities.

In the early spring of 1975, I decided to throw in the towel. The Agency had no defenders. I was cocky enough to think that I could be its champion. Unbeknownst to me, Dave Phillips, then chief of Latin America Division, had made a similar decision. He was eligible to retire. I merely resigned.

Dave's plan was to found the Association of Foreign Intelligence Officers (AFIO) to lobby for an effective intelligence capability. In retrospect, his plan was far wiser than mine, which was to champion the Agency as a lone wolf, perhaps writing a book and entering politics.

I contacted Bill Montalbano, a friend from graduate school, who at the time was covering Latin America for the *Miami Herald*, and confided to him my status as case officer and my intention to resign. He candidly advised me, for maximum impact, to "come out" in the *New York Times* or the *Washington Post*, since neither "national newspaper" would give much weight to a story from the *Herald*. I ignored his advice and stayed with the Miami newspaper, mainly because I knew that Bill and his managing editor, Larry Jinks, would give me a fair shake. It was one of a series of strategic blunders.

The *Herald* featured my story in its Sunday edition on June 8, 1975. I outlined my reasons for leaving the Agency and warned that the self-serving congressional investigation, by subjecting the Agency to intensive public scrutiny, was in effect throwing the baby out with the bathwater. No intelligence agency could possibly survive this "goldfish bowl" with its capabilities intact.

The impact of the *Herald* story was very limited. I was invited to appear on a few TV talk shows and received a very lukewarm reception. I got a handful of lecturing gigs. It was not a time to champion the Agency.

My failure to rally public opinion behind the CIA and its operatives came home to me in a very personal way on December 23, 1975. While watching the evening news, I was shocked to see the screen filled with a picture of Dick Welch, who had been shot to death by Greek leftists in Athens after having been named as the CIA station chief by *Counterspy* magazine. Months of tugging on sleeves, grasping lapels, pleading for interviews, and seeking forums had been for naught.

I went to Washington for the funeral and returned again a few weeks later to speak at a congressional hearing. President Gerald Ford had nominated George H. W. Bush to be CIA director, and I was only one of two people—the other was a representative of an extreme leftist group—to speak in opposition. While I had nothing but respect for Bush, and said so, I was concerned about the precedent of appointing to the directorship the former chairman of the Republican National Committee. The nomination, of course, sailed through, and several weeks later I was surprised to receive a gracious letter from then-director Bush applauding my stand and assuring me that he would make every effort to avoid politicizing the Agency.

I recounted my career in a book, *Street Man*. There was some interest from a couple of publishers, but only if I went ahead without the Agency's imprimatur. This I refused to do. I was—and still am—contractually obliged to obtain Agency approval for any published material dealing with intelligence sources and methods.

I decided to run in a Democratic congressional primary in Miami against Bill Lehman, a member of the Pike Committee, the House of Representatives committee that was investigating the Agency. I had been a lifelong Democrat, as were most of my peers at the Agency, though many of us had begun to have doubts about the party in 1972, with the presidential nomination of Senator George McGovern, who was astoundingly soft on communism. Still, the conventional wisdom in Miami in 1976 was that a Republican could not be elected to Congress and that the battle had to be waged in the Democratic primary.

I campaigned with virtually no financing. Pledges of assistance from Democratic hawks in Washington, some of whom subsequently achieved prominence as neoconservatives, came to naught. I was beaten—badly—and took the cure, never again venturing into politics.

I did, however, continue to do my best to champion the CIA. In a December 1978 op-ed piece in the *Miami Herald*, I warned that "one day decent people will surely ask how and why the CIA was destroyed." Eight years later, in an op-ed article in the *Los Angeles Times*, I addressed myself specifically to the need for a strong Agency, pointing out that "a dozen years ago, with astounding absence of foresight, we did away with the covert arm of our government," and warning that "there will be no more crucial test of our political system in the remaining years of this century than our response to terrorism." I guess that I was off by a year or two. In any event, I take not one whit of satisfaction in the accuracy of my warnings.

Nor do I have much hope for the revitalization of the CIA. In my view, for an intelligence service to operate effectively in a democracy, which is always something of a stretch, there must exist a broad consensus that its mission is crucial to the nation's survival. Top leaders of the executive must buy into the consensus, along with legislators, judges, and, perhaps most critically, the media, which cannot engage the service in a constant game of gotcha.

Younger people will find it hard to even conceive of such a consensus, but it did exist when I joined the CIA at the height of the cold war, and it is to our detriment that it cannot be restored in the face of the current challenge from Islamic extremism.

In any event, by 1977 reality had overtaken my hapless crusade. I was dead broke after my defeat and looking for any opportunity that might keep me afloat. I made several inquiries about positions in corporate security but was met with a chilly reception. Former CIA officers were not in great demand.

Early in the year, I received a call from Lou Palumbo, who had been an Agency security officer and was eligible to retire. He was anxious to get into security consulting and thought our respective talents would complement each other. They did, although, as previously stated, it took some time for us to get going.

Lou spearheaded the security training and security survey aspects of the company and did a good deal of the marketing, an area in which he truly excelled, while I focused on risk forecasting and emergency response. Nine months into our collaboration, we received a retainer from Chubb Corporation to do the response work for their Kidnap, Ransom and Extortion policyholders, and we were on our way.

Before long I was on the road again, doing work that was just as challenging, if not even more so, than my work in the Agency. In the CIA, I labored abroad, always a step or two away from running afoul of the government on whose turf I was working, but I had a safety net under me—the United States government. Now I was working abroad, the same step or two away from running afoul of the host government, but without a net. If I pushed the limits too far, if I screwed up, it was on me.

There was one advantage in being in the private sector. For the first time since my air force service, I could tell people what I really did for a living. Not that I necessarily wanted to! Try telling new acquaintances that you specialize in recovering kidnap victims. Mostly, I described myself as a business consultant.

The collaboration with Lou lasted until 1989, when I purchased his share of the company. By that time, I had married, at age forty-five, and my wife and I had had our first son. A second was on the way, and two daughters followed. I began to limit my time on the road, but not entirely. I still go out to meet important clients and pursue major kidnap cases, and my family has proven remarkably understanding.

It was shortly after Lou's departure that I became friendly with Dick Helms, who had sought me out to congratulate me on my success in the private sector. I was flattered by the initiative and even more honored in ensuing years when he attended some ten Terrorism Roundtables sponsored by our firm, in the process becoming my mentor and my friend. My wife insists that she always knew when I was on the phone with him, because, invariably, I stood at attention.

My kids, after helping to welcome the director several times to our home, made the natural assumption that I had hobnobbed with him during my Agency days. Nothing could have been farther from the truth. He had been in the ether, while I was in the trenches. He spoke once to my training class, and I briefed him on one occasion on a particular operation in which I was involved. My knowledge of him was limited to second-hand impressions from my seniors, who were unswervingly loyal. I knew that he much preferred classical intelligence gathering to covert political action, which he believed should be used very judiciously, and that he had been a strong critic of the Bay of Pigs operation, perhaps the Agency's most ambitious covert action program and its biggest failure, but at that time I had little appreciation of the man himself.

The man himself proved even more heroic than his reputation. Indeed, I have never met anyone with greater integrity or less pretentiousness. I experienced his integrity firsthand in the early 1990s, the heady days that followed the fall of the Soviet Union and the rise of Boris Yeltsin, a time in which it seemed that capitalism and democracy might just take root. I made several trips to Moscow to study the business-security climate and was asked to become an adviser on business security to the Yeltsin regime's National Security Council. I was even provided a visa describing me as such—an unimaginable prize for a former CIA operative. Council representatives visited our roundtable.

In my dealings with the Russian officials, it soon became clear that their interest in me was largely predicated on my access to Dick Helms, a respected adversary who perhaps was even better known in Russia than in the United States. They wanted Helms—and, to a much lesser extent, me—to bless their efforts to combat organized-crime influence in the burgeoning private sector. Helms was game to participate (you have to appreciate what a kick it was for the quintessential cold warrior to be invited to advise his former adversaries), but he added the caveat that the initiative not discredit him or the CIA. "I'm putting my honor in your hands, Mike," he said.

Well, that proved quite a burden. The Russian officials, it turned out, in addition to their governmental duties, aspired to establish themselves as corporate security consultants, and it was mainly for these pursuits that the Helms brand interested them. Also, it quickly became clear that they, like other post-Soviet Russians, were out to make their fortune and make it quickly, with little attention paid to ethics or long-term equities. They were willing to share the spoils with us, of course, but the more I dealt with them, the more uneasy I became. When I called the director to tell him that I could not in good conscience recommend that we proceed, he recalled the mandate he had given me and thanked me for fulfilling it. As to my misgivings about the Russians: "I'm not in the least bit surprised," he said.

Helms's lack of pretentiousness is less well known but is perhaps best illustrated by an incident early in our friendship. The first time I invited him to address our roundtable, I made the mistake of accepting his suggestion that he make his own airline reservations and bill the company. He spoke eloquently and, as on all subsequent occasions, paid great attention to the other speakers, anxious to learn as much as possible about the development of the terrorism phenomenon.

When he returned home and mailed in his accounting, I was chagrined to learn that he had squeezed his lanky frame into an economy seat. When I called to assure him that it had been my intention that he travel first class, he responded that it was no big deal. He opted to fly coach simply because he did not know what our policy was or what kind of financial shape the company was in. Over the years, speakers of far less stature have been far more demanding.

They all are gone now, Helms, Phillips, Flannery, and Welch, all at Arlington. I followed all four to their resting places, always awestruck that men of this caliber had befriended me. Welch, of course, died first, in 1975 at forty-five. Flannery was the last to go, in

2005, at eighty-five. We had kept in touch by phone during the years of his retirement, and it was always a treat to talk with him. It was a measure of the man that the week before he passed on he called to tell me that he was dying and to thank me for my friendship. I tried my best to convey to him how large he had loomed in my life, but, in the emotion of the moment, I'm afraid that I came up short.

Jim, Dave, Dick, Director, thank *you* for everything you did for me—and for our country. You were among the very best it has produced. I can only pray that future crises will bring to the fore public servants of comparable worth.

Chapter Twenty-Eight

A LOOK AHEAD

One of the exciting things about my business is its unpredictability. I come into work each morning not knowing what lies in store. Will we be called upon to respond to a kidnapping or extortion? Will there be an al-Qaida atrocity? Will we be asked to deal with some new wrinkle in terrorism or criminality? Will we need to stage an evacuation in the face of a military coup—or revolution?

The only certainty each morning is that I cannot possibly predict what the day ahead will bring. Indeed, I never know for sure where I will lay my head that night. My bag is always packed, my affairs always in order.

Another certainty is that new developments will require the modification of some of the "principles" discussed in this book. Some will turn out not to have been principles at all. Also, kidnap risks will shift to new countries. New methodologies and technologies will be developed for responding to terrorism.

The future of Global Jihad is a major question mark. It has proven remarkably resilient in the years since 9/11. Even with its leadership pinned down in tribal areas between Pakistan and Afghanistan, and hard put to communicate with the outside world, it has developed affiliates such as QJI in Iraq, QAP in Saudi Arabia, QIM in North Africa, LT and the jihadist tribes in Pakistan, and JI in Southeast Asia, and it has inspired countless self-generated cells of young Muslim extremists with only the most tenuous of ties to the core movement.

As stated earlier, these self-generated cells for the most part have failed to stage significant attacks. But if the al-Qaida core

solves the problem of seeding into them experienced operatives, it will become a far more dangerous movement.

The country to watch most closely in this regard is Pakistan. It is too soon to know whether the traditional parties voted into power in the February 2008 elections will permit Pakistani intelligence services to continue to interdict extremists transiting their country, as they did so effectively when Musharraf reigned supreme. Another unknown is their will to engage the al-Qaida core and its tribal allies in the northwest. If the Pakistanis falter, we'll be right back where we were in the years preceding 9/11.

Another major concern is the thousands of foreign jihadists who have passed through Iraq, acquiring operational experience and explosives expertise.

It could be argued that al-Qaida itself developed as a reaction to the Soviet occupation of Afghanistan. Having expelled the Soviets, the Islamists established themselves in that country and set about to engage Western civilization on a grand scale. Islamist opposition to the American occupation of Iraq could have—should have—been foreseen. For some time, it appeared that QJI and the allied Sunni extremists who had succeeded in establishing themselves in western Iraq's Anbar Province might turn it into a new Afghanistan, a new impermeable base for terrorist adventures abroad. Now, that threat appears to have dissipated. Iraqi Sunnis, with encouragement from American forces, have turned against QJI, and the al-Qaida affiliate has been placed on the defensive. It remains to be seen, however, whether the United States will have the fortitude to maintain sufficient troop levels in Iraq to hold them in check. Also, countless jihadists trained in Iraq are still out there, dispersed across the Middle East, Europe, even the United States—a time bomb if there ever was one.

Yet another concern is the durability of our stalwart Muslim allies—the aging Mubarak in Egypt, the Saud Dynasty in Saudi Arabia, King Abdullah in Jordan, all of whom have been so effective in opposing al-Qaida. But each of them governs by virtue of the might and loyalty of their security forces, and not the will of their people.

The contribution of these regimes to stemming Global Jihad cannot be overstated. Their success in suppressing radicals in their home countries has exceeded the expectations of even the most optimistic analysts. If any of these regimes were to be overturned, it would severely undermine the War on Terrorism.

In coming years, Sunni militancy will take new turns, open new fronts, develop new techniques. It most likely will ebb and flow. We all earnestly hope that 9/11 will be its high watermark, but chances are that it will not be. A religious imperative is impossible to kill. Indeed, it can be argued that militant Islam as we know it today is the descendent of a bellicose strain of the faith that has reasserted itself countless times in the fourteen centuries since Muhammad.

Religious zealotry, while it may see periods of remission, always seems to eventually reassert itself with renewed vigor. In Algeria, we have seen a succession of radical Islamic groups evolve over nearly twenty years. They have suffered from debilitating factionalism and in the early part of this decade appeared to be on the ropes, but in the past couple of years they have made a stunning comeback.

Meanwhile, in Egypt, though Gama'a shows few signs of life, it clearly has inspired other radical Islamists to follow in its path.

Chances are that history will look back upon the years since 9/11 as an ebb tide for al-Qaida, a time of regrouping for its minions, who will reclaim center stage with even greater ferocity.

Or, will the greater risks emanate from Iran-backed Shia Muslim extremists, who may be poised to sue for control of much of Iraq's territory and oil? Will Hizbollah, which hijacked TWA Flight 847 and staged mega-bombings against Israeli and local Jewish targets in Buenos Aires that killed scores in the early 1990s, and like-minded Shia extremists return to transnational terrorism? Will an axis of Tehran's Mahmoud Ahmadinejad, Iraq's Muqtada al-Sadr, and Lebanon's Hassan Nasrallah rival—or even replace—al-Qaida as the scourge of the West?

One of my major concerns relative to corporate decision making in the security sector is its chronic Attention Deficit Dis-

order (ADD). One of the bedrock principles of security is the need for constancy, but corporate governance has a hard time with this concept. Budgets rise and budgets fall. When economies are called for, the security department, whose contribution to profitability is more nuanced than many other divisions of the corporation, is often considered a good place to start.

Decision makers by and large tend to react to developments. Security budgets were flush after 9/11 and became even more bloated after the anthrax scare. Indeed, numerous security directors were summoned into the CEO's office and given a virtual blank check. Then, after a few years passed without a significant domestic attack, many budgets were cut dramatically.

In the immediate aftermath of 9/11 and the anthrax scare, much of the money pumped into security was spent foolishly. I remember a call from the properties manager of a medium-sized company who bore the security responsibility. He was seeking a recommendation for an x-ray machine, which he intended to use to screen mail for anthrax.

I made two comments. First, the x-ray machine would not detect anthrax. Second, while the machine might assist in the detection of letter-bombs, his company was not in the kind of controversial business that would normally come to the attention of potential mail-bombers. I advised that it would be much more cost-effective and, in the case of anthrax, simply more beneficial, to train his mailroom clerks to detect suspicious packages, which could then be turned over to the local police for analysis.

He wasn't at all interested in this option. "You don't understand," he said. "I have the budget and I have to appear to be taking some action." Well, at least he was honest.

While security programs need to be a constant, they also need to be flexible. We need to anticipate change and stay nimble enough to cope with changes when they come.

The biggest mistake a terrorism analyst can make is to marry his analysis—to make developments fit his analytical framework rather than vice versa.

The biggest mistake a security planner can make is to assume that the next attack will take the same form as the last.

The biggest mistake that a responder can make is to assume that his next kidnapping will play out exactly like the others in which he has been involved.

The biggest mistake a corporate leader can make is to fail to keep abreast of new developments and new analysis, for globalization has brought challenges that could have scarcely been imagined a decade ago. Terrorism, one way or another, is going to intrude on plans, require unexpected course alterations, and dramatically affect chances for success.

ADDENDA

MAJOR GLOBAL JIHAD ATTACKS AND ATTEMPTS POST-9/11

A
Direct Attacks on Commercial Targets

Date	Country	Event
1. May 8, 2002	Pakistan	Suicide car bombing targeting French technicians outside Sheraton Hotel in Karachi
2. October 6, 2002	Yemen	Attack on French super-tanker *Limburg* off Yemen
3. May 12, 2003	Saudi Arabia	Bombings at three housing complexes in Riyadh
4. November 20, 2003	Turkey	Suicide bombing at HSBC building in Istanbul
5. May 1, 2004	Saudi Arabia	Shooting attack on ABB Lummus in Yanbu
6. May 29, 2004	Saudi Arabia	Massacre at oil complex in al-Khobar
7. June 8–12, 2004	Saudi Arabia	Murder spree against US defense contractors in Riyadh
8. February 24, 2006	Saudi Arabia	Attempt to bomb giant oil refinery in Abqaiq
9. September 15, 2006	Yemen	Attempt to bomb two oil facilities in Yemen

10. December 10, 2006	Algeria	Attack on bus carrying employees from Brown & Root-Condor in Algiers
11. March 3, 2007	Algeria	Roadside-bomb attack against minibuses carrying Stroitransgas employees in Algiers
12. September 21, 2007	Algeria	Suicide car-bomb attack against Razel construction company convoy in Algeria
13. June 8, 2008	Algeria	Murder of French engineer from Razel in roadside bombing

B
Commercial Aviation Targets

	Date	Country	Event
1.	December 22, 2001	United Kingdom	Attempt by Richard Reid to bomb American Airlines jet
2.	November 28, 2002	Kenya	Attempt to shoot down an Israeli airliner in Mombasa
3.	February 13, 2003	Venezuela/ United Kingdom	Attempt to blow up a British Airways flight from Caracas to London's Gatwick Airport
4.	May 20, 2003	Saudi Arabia	Attempt to hijack an aircraft from Jiddah
5.	August 10, 2006	United Kingdom	Attempt to blow up multiple US airliners over the Atlantic
6.	June 30, 2007	United Kingdom	Attempt to drive a car-bomb into Glasgow Airport

C
Train and Subway Targets

Date	Country	Event
1. March 11, 2004	Spain	Bombings on four commuter trains in Madrid
2. July 7, 2005	United Kingdom	Suicide bombings aboard three subway trains and a bus in London
3. February 19, 2006	India	Bombing of Ahmadabad, India, train station
4. July 11, 2006	India	Bombings of seven commuter trains and railway stations in Mumbai
5. February 18, 2007	India	Bombing of Delhi to Lahore "Friendship Express" train

D
Hotels

Date	Country	Event
1. November 28, 2002	Kenya	Suicide bombing at Paradise Hotel in Mombasa
2. August 5, 2003	Indonesia	Suicide car bombing at JW Marriott in Jakarta
3. October 7, 2004	Egypt	Bombing at Hilton in Taba
4. October 28, 2004	Pakistan	Bombing in lobby of Islamabad Marriott
5. November 9, 2005	Jordan	Bombings at three hotels in Amman
6. January 26, 2007	Pakistan	Suicide bombing at Islamabad Marriott

E
Tourism-Related Targets

	Date	Country	Event
1.	April 11, 2002	Tunisia	Suicide truck bombing outside the historic el-Ghriba synagogue in Jerba
2.	October 12, 2002	Indonesia	Mega-bombing at Bali
3.	April 7 and 30, 2005	Egypt	Attacks on tourists in Kahn al-Khalili Bazaar in Cairo
4.	July 23, 2005	Egypt	Suicide bombings in Sharm al-Sheikh
5.	October 1, 2005	Indonesia	Restaurant bombings in Bali
6.	April 24, 2006	Egypt	Suicide bombings at restaurants and a market in Dahab
7.	July 2, 2007	Yemen	Attack on Spanish tourists at Queen of Sheba Temple

F
Governmental and Military Targets

Date	Country	Event
1. June 14, 2002	Pakistan	Suicide car bombing at US Consulate in Karachi
2. November 20, 2003	Turkey	Suicide car bombing at British Consulate in Istanbul
3. December 14, 2003	Pakistan	Attempt to strike convoy carrying President Pervez Musharraf in Rawalpindi with remote-control bomb
4. December 25, 2003	Pakistan	Attempt to assassinate President Pervez Musharraf in suicide car bombing in Rawalpindi
5. April 21, 2004	Saudi Arabia	Suicide car bombing at Saudi security service HQs in Riyadh
6. September 9, 2004	Indonesia	Suicide car bombing at Australian Embassy in Jakarta
7. March 2, 2006	Pakistan	Suicide car bombing at US Consulate in Karachi
8. April 11, 2007	Algeria	Suicide car bombing at Prime Minister Abdelaziz Belkhadem's office in Algiers
9. July 6, 2007	Pakistan	Weapon fired at President Pervez Musharraf's plane in Rawalpindi
10. September 4, 2007	Pakistan	Suicide-bombing against a

		Pakistani military bus in Rawalpindi
11. October 18, 2007	Pakistan	Attempt to assassinate opposition leader Benazir Bhutto in suicide-bombing attack against her convoy traveling from airport in Karachi
12. November 24, 2007	Pakistan	Twin bombings against military and intelligence targets in Rawalpindi
13. December 11, 2007	Algeria	Simultaneous suicide car bombings against the constitutional court building and United Nations offices in the Hydra district of Algiers
14. December 21, 2007	Pakistan	Unsuccessful attempt to murder former interior minister Aftab Ahmed Khan Sherpao in suicide bombing at a mosque near Peshawar
15. December 27, 2007	Pakistan	Assassination of opposition leader Benazir Bhutto in Rawalpindi
16. March 3, 2008	Pakistan	Suicide bombing at Naval College in Lahore
17. March 11, 2008	Pakistan	Suicide car bombing at Federal Investigative Agency (FIA) in Lahore

TRAVEL GUIDES

1. Air Travel

T ravel on private jets is inherently safer than travel on commercial airliners. All commercial airline choices involve some degree of terrorism-related risk. American, British, and Israeli carriers probably bear the greatest dangers of an in-flight bombing or attack by a surface-to-air missile, despite their superior security practices. Other airliners considered at high risk of such attacks are flag carriers from Muslim countries with secular governments, such as Egypt.

On the other hand, any airline, even the most neutral, must be considered a candidate for a 9/11-type hijacking, since the objective of the hijackers is to crash a plane, any plane, into a specific ground target. Indeed, it can be argued that, because of their superior security practices, American, British, and Israeli carriers are the least susceptible to hijacking.

Conventional hijackings are less likely today because few countries are willing to receive hijacked planes, but this risk cannot be written off entirely.

For US domestic travel and short hops elsewhere, smaller aircraft, such as 737s, should be used to the extent possible, on the theory that Global Jihad, which always goes for the greatest possible impact, would be inclined to target wide-bodies.

PLANNING THE TRIP

- To the degree possible, avoid carriers that are either high risk or lax in their security, especially when departing developing countries.

257

- Choose flights with the fewest number of intermediate stops. Intermediate stops provide terrorists not inclined toward suicide with opportunities to plant explosives and then deplane.
- Select your seat carefully. A seat next to an over-the-wing emergency exit is best, but a position near an alternate exit is also acceptable. To put a little distance between yourself and any confrontation in the aisle, select a window seat whenever possible.

PACKING

In conventional hijackings, assailants often seize documents on a passenger's person or in his or her carry-on baggage. Potentially provocative items should be dispensed with or, if essential to the purpose of the trip, relegated to checked luggage.

The following items are potentially provocative:

- A passport that shows travel to controversial countries such as Israel. Passports with visa stamps from such countries should be replaced. United States passports can be turned in at US Department of State passport offices and new, "clean" passports obtained.
- ID cards for the military reserve or cards showing membership in a political party, political action group, veterans' organization, or any group that can be considered controversial.
- Business cards or letterhead—your own or those of associates— citing companies in controversial industries, especially cards indicating titles such as "Director, Weapons Sales" or "Manager, Special Weapons Development Group." If carried at all, they should be relegated to checked baggage.
- Any other materials linking you to your company, if your company is in a controversial industry. This includes company literature such as annual reports, polo shirts, luggage tags, and other items bearing the company's logo—even credit cards issued in the company name.

- Expensive jewelry such as large diamond rings or pins, gold chains or medallions, and gold watches.
- Clothing that sets you apart from the crowd.
- Reading matter that may be offensive (such as racy magazines) or provocative to terrorists (this book, for example).

AT THE AIRPORT

- Know the scheduled time of departure for your flight and plan your arrival at the airport so that you have enough time for processing. Take into consideration baggage check-in and security inspections.
- Spend a minimum of time in the public lobby areas, which carry the highest risks of bombings and other terrorist incidents. Proceed as soon as possible to the security checkpoint and pass into the "sterile area" of the departure gates.
- Avoid people who are receiving special attention from airline employees or the press, as well as those who appear to be holding unusually animated conversations. *Avoid disturbances of any kind. Move away from potential trouble, not toward it, as many people are inclined to do.*
- Be alert to an influx of uniformed security or police officers or to airline personnel milling about with two-way radios. If airport officials order an evacuation of the area, take a position in the center of the group with as many people around you as possible. Do not take the lead or straggle.
- Never ignore "gut" feelings. If something feels amiss, it very well may be. Follow your instincts to a safe harbor.
- If a fellow passenger appears to be acting in an unusual manner, report your suspicions to an airline employee or to the authorities.

IN THE EVENT OF A HIJACKING

The events of September 11, 2001, dramatically changed strategies for surviving hijackings. Previously, the idea was to become as "invisible" as possible during a hijacking so as not to be singled out and to await resolution of the crisis, either through satisfaction of the hijackers' demands, their surrender, or the storming of the aircraft by authorities.

This passive approach was of little use to passengers involved in the 9/11 hijackings. Indeed, the passengers aboard the fourth flight who, having been apprised of the earlier crashes by telephone, decided to confront the hijackers, might have saved countless lives on the ground.

The main challenge confronting victims of future hijackings will be to determine whether the hijackers are suicidal and bent on crashing the plane or merely attempting to achieve some lesser political—or personal—objective. Although this assessment may be impossible to make in certain circumstances, there may be instances when it is relatively easy to determine the intent of the hijackers. For example, a Chinese national hijacking an aircraft over China is likely to have a personal objective—safe haven in Taiwan. Colombian guerrillas, on the other hand, may have political motives but are not necessarily suicidal. In fact, only a few terrorist groups have a history of suicidal attacks: among them are Islamic extremists, Palestinian nationalists, and Chechen and Sri Lankan Tamil separatists.

The pilot, assuming he remains insulated from the hijackers (a reasonable assumption when cockpit doors are reinforced), may communicate to passengers the hijackers' goals; it would be wise to take your cues from him.

NONSUICIDAL HIJACKING

If you believe the hijackers are not suicidal, the passive response remains the most appropriate. Realistically speaking, however, in the aftermath of the 2001 attacks, other passengers may be disposed to take matters into their own hands. In addition, sky marshals may be aboard the flight and they, too, will be inclined to take action. Be prepared to follow a course of action that gives you the greatest chance of survival.

The following suggested guidelines pertain to nonsuicidal hijackings:

- Even though you may be accustomed to being "in charge," do not display authority or impatience. Be as neutral as possible.
- Avoid making eye contact with any of the perpetrators, especially during the first twenty to thirty minutes of the incident. The initial stages of a hijacking, when the perpetrators are particularly nervous and agitated, are the most dangerous.
- If the hijackers collect valuables, documents, or other personal items from passengers, do not hide or attempt to withhold anything. Do not ask that certain items—watches, rings, and so forth—be retained for sentimental reasons.
- Do not ask special permission to do anything, such as smoke, change seats, or go to the lavatory, unless absolutely necessary. Consume liquids in moderation to cut down on the need for lavatory visits.
- Unless absolutely necessary, do not talk with the passengers around you. The hijackers may think you are plotting something and take action against you.
- Trust no one on the aircraft with your thoughts, opinions, emotions, or plans. The passenger in whom you confide may be a hidden accomplice of the hijackers or may offer information about you in the hope of ingratiating himself or herself with the hijackers.
- Remain as calm as you can throughout the incident and conserve your strength. Although you may feign sleep, you should remain awake and alert to everything going on around you. If the incident is prolonged and you need to sleep, do so for brief periods.
- Accept all food and beverages offered to you by the hijackers. If

you are offered an alcoholic beverage, accept it but do not consume it. Do not ask for special foods, drink, or utensils, but take what you are given. Be quietly gracious.

- Prepare yourself mentally for questioning by the hijackers. Consider whether any of your personal effects could draw attention to you. Formulate reasonable answers to explain your position and effects. If you are questioned, be as truthful as you can without revealing information that may cause the hijackers to take action against you.

- Do not offer political opinions or make comments either for or against the hijackers' cause. If you are asked for an opinion, say that you are not knowledgeable enough to comment. If the hijackers wish to talk about their cause, listen attentively but without volunteering agreement or disagreement.

- Use your time to assess the situation and plan various reactions to situations that might arise. Note the location of the emergency exits and the movements of the hijackers, crew, and other passengers. Mentally rehearse your actions in the event the situation deteriorates into violence and you have to move quickly.

- Keep the floor area between you and the seat in front of you clear of clutter, as you may have to crouch down there for safety in the event of gunfire. Wear as much clothing as you can tolerate—it will provide some protection if an explosive is detonated. Try to have a coat or a blanket handy for covering and protecting your head.

- At the sound of gunshots or other disturbance, crouch as low as possible and remain in that position until you have no doubt that it is safe to sit back up or that you must take other action for your safety.

- A few words about escape: Statistically, your best chances lie in a negotiated release. However, if you have a good opportunity to escape, take advantage of it. The decision to escape must be based upon a careful analysis of your situation, the danger you are facing, and the possibilities open to you. Remember that strong emotions may affect your thinking in these circumstances. Calmly evaluate all factors affecting a safe escape and reach a reasoned conclusion. You have nothing to gain by remaining captive unnecessarily if you can get away. Once you have made the decision to escape, do not vacillate. Move fast.

SUICIDAL HIJACKING

If you become convinced that the hijackers are suicidal, it is probably wise to allow some time to pass, to let any sky marshals aboard the flight initiate action. If they do, there is apt to be gunfire, and if there is you should crouch as low as possible and remain in that position until you have no doubt that it is safe to sit back up. If there is no action by sky marshals, it is probably wise to consider joining other passengers in attempting to overpower the hijackers. Make use of any implements at hand.

2. Travel by Senior Officers with Protective Details

This checklist is designed specifically for senior officers and others traveling to high-risk destinations. It also may be pertinent for senior officers traveling to lower-risk destinations, since many corporations require that they be accompanied by protective details any time they travel abroad.

PREPARATIONS FOR THE SENIOR OFFICER OR HIS SECURITY DESIGNEE

- Determine if it is absolutely necessary for you to take this trip. Could a subordinate go in your place?

- Limit knowledge of your schedule to persons with an absolute need to have this information.
- Curtail pretravel publicity about your trip to the extent feasible. Curtail publicity during the trip as well, since publicity of any sort increases risks.
- Ensure that your passport is valid and will not expire while traveling and for six months thereafter, and obtain necessary visas.
- Provide only generic information when filling out landing cards and hotel registration forms. Describe yourself as a manager instead of a vice president.
- Register your travel plans with your country's local diplomatic mission. The US State Department provides online registration at http://www.travel.state.gov.
- Pack clothing compatible with local customs.
- Do not take clothing with company logos and do not use brief-cases or suitcases with company logos.
- Use only luggage tags with flaps that must be opened to determine ownership. Do not use your business card as a luggage tag. Use your business address instead of your home address on all luggage tags.
- Submit to your security director or travel coordinator details of any existing medical conditions and any prescription drugs you require. Remember to take extra eyeglasses and contact lenses.
- Be certain to carry prescription drugs in their original containers and take sufficient amounts (and a little extra) for your trip.
- Educate yourself about current criminal and terrorism risks, political instability issues, business practices, and social customs in the area(s) to be visited. *(Suggested Web sites for pretravel information: http://www.risknet.com provided by subscription by The Ackerman Group LLC and http://www.travel.state.gov provided by the US State Department.)*
- Arrange to be briefed on your company's operations in the country/region to be visited. The briefing should highlight particular problems confronting the company, such as labor or environmental issues.

- Obtain a plasticized card with the telephone numbers of key local contacts.
- Ascertain the name and background (professional experience, geographic area knowledge, language skills) of the protective-detail leader.
- Obtain a photograph of the protective-detail leader.
- Ascertain where the protective detail will meet you (at plane-side, outside of customs, etc.) and what recognition signs will be used to establish the leader's bona fides. (Company names or logos should not be used.)
- Furnish the protective-detail leader with a prospective agenda.

WORKING WITH YOUR PROTECTIVE DETAIL

- Upon arrival at your destination, you and/or your security director, if he is accompanying you, should plan to have a short, private meeting with the protective-detail leader. He will provide you with a brief explanation of how the detail will work and what he expects from you. Among other things, he will explain the following:

  —He has responsibility for your safety and is thus outside the chain of command of your company's trip-support team. The protective-detail leader, when necessary, will make instantaneous decisions regarding your security. When time permits, he will make recommendations regarding suggested courses of action to you and/or your security designee. His recommendations should be given due weight.

  —Within the parameters of your agenda and in consultation with you or your security designee, the protective-detail leader will attempt to avoid the establishment of a predictable routine.

  —The protective-detail leader will request that you keep him apprised of all of your intended personal movements. If you wish to do something that is not on the submitted agenda, please inform him so that he can make the necessary arrangements.

—Inform the protective-detail leader of any special needs or potential problem areas, such as attendance at publicized events.

—The protective-detail leader will provide you with a cell phone that works in the local area, with his cell phone number programmed on the speed dial. He will let you know where he will be at all times.

—If you have a pertinent medical condition, inform the protective-detail leader and provide him with extra prescription medications, which he will place in the emergency medical kit that he carries in your vehicle.

- The protective-detail leader and the other bodyguards will address you as "sir" or "ma'am" and as "Mr. or Ms. *Surname*," even if you ask them to address you by first name. They will be cordial but will have been instructed not to be familiar or intrusive.
- The protective-detail leader will sit in the front passenger seat of your vehicle. You will be directed to a rear seat.
- Never open the door of your vehicle yourself. The protective-detail leader will ascertain conditions on the street upon arrival at your destination and will open your door only when he is satisfied that it is safe for you to alight.

IF YOU COME UNDER ATTACK

- If an attack occurs while you are in a moving vehicle, get as low as possible in the vehicle and follow all commands from the detail leader.
- If gunfire occurs while you are moving to or from your vehicle, the detail leader will physically bring you down for your protection. Do not resist this.

GENERAL SECURITY GUIDELINES

- Your hotel should be selected with an eye to security. Your room or suite should be as far as possible from streets and from the front entrance. It should not be accessible from balconies of adjoining rooms.
- Although your protective detail will inspect your hotel room from a security perspective, you or your security designee should personally ensure that the door's deadbolt lock works properly and that the u-bar or chain also functions properly.
- All valuables and sensitive documents should be placed in a front-desk safe-deposit box, not in your room safe.
- Study the fire escape map in your room and be sure you know how to move to the closest exit in the event of a fire.
- Travel with a small flashlight and place it in the same location before retiring at night. Fires and other emergencies often occur at night, and hotel electricity often fails.
- If private meetings are to be held with individuals you do not know, a hotel meeting room or a public area should be used instead of your room or suite.

3. Solo Travel to Countries with High Terrorism or Crime Risks

Police in countries with high crime risks are apt to be swamped by high levels of crime and/or terrorism with their operations being reactive rather than preventive. Responsibility for keeping trouble at bay generally rests with you and your company. As the guidelines below indicate, the best defense is anonymity.

TRAVEL PREPARATIONS

- Learn as much as possible about recent terrorist or criminal activity in the areas you will be visiting.
- Limit knowledge of your visit to trusted people who have a legitimate need for this information.
- Avoid pretravel publicity about your trip.
- Request airline reservations and tickets in your own name. Corporate affiliation should not appear on your ticket or travel itinerary. Follow the same rules when reserving hotel rooms, even if you must forfeit discounts.
- Provide your travel itinerary to a corporate security representative or travel coordinator. It should include travel dates, flight numbers, arrangements for ground transportation, and local points of contact. Advise your security representative of any change in plans.
- Submit to your security director or travel coordinator details of any existing medical conditions and any prescription drugs you require.
- Ensure that your passport is valid and will not expire while traveling and secure the necessary visas.
- Register your travel plans with your country's local diplomatic mission. The US State Department provides online registration at the Web site listed below.
- Prepare clothing compatible with local customs.
- Do not carry valuables that are not essential for the trip. Expensive watches and jewelry will cause you to be noticed and perhaps targeted for a robbery.
- Do not take clothing with company logos and do not use briefcases or other carry-on bags with company logos.
- Use luggage tags with flaps that must be opened to determine ownership. Do not use your business card as a luggage tag. Use your business address instead of your home address on all luggage tags.

- Educate yourself about current criminal and terrorism risks, political instability issues, business practices, and social customs in the area(s) to be visited. *(Suggested Web sites for pretravel information: http://www.risknet.com provided by subscription by The Ackerman Group LLC and http://www.travel.state.gov provided by the US State Department.)*
- Arrange to be briefed on your company's operations in the country/region to be visited. The briefing should highlight particular problems, such as labor issues, that are confronting the company.
- Obtain a plasticized card with the telephone numbers of key local contacts.
- If you are not being picked up at the airport, arrange with your hotel or a reputable limo company to provide transportation from the airport. If you intend to utilize an airport taxi, check *Risknet* or a comparable service to make sure that it is safe to do so.

ON THE DAY YOU TRAVEL

- Dress casually. Try to look more like a tourist than a businessperson while in transit. Terrorists or criminals interested in large ransoms rarely kidnap tourists.
- While aboard the aircraft, do not provide new acquaintances with a lot of information about yourself.
- You will be asked to fill out a landing card prior to arrival. Provide only required information, avoiding company affiliation. Under occupation, use generic terms, such as "businessperson" or "salesperson."
- If the country of your destination has a significant kidnapping problem, you should not be met at the airport by a high-profile, high-risk resident associate in a company car.
- If you are to be met by a company driver or a junior staff member, you should confirm his or her identity before getting

into the car. Ideally, you should have been provided with his picture. The driver under no circumstances should carry a sign with your name or your company's name on it. Coded signs are the preferred means for establishing contact.

- If you are traveling to your hotel by taxi, select a franchised cab as opposed to an independent or gypsy cab. If you have misgivings about a particular taxi, turn it down.

HOTEL SELECTION

- Select your hotel with an eye to security. Your room or suite should be as far as possible from streets and from the front entrance. It should not be accessible from balconies of adjoining rooms.
- Ensure that the door's deadbolt lock works properly and that the u-bar or chain also functions properly.
- Place all valuables and sensitive documents in a front-desk safe-deposit box, not in your room safe.
- Study the fire escape map in your room and be sure you know how to move to the closest exit in the event of a fire.
- Travel with a small flashlight and place it in the same location before retiring at night. Fires and other emergencies often occur at night, and hotel electricity often fails.
- If private meetings are to be held with individuals whom you do not know, a hotel meeting room or a public area should be used instead of your room or suite.
- Do not discuss your plans with hotel staff members, who may be terrorist or criminal informants.
- Be alert to pretext phone calls and unexplained coincidences. Be suspicious of chance acquaintances made in or around the hotel. Do not accept a ride or leave the hotel with a new acquaintance.

IN GENERAL

- Watch local television or use local contacts to stay abreast of current events during your visit.
- Within the parameters of your agenda, vary your daily routine as much as possible.
- Vary the times you leave your hotel each day. If your hotel has more than one entrance, make use of each on a random basis. Schedule your workday so that you are back in your hotel by sundown.
- Move around in a corporate vehicle or by a hotel-provided limo or taxi. Do not flag taxis on the street.
- Be surveillance conscious even when traveling by vehicle. Stay aware of your surroundings, observe the people around you, move away from street demonstrations, protest marches, political rallies, accidents, and all crowds.
- If you believe that you are being followed, report your observations to your local office or to the police. Under no circumstances should you confront suspected surveillants.
- When planning your business meetings, make sure that you have addresses and directions ahead of time. If you are going by taxi, ask the hotel to call one for you.
- If you are visiting a location outside the city, apprise yourself of the perils before you depart. Most US embassies have a Regional Security Officer (RSO) who can provide you with information.
- Carry two telephone numbers: the police emergency number and that of your embassy or consulate. Use them in the event of a problem.
- Use ATMs only in secure locations, such as hotel lobbies and bank interiors.
- If confronted by armed assailants, do not resist. Follow their instructions within reason and give them what they are demanding.

TRAIN TRAVEL

Train travel, particularly overnight travel, is hazardous in several parts of the world. Criminals, in some cases rogue conductors, may offer passengers food or drinks laced with drugs or they may spray soporific agents into compartments with a view toward stealing cash and valuables. If you must travel by train, the following are suggested precautions:

- When undertaking an overnight trip, arrange for the entire sleeping compartment. Secure it with a portable alarm and/or a portable lock. Do not allow other passengers to enter.
- Board the train with enough food and water for the journey. Do not purchase either snacks or drinks from vendors onboard.
- Treat chance acquaintances with suspicion; decline offers of food or drinks from them.

4. Travel to Moderate-Risk Destinations

TRAVEL PREPARATIONS

- Limit knowledge of your schedule to persons with a need to have this information.
- Curtail pretravel publicity about your trip to the extent feasible.
- Ensure that your passport is valid and will not expire while traveling and secure the necessary visas.
- Register your travel plans with your country's local diplomatic mission. The US State Department provides online registration at the Web site listed below.
- Prepare clothing compatible with local customs.
- Leave expensive watches and jewelry at home.

- Do not take clothing with company logos and do not use brief-cases or other carry-on bags with company logos.
- Use luggage tags with flaps that must be opened to determine ownership. Do not use your business card as a luggage tag. Use your business address instead of your home address on all luggage tags.
- Submit to your security director or travel coordinator details of any existing medical conditions and any prescription drugs you require. Remember to take extra eyeglasses and contact lenses.
- Be certain to carry prescription drugs in their original containers and take sufficient amounts (and a little extra) for your trip.
- Educate yourself about current criminal and terrorism risks, political instability issues, business practices, and social customs in the area(s) to be visited. *(Suggested Web sites for pretravel information: http://www.risknet.com provided by subscription by The Ackerman Group LLC and http://www.travel.state.gov provided by the US State Department.)*
- Arrange to be briefed on your company's operations in the country/region to be visited. The briefing should highlight particular problems, such as labor issues, that are confronting the company.
- Obtain a plasticized card with the telephone numbers of key local contacts.
- If you are not being picked up at the airport, arrange with your hotel or a reputable limo company to provide transportation. If you intend to utilize an airport taxi, make certain to select one from the line of authorized cabs. Do not use unmarked gypsy cabs.

UPON ARRIVAL

- Provide only generic information when filling out landing cards and hotel registration forms. Describe yourself as a manager instead of a vice president.

- Select your hotel with an eye to security. Your room or suite should be as far as possible from streets and from the front entrance. It should not be accessible from balconies of adjoining rooms.
- Ensure that the door's deadbolt lock works properly and that the u-bar or chain also functions properly.
- Place all valuables and sensitive documents in a front-desk safe-deposit box, not in your room safe.
- Study the fire escape map in your room and be sure you know how to move to the closest exit in the event of a fire.
- Travel with a small flashlight and place it in the same location before retiring at night. Fires and other emergencies often occur at night, and hotel electricity often fails.
- If private meetings are to be held with individuals whom you do not know, a hotel meeting room or a public area should be used instead of your room or suite.

IN GENERAL

- Watch local television or use local contacts to stay abreast of current events during your visit.
- Within the parameters of your agenda, vary your daily routine as much as possible.
- Move around in a corporate vehicle, hotel-provided limo or taxi, or radio taxi. Do not flag taxis on the street.
- Be surveillance-conscious whenever you are on the street. Stay aware of your surroundings, observe the people around you, move away from street demonstrations, protest marches, political rallies, accidents, and all crowds.
- Attempt to maintain a low profile during your visit. Dress down if you are going to walk city streets. Do not flash cash when making purchases.
- Use ATMs only in secure locations, such as hotel lobbies and bank interiors.

- Use money belts or other concealment devices to protect cash, credit cards, and other valuables from pickpockets.
- Walk with purpose (look like a local if possible) and never stop to talk to strangers.
- If confronted by an armed assailant, do not resist. Follow his instructions within reason and give him what he is demanding.

5. Travel to the Muslim World

Travel to Muslim countries and countries like India and Kenya with large Muslim minorities, where attacks by al-Qaida—its regional affiliates or self-generated groups of sympathizers—are most likely to take place, requires special precautions.

HOTEL SELECTION

The penchant of al-Qaida, its regional affiliates, and like-minded groups to attack business-class hotels requires careful attention to hotel selection.

- The ideal hotel choices are situated within well-protected, walled compounds, with guest rooms some distance from street traffic. Compound entrances should feature both armed security personnel and stout physical barriers to attempts at intrusion by would-be suicide-bombers. The best barriers are hydraulic wedges or bollards that permit guards to admit vehicles one at a time, after vetting and inspection. Ideally, the driveway to the hotel should have stout zigzag barriers, to prevent a high-speed approach.
- Few hotels have these state-of-the-art barriers, however, so in most instances guests have to settle for the best combination of armed guards and barriers that is available. (Armed guards are

of some value even without stout barriers, though determined suicide-assailants can overcome them.)

- In areas in which facilities with strong perimeters are not available, one suitable alternative is the smaller, "boutique" hotel, which most likely will not be on the terrorists' radar.
- Another option is a low-rise hotel with several out-buildings. In a property of this sort, it is best to obtain a room as far from the lobby as possible, since suicide-bombers almost always set off their explosives at the main entrance to the hotel or in the lobby.
- Where high-rise hotels lacking strong perimeters are the only option, it is important that travelers request rooms on higher floors that do not face the street and especially the main entrance.
- Underground garages are a strong negative in hotel selection, because of the opportunities afforded to terrorists to park explosives-laden vehicles in them. Entry-point inspections of vehicles mitigate these risks to some degree, but it is worth keeping in mind that inspectors can be suborned or distracted.

OTHER TERRORISM RISKS

In high-risk countries, it is wise to steer clear of places, other than hotels, in which Westerners congregate. These include:

- bars (where permitted)
- restaurants, especially those that serve alcohol
- clubs
- trendy shopping malls
- tourist attractions
- Christian and Jewish places of worship

Tourist attractions are a special problem because they often are of keen interest to corporate travelers visiting a country for the first time. Visiting points of interest, however, is not central to the business mission at hand, and, owing to Global Jihad's track record of attacking such sites, they should be given a pass.

NONTERRORISM-RELATED RISKS

Travel to Muslim countries, including Persian Gulf states not currently experiencing high levels of terrorism, requires more extensive preparation and greater discretion than normal business travel. The watchword is prudence, as well as an awareness that you are operating in a distinctly different culture and are obliged to obey its norms. Because there is a good deal of variation in both law and practice in Muslim countries, it is a good idea for travelers to familiarize themselves with laws and mores of the particular countries to be visited well before setting out.

PACKING

Anticipate a thorough search of your luggage and your person on arrival. If you carry prohibited items, you risk not only their confiscation but also your arrest. The following are some do's and don'ts:

- Do not carry alcoholic beverages of any kind.
- Do not carry racy magazines, books, or videos.
- Do not carry books offensive to Islam.
- Carry medicines in their original containers with copies of the original prescriptions.
- Do not honor requests to carry letters or packages from persons not intimately known to you, however innocent they may appear.
- Pack conservative clothing. Women in particular should pack long-sleeved blouses and long dresses. (Slacks are acceptable in some Muslim countries but not in the Persian Gulf region.)

- It may be wise for women to pack head scarves as well for countries such as Iran.
- If traveling to Saudi Arabia, women should pack a black cloak as well as a head scarf.

ONCE YOU HAVE ARRIVED

- Review laws and mores with local contacts.
- Make no attempt to obtain or consume alcoholic beverages in countries in which they are banned.
- Turn down invitations to parties at which alcohol may be present.
- Wear clothing appropriate to the country of destination.
- Do not jog in exercise outfits that may be offensive.
- Men should avoid socializing with Muslim women.
- In Saudi Arabia, be mindful that men and women who venture out in public together need to carry proof that they are married.

6. Travel to Hostile Countries

Travel to countries hostile to the United States and the West in general requires a much higher level of both preparation and discretion than normal business travel. You must constantly be aware that you are in unfriendly territory and that the police cannot be relied on to protect you. On the contrary, the authorities may well be out to embarrass, compromise, and/or exploit you.

PACKING

Anticipate a thorough search of your luggage and your person on arrival. If you carry prohibited items, you risk not only their confiscation but also your arrest. The following are general guidelines on prohibited items, as well as items that will attract the attention of immigration and security officials:

- Do not carry books by prominent dissidents or other controversial literature.
- Do not honor requests to carry letters or packages of any sort, however innocent they may appear.
- Do not take cameras or microcassette recorders. Both may be looked upon as "spy gear."
- Carry medicines in their original containers with copies of the original prescriptions.
- If you need to take along a laptop computer, be prepared to supply access codes to authorities.
- Be aware of the legal limits of cash, both US and local, that you are permitted to carry into a hostile country. It is inadvisable to enter the country with large amounts of cash, since it may be confiscated upon entry or departure. Credit cards should be used when possible.
- Do not travel with large amounts of designer clothing, perfume, or other potential "black market" items.
- Leave expensive jewelry at home. Items that you choose to carry with you, such as watches or rings, should be declared upon entry. Otherwise, they may be confiscated upon departure.

ONCE YOU HAVE ARRIVED

Visitors who violate laws or regulations in hostile countries face arrest and imprisonment. Rules of prudent behavior include the following:

- If your visa limits you to certain activities or specific geographic areas, respect those caveats.
- Do not try to compile information on the country you are visiting.

No matter how innocuous a market survey may seem to you, information gathering of any sort is likely to raise suspicions.

- Never engage in political discussion and keep away from all controversial subjects.
- If you have brought a camera, do not photograph government buildings or objects with possible military applications.
- Assume that your hotel room is bugged and that your telephone conversations and Internet communications are being monitored.
- Do not reveal personal information to casual acquaintances. Be suspicious of everyone. Chambermaids, taxi drivers, and the like all report to the police. Be especially suspicious of attractive, flirtatious men or women. They are often intelligence operatives.
- Never give authorities false information of any kind.
- If you suspect that you are under surveillance, do not try to avoid it. Carry on business as usual. An attempt to "lose" surveillance would arouse suspicion. Surveillances often are undertaken by teams of people and may be difficult to detect.
- Communicate on at least a daily basis with your home office to assure them that you are okay.
- Do not utilize rental cars, since you may be subjected to exorbitant fines, even detention, for minor traffic offenses and accidents.
- Convert currency only in officially sanctioned exchanges and retain all receipts. Never convert currency on the "black market."
- Do not sell personal items. Transactions of this sort may be a criminal offense.
- If you purchase antiques, do so in stores that can provide you with a certificate of export.
- Do not agree to carry anything out of a hostile country for a local contact, no matter how innocent the item may appear.
- Depart as soon as you have finished your business. The longer you stay, the greater the risk.

7. Travel to Unstable Countries

The watchword for travel to unstable countries is vigilance.

- Use on-the-ground contacts, embassies, private analytical services, and local and international media to monitor internal developments.
- Also, monitor the state of relations between your own country and the one you are visiting.
- If matters turn especially tense, depart immediately. Your best chance of departing the country safely is by commercial aviation—before the crisis boils over.
- Some emergencies, such as coups, erupt with no warning. If taken by surprise, the best thing to do at the first sound of gunfire or report of hostilities is to take shelter inside a hotel or another neutral building, in other words, one that is not apt to be a military target. Government facilities of any sort are likely military targets, as are television stations and other communications centers.
- Remain in that safe harbor, assuming sufficient water and food, unless:

  —there is imminent danger of its becoming engulfed in hostilities
  —a military force, embassy, or humanitarian organization organizes an evacuation
  —authoritative word is received that hostilities have been suspended or terminated

- Do not attempt to follow the action from a window or balcony. Stay in an interior area of the building.
- If you must move out of safe harbor, it is generally best to move in a direction away from hostilities—away from the troops, tanks, and/or circling helicopters.
- Under most circumstances it is inadvisable to make a run for the airport with hostilities still in progress. The airport probably will be closed. Moreover, it is likely to be a magnet for fighting, and,

in any case, your path to it probably will be impeded by military roadblocks manned by nervous soldiers.

- Overland evacuations, likewise, can be dangerous during periods of hostility.

8. Travel Tips for Women

In general, the same commonsense rules that should be followed by men traveling overseas also apply for women. Women, however, should be cognizant of some unique problems, most notably a rise in the incidence of molestation of women travelers by taxi drivers in developing countries.

- Dress modestly, especially in developing countries.
- Avoid gypsy cabs entirely. When arriving at the airport, utilize cabs from the regular taxi line; otherwise, use hotel cabs or radio taxis.
- Never allow the driver to guide you into the front passenger seat. (Some drivers may place your luggage in the back seat in an attempt to oblige you to sit up front; insist that they place luggage in the trunk.)
- In general, follow your instincts about the driver (and all other people you encounter). If you sense that something is amiss, do not get into the vehicle.
- Do not allow the driver to pick up additional passengers. Put up a fuss, if necessary.
- If traveling alone in a questionable country, take your meals in your hotel.
- Avoid being out on the streets alone after dark.
- Even during the day, stick to the beaten commercial paths.
- If harassed verbally on the street, do not confront the harasser. Instead, duck into a nearby store or other safe harbor.
- If no safe harbor is available nearby, appeal for help to older men and women in the vicinity.

- Always keep in mind that in developing countries Western women have been stereotyped by Hollywood as promiscuous, and that even an innocuous conversation with a local man may be interpreted by him as a sexual come-on.

9. Travel Tips for Nonwhites

Nonwhites face some unique security problems, primarily in several countries of central and eastern Europe and in Russia. Xenophobic "skinhead" gangs beat men, and in some cases even women, they perceive to be immigrants, and in Germany racists on occasion also assault American servicemen.

To reduce the risk of an encounter of this sort:

- Dress "up" instead of down, choosing normal business attire as much as possible.
- In general, stick to the beaten paths of the business community, confining your activities to the business districts of large cities.
- Be mindful of your surroundings, avoiding for the most part public transportation and strolls through neighborhoods with which you are unfamiliar, especially after dark.
- Do not enter parks, which often are skinhead hangouts.
- Eat, drink, and socialize only in hotel restaurants and bars, and those recommended by colleagues or concierges.

10. Surviving an Abduction

In the event you are abducted, the following are suggested guidelines:

- Remain calm.
- Follow instructions. Do not give your abductors cause to hurt you.

- Provide a *local* phone contact (a company field office or the home or office of a vendor, distributor, or other business contact) if one is solicited.
- Anticipate feelings of denial and disorientation during the early days of your captivity. After that, depression may set in. You may suffer sleep loss and intestinal disorders as well. These symptoms will recede if you are able to reduce stress and adapt to captivity.
- Eat, rest, and exercise as much as possible.
- Adapt by dealing with your abductors in a respectful but not subservient manner. Attempt to win their respect and sympathy by developing a person-to-person relationship with them. Tell them about your family. Show pictures if you have them.
- Avoid political discussion. If your captors wish to talk about their cause, hear them out but without indicating agreement or disagreement. If asked for an opinion, say that you are not knowledgeable enough to comment.
- Do not attempt to remove a blindfold if one is placed on your eyes, or make other efforts to observe your captors. Assume that they do not want you to be able to describe them.
- Do not attempt to negotiate your release. Understand that you are under duress and thus at a severe disadvantage in any negotiation. Leave the negotiating to others.
- Do not be concerned by the so-called Stockholm Syndrome, that is, developing strong positive feelings toward your captors, if it occurs. It is common, normal, and may help improve your chances for survival.
- If you have a clear opportunity to escape, take it, but be mindful that your abductors might have laid a trap for you. Statistically, your best chances lie in a negotiated release.
- Remember that efforts are being made to secure your safe release. Keep a positive frame of mind.

RESIDENTIAL SECURITY CHECKLISTS

1. Apartment—High-Risk Area

SELECTING A NEIGHBORHOOD

- Have there been home invasions or burglaries in this neighborhood? Have there been classical or express kidnappings?
- Is there a police precinct and fire station in or near the neighborhood?
- What is the distance from the neighborhood to the closest trauma-care hospital?

SELECTING AN APARTMENT COMPLEX

Perimeter

- Is the perimeter of the property protected by a significant wall or fence at least ten feet high?
- Does the perimeter barrier have a topguard made up of glass shards, barbed wire, concertina wire, or electrified wire?
- Is there a cleared buffer of at least twenty feet around the perimeter barrier and is that buffer area well lit?
- Are there any trees on either side of the perimeter barrier that would allow an intruder to scale it?
- What kinds of perimeter gates (pedestrian and vehicular) are installed in the perimeter barrier?

—Are the gates of equal height to the rest of the barrier?

—Do the gates have adequate topguards?

- Do guards admit all visitors? Do they check with residents before admitting them?
- Are guards in a protected location—behind a bullet-resistant glass barrier?
- Is the building itself well lit?

Parking

- Is there an enclosed garage in which residents may park vehicles?
- Do armed guards control access to the garage?
- If not, is the garage door or gate controlled by electronic access-card readers?
- Is CCTV used generously in the garage?
- Is there interior access via the elevator or stairwell from the garage to the building itself?
- Do the elevators require access cards?
- Do the elevators lead to the building lobby or directly to upper floors? *The former is preferred.*
- Is there a separate parking area for guests?
- Do guests have to pass through the lobby in order to be admitted to upper floors?

Building Entrance Lobby

- Is the entrance door to the building lobby closed and secured at all times?

—Is access controlled 24/7 by guards stationed in the lobby?

—Do guards recheck with householders before admitting visitors?

—Do the guards control the use of elevators by guests?

—Can guards direct the elevators to one specific floor?

—Can residents open the entrance door by using electronic access cards?

PHYSICAL SECURITY OF APARTMENT UNIT

- Is the unit above the second floor? *Lower units are accessible from the outside.*
- Is the unit accessible by local fire equipment?
- Do entry doors have solid-wood cores at least two inches thick or are they constructed of fire-rated metal? *Either option is acceptable.*
- Do entry doors have deadbolt locks and 190-degree optical viewers?
- Do any entry doors have glass panels or are they in close proximity to glass panels?

> —If so, are they equipped with double-cylinder deadbolt locks (with keyways on both sides of the door) to prevent a burglar from cutting or breaking the glass and reaching in to a thumb-turn knob, as would be the case with a single-cylinder lock?
> —If double-cylinder deadbolt locks are used, are keys routinely removed from the interior keyways?

- Are there any balconies in the apartment? If so, are they accessible from neighboring apartments or from the building's roof?
- Are doors leading to accessible balconies solid-core, French doors, or sliding-glass doors? *If they are solid-core, they require deadbolt locks. If they are French doors, they should be equipped with double-cylinder deadbolt locks and grilled. If they are sliding-glass doors, they should be equipped with key-operated antislide bolts and grilled. Residents reluctant to grill doors for aesthetic reasons should, at a minimum, equip them with intrusion-detection alarms.*

- Are there windows on accessible balconies? *Windows on accessible balconies also should be grilled or, at a minimum, be equipped with intrusion-detection alarms.*
- Is there a rooftop skylight? If so, is it grilled or equipped with a stout locking device?

INTRUSION-DETECTION ALARM SYSTEM

- Does the unit have an intrusion-detection alarm system?
- Does it have magnetic contacts on doors, windows, and skylights, glass-break sensors on all glass surfaces, and motion sensors? *All three are recommended.*
- Are there multiple control panels for the system so that residents can access it from more than one room?
- Is there an audible annunciator (siren, claxon, etc.) located inside or outside the unit? *Ideally, there should be annunciators both inside and outside the residence.*
- Are smoke detectors wired into the system?
- Is the intrusion-detection alarm system linked to building guards?
- Does the system provide fixed and/or portable duress alarm devices? *Both are desirable.*

ASSESSMENT OF A POTENTIAL INTERIOR SAFE HAVEN

- One room in the unit should be selected as a safe haven to which family members can retreat in the event that an intruder gains access to the apartment. It is always advisable for family members to avoid confrontation and to retreat to an area in which they can safely summon guards and/or police assistance and wait for help.

- Typically, the master bedroom, the master bath, or a walk-in closet in the master suite is selected as the safe haven. However, if all bedrooms are located on the upper floor of a duplex apartment, it may be possible to install a solid-core or metal-backed door at the entry point to those quarters to effectively turn the entire floor into a safe haven.
- Specifications for converting the selected room or area into a safe haven include the following:

  —The room or area selected should have a stout door that cannot be easily kicked in by the intruder. It should be solid-wood core at least two inches thick or metal-backed wood and mounted in a metal frame and equipped with a single-cylinder deadbolt lock with the keyway on the outside.

  —A control panel and panic/duress alarm for the intrusion detection system should be located within the safe haven.

  —A dedicated cellular telephone with a trickle charger should be placed in the safe haven and never removed. *Landline telephones are not recommended because they can be easily disabled by cutting the line or lifting a receiver off-hook in another area of the house.*

  —A list of emergency telephone numbers should be kept in the safe haven.

  —An all-purpose A-B-C fire extinguisher, a flashlight (with extra batteries), and some food and water should be stored in the safe haven.

DOMESTICS

- Are new hires vetted with law-enforcement authorities?
- Are references required and checked thoroughly?
- If domestics are to be provided with keys, have they been instructed in the proper means of safeguarding those keys?
- Are locks rekeyed after domestics quit or are dismissed?

- Have domestics been instructed on how to screen visitors?

    —Have they been instructed to admit to the home only individuals known to them and maintenance personnel, including utility personnel, who have been summoned and who present proper identification?
    —Have they been instructed not to provide any information about the residents to persons calling on the telephone?

2. Apartment—Moderate-Risk Area

SELECTING A NEIGHBORHOOD

- Have there been home invasions or burglaries in this neighborhood?
- Is there a police precinct, fire station, and hospital in or near the neighborhood?
- What is the distance from the neighborhood to the closest trauma-care hospital?

SELECTING AN APARTMENT COMPLEX

Perimeter

- Is the property fenced?
- Is the perimeter well lit?
- What kinds of perimeter gates (pedestrian and vehicular) are installed in the perimeter barrier?

    —Do guards admit all visitors? Do they check with householders before admitting them?
    —Are guards in a protected location?

—Is the residents' vehicular gate equipped with a remote transmitter to allow it to be opened and closed from within the vehicle?

- Is the building itself well lit?

Parking

- Is there an enclosed garage in which residents may park vehicles?
- Is the garage door or gate controlled by electronic access-card readers?
- Is CCTV used generously in the garage?
- Is there interior access via the elevator or stairwell from the garage to the building itself?
- Do the elevators require access cards?
- Do the elevators lead to the building lobby or directly to upper floors? *The former is preferred.*
- Is there a separate parking area for guests?
- Do guests have to pass through the lobby in order to be admitted to upper floors?

Building Entrance Lobby

- Is the entrance door to the building lobby closed and secured at all times?

    —Is access controlled 24/7 by concierges stationed in the lobby?
    —Do the concierges check with householders before admitting visitors? *Checks may be made either by gate guards or concierges.*
    —Do the concierges control the use of elevators by guests?
    —Can concierges direct the elevators to one specific floor?
    —Can residents open the entrance door by using electronic access cards?

PHYSICAL SECURITY OF APARTMENT UNIT

- Is the unit above the second floor? *Lower units are accessible from the outside.*
- Is the unit accessible by local fire equipment?
- Do entry doors have solid-wood cores at least two inches thick or are they constructed of fire-rated metal? *Either option is acceptable.*
- Do entry doors have deadbolt locks and 190-degree optical viewers?
- Do any entry doors have glass panels or are they in close proximity to glass panels?

   —If so, are they equipped with double-cylinder deadbolt locks (with keyways on both sides of the door) to prevent a burglar from cutting or breaking the glass and reaching in to a thumb-turn knob, as would be the case with a single-cylinder lock?
   —If double-cylinder deadbolt locks are used, are keys routinely removed from the interior keyways?

- Are there any balconies in the apartment? If so, are they accessible from neighboring apartments or from the building's roof?
- Are doors leading to accessible balconies solid-core, French doors, or sliding-glass doors? *If they are solid-core, they require deadbolt locks. If they are French doors, they should be equipped with double-cylinder deadbolt locks. If they are sliding-glass doors, they should be equipped with key-operated antislide bolts.*
- Is there a rooftop skylight? If so, is it equipped with a stout locking device?

INTRUSION-DETECTION ALARM SYSTEM

- Does the unit have an intrusion-detection alarm system?
- Does it have magnetic contacts on doors, windows, and skylights, glass-break sensors on all glass surfaces, and motion sensors? *All three are recommended.*
- Are there multiple control panels for the system so that residents can access it from more than one room?
- Is there an audible annunciator (siren, claxon, etc.) located inside or outside the unit? *Ideally, annunciators should be both inside and outside the residence.*
- Are smoke detectors wired into the system?
- Is the intrusion-detection alarm system linked to building guards or concierges?
- Does the system provide fixed and/or portable duress alarm devices? *Ideally, it should have both.*

DOMESTICS

- Are new hires vetted by law-enforcement authorities?
- Are references required and checked thoroughly?
- If domestics are to be provided with keys, have they been instructed in the proper means of safeguarding those keys?
- Are locks rekeyed after domestics leave?
- Have domestics been instructed on how to screen visitors?

  —Have they been instructed to admit to the home only individuals known to them and maintenance personnel, including utility personnel, who have been summoned and who present proper identification?

  —Have they been instructed not to provide any information about the residents to persons calling on the telephone?

3. Single-Family Dwelling in Walled, Gated Community—High-Risk Area

SELECTING A NEIGHBORHOOD

- Have there been home invasions or burglaries in this community? Have there been classical or express kidnappings?
- Is the community gated?
- Is it also walled? *Gated communities that are not walled are only a marginal improvement over homes on public streets. If the community is not walled, see the checklist for homes on public streets.*
- Is there a security guard post at the entry(ies) to the community? Are the guards armed?
- Is a private security company employed to patrol the community?
- Do prominent local politicians and businesspeople who employ private security personnel live in this neighborhood? *In general, the more private security personnel, the better.*
- Is there a police precinct and station in or near the community?
- What is the distance from the neighborhood to the closest trauma-care hospital?
- Is there new construction in the area? *Construction crews often serve as spotters for burglars.*

SELECTING A HOME

Perimeter

- Is the perimeter of the property protected by a significant wall or fence at least ten feet high? *There may be some walled communities in high-risk areas in which security arrangements are so strong that they obviate the necessity for a perimeter wall or fence around the property, but these are the exception.*

- Does the perimeter barrier have a topguard made up of glass shards, barbed wire, concertina wire, or electrified wire?
- If the property is surrounded by other homes, do they have comparable barriers?
- If the property is not surrounded by other homes, is there a cleared buffer of at least twenty feet around the perimeter barrier and is that buffer area well lit? Are there any trees on either side of the perimeter barrier that would allow an intruder to scale the barrier?
- What kinds of perimeter gates (pedestrian and vehicular) are installed in the perimeter barrier?

  —Are those gates of equal height to the rest of the barrier?
  —Do the gates have adequate topguards?
  —Is the pedestrian gate equipped with a CCTV camera and intercom to communicate with and identify visitors?
  —Is the vehicular gate equipped with remote controls to allow it to be opened and closed from within the vehicle?

- Is the interior side of the perimeter barrier and the area between it and the house well lit?
- Are there bushes or other foliage close to the house itself that could provide concealment for an intruder?
- Are utility/telephone boxes outside the house vulnerable to tampering?
- Is the structure itself well lit?
- Does the exterior lighting need to be activated by manual switch or is it wired to an automatic timer or photocell sensor? *The latter two options are preferable, since it is easy to forget to throw the switch. Activating lighting by means of motion detectors, while it affords some protection, is not as effective as having the lights on constantly during hours of darkness.*

Parking

- Is there an enclosed garage in which to park vehicles?
- Is the garage door equipped with remote controls to allow it to be opened and closed from within the vehicle? Do the openers operate quickly?
- Is the garage connected to the house, or is it necessary to walk outside in order to enter the house? *The connected garage affords greater security.*

Exterior Doors/Windows/Patios/Balconies/Skylights

- Do entry doors have solid-wood cores at least two inches thick or are they constructed of fire-rated metal? *Either option is acceptable.*
- Are entry doors equipped with deadbolt locks and 190-degree optical viewers?
- Do entry doors have glass panels or are they adjacent to glass panels?

  —If so, are they equipped with double-cylinder deadbolt locks (with keyways on both sides of the door) to prevent a burglar from cutting or breaking the glass and reaching in to a thumb-turn knob, as would be the case with a single-cylinder lock?
  —If double-cylinder deadbolt locks are used, are keys routinely removed from the interior keyways?

- Are all accessible windows equipped with stout locking devices?
- Are doors leading to ground-floor patios and accessible balconies solid-core, French doors, or sliding-glass doors? *If they are solid-core, they require deadbolt locks. If they are French doors, they should be equipped with double-cylinder deadbolt locks. If they are sliding-glass doors, they should be equipped with key-operated antislide bolts.*

- Is there a rooftop skylight? If so, is it equipped with a stout locking device?

INTRUSION-DETECTION ALARM SYSTEM

- Does the house have an intrusion-detection alarm system?
- Does it have magnetic contacts on doors and windows, glass-break sensors, and motion sensors? *All three are recommended.*
- Are there multiple control panels for the system so that residents can access it from the ground floor and from upper floors?
- Is there an audible annunciator (siren, claxon, etc.) located inside or outside the house? *Ideally, annunciators should be both inside and outside the residence.*
- Are smoke detectors wired into the system?
- Is there also a strobe light outside the house? *The strobe light is another useful indicator of trouble.*
- Is the intrusion-detection alarm system monitored by a central station?
- Is the system tied to the central station by a telephone or radio signal? *The radio signal is the optimum. If a telephone line is to be used, it should be stoutly protected and should alert the central station if cut.*
- Is the central station tied into roving security patrols in the community?
- Does the system provide fixed and/or portable duress alarm devices? *Both are desirable.*

ASSESSMENT OF A
POTENTIAL INTERIOR SAFE HAVEN

One room should be selected as a safe haven to which family members can retreat if an intruder should gain access to the house. It is always advisable for family members to avoid confrontation and to retreat to an area in which they can safely summon police assistance and wait for help. *There may be some walled communities in high-risk areas in which security arrangements are so strong that they obviate the need for a safe haven, but these are the exception.*

- Typically, the master bedroom, the master bath, or a walk-in closet in the master suite is selected as the safe haven. However, if all bedrooms are located on the upper floor, it may be possible to install a solid-core or metal-backed door at the entry point to those quarters to effectively turn the entire floor into a safe haven.
- Specifications for converting the selected room or area into a safe haven include:

  —The room or area selected should have a stout door that cannot be easily kicked in by the intruder. It should be solid-wood core at least two inches thick or metal-backed wood and mounted in a metal frame and equipped with a single-cylinder deadbolt lock with the keyway on the outside.
  —The selected room or area should have no windows accessible to the intruder.
  —A control panel and panic/duress alarm for the intrusion detection system should be located within the safe haven.
  —A dedicated cellular telephone with a trickle charger should be placed in the safe haven and never removed. *(Landline telephones are not recommended because they can be easily disabled by cutting the line or lifting a receiver off-hook in another area of the house.)*
  —A list of emergency telephone numbers should be kept in the safe haven.
  —An all-purpose A-B-C fire extinguisher, a flashlight (with extra batteries), and some food and water should be stored in the safe haven.

Domestics

- Are new hires vetted by law-enforcement authorities?
- Are references required and checked thoroughly?
- If domestics are to be provided with keys, have they been instructed in the proper means of safeguarding those keys?
- Are locks changed when domestics quit or are dismissed?
- Have domestics been instructed on how to screen visitors?

  —Have they been instructed to admit to the home only individuals known to them and maintenance personnel, including utility personnel, who have been summoned and who present proper identification?
  —Have they been instructed not to provide any information about the residents to persons calling on the telephone?

4. Single-Family Dwelling on Public Street—High-Risk Area

Note: In high-risk areas, personnel insofar as possible should live in apartments of single-family homes in walled, gated communities. Dwellings on public streets are acceptable only if there is no other option.

SELECTING A NEIGHBORHOOD

- Have there been home invasions or burglaries in the neighborhood? Have there been classical or express kidnappings?
- Is a private security company employed to patrol the neighborhood?
- Do prominent local politicians and businesspeople who employ private security personnel live in this neighborhood? *In general, the more private security personnel, the better.*

- Is there a police precinct and fire station in or near the neighborhood?
- What is the distance from the neighborhood to the closest trauma-care hospital?
- Is there new construction in the area? *Construction crews often serve as spotters for burglars.*

SELECTING A HOME

Perimeter

- Is the perimeter of the property protected by a significant wall or fence at least ten feet high?
- Does the perimeter barrier have a topguard made up of glass shards, barbed wire, concertina wire, or electrified wire?
- Is the property surrounded by other homes, and do they have similar barriers?
- If the property is not surrounded by other homes, is there a cleared buffer of at least twenty feet around the perimeter barrier and is that buffer area well lit? Are there any trees on either side of the perimeter barrier that could allow an intruder to scale the barrier?
- What kinds of perimeter gates (pedestrian and vehicular) are installed in the perimeter barrier?

    —Are those gates of equal height to the rest of the barrier?
    —Do the gates have adequate topguards?
    —Is the pedestrian gate equipped with a CCTV camera and intercom to communicate with and identify visitors?
    —Is the vehicular gate equipped with remote controls to allow it to be opened and closed from within the vehicle?

- Is the interior side of the perimeter barrier and the area between it and the house well lit?

- Are there bushes or other foliage close to the house itself that could provide concealment for an intruder?
- Are utility/telephone boxes outside the house vulnerable to tampering?
- Is the structure itself well lit?
- Does the exterior lighting need to be activated by manual switch or is it wired to an automatic timer or photocell sensor? *The latter two options are preferable, since it is easy to forget to throw the switch. Activating lighting by means of motion detectors, while it affords some protection, is not as effective as having the lights on constantly during hours of darkness.*

Parking

- Is there an enclosed garage in which to park vehicles?
- Is the garage door equipped with remote controls to allow it to be opened and closed from within the vehicle? Do the openers operate quickly?
- Is the garage connected to the house, or is it necessary to walk outside in order to enter the house? *The connected garage affords greater security.*

Exterior Doors/Windows/Patios/Balconies/Skylights

- Do entry doors have solid-wood cores at least two inches thick or are they constructed of fire-rated metal? *Either option is acceptable.*
- Are entry doors equipped with deadbolt locks and 190-degree optical viewers?
- Do entry doors have small glass panels or are they adjacent to small glass panels?

   —If so, are they equipped with double-cylinder deadbolt locks (with keyways on both sides of the door) to prevent a burglar

from cutting or breaking the glass and reaching in to a thumb-turn knob, as would be the case with a single-cylinder lock?
—If double-cylinder deadbolt locks are used, are keys routinely removed from the interior keyways?

- Are all accessible windows equipped with stout locking devices and grilled? *Bars should be manufactured of solid steel and should be at least .6 inches (1.5 centimeters) in diameter. Spaces between bars should not be more than 6 inches (15 centimeters). Bars should be grouted at least 3 inches (7.5 centimeters) into exterior walls. A sufficient number of grilles should be hinged (and secured with padlocks) to permit emergency egress in the event of a fire. The keys to the padlocks should be stored in a safe place close to the windows to ensure quick egress in case of fire.*
- Are doors leading to patios and accessible balconies solid-core, French doors, or sliding-glass doors? *If they are solid-core, they require deadbolt locks. If they are French doors, they should be equipped with double-cylinder deadbolt locks and grilled. If they are sliding-glass doors, they should be equipped with key-operated antislide bolts and grilled.*
- Is there a rooftop skylight? *If so, it should be equipped with a stout locking device and grilled.*

INTRUSION-DETECTION ALARM SYSTEM

- Does the house have an intrusion-detection alarm system?
- Does it have magnetic contacts on doors and windows, glass-break sensors on all glass surfaces, and motion sensors? *All three are recommended.*
- Are there multiple control panels for the system so that residents can access it from the ground floor and from upper floors?
- Is there an audible annunciator (siren, claxon, etc.) located

inside or outside the house? *Ideally, annunciators should be both inside and outside the residence.*

- Are smoke detectors wired into the system?
- Is there also a strobe light outside the house? *The strobe light is another useful indicator of trouble.*
- Is the intrusion-detection alarm system monitored by a central station?
- Is the system tied to the central station by a telephone or radio signal? *The radio signal is the optimum. If a telephone line is to be used, it should be stoutly protected and should alert the central station if cut.*
- Does the system provide fixed and/or portable duress alarm devices?
- Is the central station tied into roving security patrols in the community?

ASSESSMENT OF A POTENTIAL INTERIOR SAFE HAVEN

- One room should be selected as a safe haven to which family members can retreat if an intruder should gain access to the house. It is always advisable for family members to avoid confrontation and to retreat to an area in which they can safely summon police assistance and wait for help.
- Typically, the master bedroom, the master bath, or a walk-in closet in the master suite is selected as the safe haven. However, if all bedrooms are located on the upper floor, it may be possible to install a solid-core or metal-backed door at the entry point to those quarters to effectively turn the entire floor into a safe haven.
- Specifications for converting the selected room or area into a safe haven include:

    —The room or area selected should have a stout door that cannot be easily kicked in by the intruder. It should be solid-wood core at least two inches thick or metal-backed wood and mounted in a metal frame and equipped with a single-cylinder deadbolt lock with the keyway on the outside.

—The selected room or area should have no windows accessible to the intruder.

—A control panel and panic/duress alarm for the intrusion detection system should be located within the safe haven.

—A dedicated cellular telephone with a trickle charger should be placed in the safe haven and never removed. *(Landline telephones are not recommended because they can be easily disabled by cutting the line or lifting a receiver off-hook in another area of the house.)*

—A list of emergency telephone numbers should be kept in the safe haven.

—An all-purpose A-B-C fire extinguisher, a flashlight (with extra batteries), and some food and water should be stored in the safe haven.

DOMESTICS

- Are new hires vetted by law-enforcement authorities?
- Are references required and checked thoroughly?
- If domestics are to be provided with keys, have they been instructed in the proper means of safeguarding those keys?
- Are locks rekeyed after domestics quit or are dismissed?
- Have domestics been instructed on how to screen visitors?

—Have they been instructed to admit to the home only individuals known to them and maintenance personnel, including utility personnel, who have been summoned and who present proper identification?

—Have they been instructed not to provide any information about the residents to persons calling on the telephone?

5. Single-Family Dwelling— Moderate-Risk Area

SELECTING A NEIGHBORHOOD

- Have there been any home invasions or burglaries in this neighborhood? Have there been classical or express kidnappings?
- Is there a police precinct and fire station in or near the neighborhood?
- What is the distance from the neighborhood to the closest trauma-care hospital?
- Is there new construction in the area? *Construction crews often serve as spotters for burglars.*

SELECTING A HOME

Perimeter

- Is the perimeter of the property protected by a significant wall or fence, or by a hedge?
- Is the perimeter well lit?
- Is the exterior lighting wired to an automatic timer or photocell sensor? Is it activated by a motion detector? Does it need to be activated by a manual switch? *The former is the most desirable, the latter the least.*
- Is there foliage close to the house that could provide concealment for a burglar?
- Are utility/telephone boxes outside the house vulnerable to tampering?

Parking

- If there is a wall, is there a gate that can be activated remotely from inside a vehicle? Does it operate reasonably quickly?
- Is there an enclosed garage?
- Is the garage door equipped with a quick-opening, remote-control opener?
- Is the garage connected to the house, or is it necessary to walk outside in order to enter the house? *The connected garage affords greater security.*

Exterior Doors/Windows/Patios/Balconies/Skylights

- Do entry doors have solid-wood cores at least two inches thick or are they constructed of fire-rated metal? *Either option is acceptable.*
- Are entry doors equipped with deadbolt locks and 190-degree optical viewers?
- Do entry doors have glass panels or are they adjacent to glass panels?

    —If so, are they equipped with double-cylinder deadbolt locks (with keyways on both sides of the door) to prevent a burglar from cutting or breaking the glass and reaching in to a thumb-turn knob, as would be the case with a single-cylinder lock?
    —If double-cylinder deadbolt locks are used, are keys routinely removed from the interior keyways?

- Are all accessible windows equipped with adequate locking devices?
- Are doors leading to ground-floor patios and accessible balconies solid-core, French doors, or sliding-glass doors? *If they are solid-core, they require deadbolt locks. If they are French doors, they should be equipped with double-cylinder deadbolt*

locks. If they are sliding-glass doors, they should be equipped with key-operated antislide bolts.

- Is there a rooftop skylight? If so, is it equipped with a stout locking device?

INTRUSION-DETECTION ALARM SYSTEM

- Does the house have an intrusion-detection alarm system?
- Does it have magnetic contacts on doors and windows, glass-break sensors on all glass surfaces, and motion sensors? *All three are recommended.*
- Are there multiple control panels for the system so that residents can access it from the ground floor and from upper floors?
- Is there an audible annunciator (siren, claxon, etc.) located inside or outside the house? *Ideally, annunciators should be both inside and outside the residence.*
- Are smoke detectors wired into the system?
- Is the intrusion-detection alarm system monitored by a central station?
- Is the system tied to the central station by a telephone or radio signal? *The radio signal is the optimum. If a telephone line is to be used, it should be stoutly protected and should alert the central station if cut.*
- Does the system provide fixed and/or portable duress alarm devices?
- Is the central station tied into roving security patrols in the community?

DOMESTICS

- Are new hires vetted by law-enforcement authorities?
- Are references required and checked thoroughly?

- If domestics are to be provided with keys, have they been instructed in the proper means of safeguarding those keys?
- Are keys changed when domestics quit or are dismissed?
- Have domestics been instructed on how to screen visitors?

    —Have they been instructed to admit to the home only individuals known to them and maintenance personnel, including utility personnel, who have been summoned and who present proper identification?

    —Have they been instructed not to provide any information about the residents to persons calling on the telephone?

INDEX

ABB Lummus, 67, 249
Abd-al-Rahman, Umar. *See*
  Rahman, Umar Abd-al-
Abdullah (king), 242
Abqaiq refinery, 53, 69, 70, 249
Abu Nidal Organization. *See* ANO
Ackerman, Mike, 13, 14, 16,
  223–29
  Ackerman Principles, 17–18
Ackerman Group, 13, 143, 210,
  264, 269, 273
Adams, Sherman, 225
Advanced Electronics, 68
advance work before trips, 197, 200
Afghanistan
  al-Qaida in, 37, 55, 61, 65, 81,
    91, 97, 241, 242
  future of terrorism in, 241–42
  Soviet-Afghan War, 16, 242
  US led war in, 34, 37, 44
AFIO. *See* Association of Foreign
  Intelligence Officers
Africa, carjackings and express kid-
  napping activities in, 155
Ahmadabad train station, 83,
  88–89, 252
Ahmadinejad, Mahmoud, 243
Ahsan, Aitzaz, 50

aircraft, attacks on, 53, 63, 75–82
Air France, 61, 63, 79, 84
airports
  attacks on, 39–40, 73, 77, 81, 146
  screening passengers, 81
  security measures for traveler,
    259–60
  workers as potential security
    danger, 81–82
air travel, security measures for, 82,
  257–63
alarm systems for apartments and
  homes, 288, 293, 297,
  302–303, 307
al-Gama'a al-Islamiya. *See* Gama'a
Algeria, 60–61
  assassinations in, 61
  attacks on commercial aviation
    targets, 61, 63
  attacks on commercial targets, 72,
    73, 74, 250
  attacks on governmental and mili-
    tary targets, 62, 73–74, 255,
    256
  Risknet analysis of, 62
al-Jazeera, 44
· al-Jihad, 55
al-Khobar massacre, 68, 249

al-Qaida, 15, 37–41
    difficulties of working with far-
        flung cells, 41
    favoring multiple, simultaneous
        attacks, 30–31
    future of, 241–45
    objectives of, 43–46
    reasons for attacks in Pakistan,
        45, 47–52
    See also Global Jihad; regional
        affiliates of al-Qaida; terrorist
        cells with links to al-Qaida
al-Qaida in the Arabian Peninsula.
    See QAP
al-Qaida Organization for Jihad in
    Iraq. See QJI
al-Qaida Organization of the
    Islamic Maghreb. See QIM
al-Tawhid wal-Jihad. See TJ
American Society of Travel Agents,
    56
ANO, 77–78
anthrax scare, 244
anti-Zionist attacks on Israel, 58,
    75–78, 80, 92, 98, 99, 243, 251
ANYO, 77–78
apartment complexes, 171–73
    safety checklist for high-risk
        areas, 285–90
    safety checklist for moderate-risk
        areas, 290–93
Arab Armed Struggle, 83–84
Arab Nationalist Youth Organiza-
    tion. See ANYO
Aramco, 69, 70

Araujo, Fernando, 109–10
Arbenz, Jacobo, 228
Argentina
    bombings in, 243
    carjackings and express kidnap-
        ping activities in, 157–58
    gated communities in, 171
    kidnappings in, 107, 118, 125–26
    robberies in restaurants, 167
Armed Islamic Group. See GIA
Armed Islamic Movement. See MIA
armed robbery, 161–62
    armed robbery of motorists,
        158–60
Armenian Secret Army for the Lib-
    eration of Armenia. See
    ASALA
armored cars, 18, 109, 189–93
Army of the Pure. See LT
ASALA, 14
assassinations, 28, 44, 49–50, 55,
    61, 229, 232, 255, 256
Association of Foreign Intelligence
    Officers, 233
ASTA. See American Society of
    Travel Agents
Atkinson, Jim, 209
ATM cards, 155, 157, 158, 271,
    274
attack, security measures if under,
    266–67
AUC, 24–25, 138–39
Australian Embassy in Jakarta, 255
authority of corporate security
    director, 215–20

avoidance of terrorist threats. *See* counterterrorism strategies; risk avoidance; security enhancements; security measures

awareness as a key to safety, 185–87

Aznar, José Maria, 85

background investigations on employees. *See* preemployment screening

Baitullah Mahsud. *See* Mahsud, Baitullah

Bali bombings, 15, 98–99, 254

Basque Land and Liberty. *See* ETA

behavior modification as a protection from violence, 181–87

Belkhadeem, Abdelaziz, 73, 255

Bhutto, Benazir, 44, 48–50, 51, 256

bin Ladin, Usama, 15, 37, 44, 55

Black September uprising, 76

"blind sheikh." *See* Rahman, Umar Abd-al-

bodyguards, 18, 109, 195–203
   security measures for travel with bodyguards, 263–67

Bodyguard's Story, The (Rees-Jones), 202

Bolivia, kidnappings in, 122

bombings. *See* car bombings; roadside bombs; suicide-bombers

boutique establishments, 94

brands, threats to corporations about, 137, 140

Brazil
   extortion activities in, 137, 139, 140, 168
   favelas in Rio de Janeiro, 162
   home invasions/burglaries in, 169

British Airways, 77, 80, 251

British Consulate in Istanbul, 71, 255

Brown & Root-Condor, 72, 250

burglary, 169–77

burundanga, 161

Bush, George H. W., 234

business acumen of corporate security director, 215–20

Canada, 105
   extortion activities in, 141–42, 143–44

car bombings, 39, 49, 65, 66, 68, 73–74, 92, 100, 249, 250, 253, 255–56

cargo-security, 24

carjackings, 155, 156, 158, 159–60, 175, 191, 195

"Carlos." *See* Sanchez, Illich Ramirez

Carnegie Corporation, 225

Carter, Jimmy, 27, 29

Castro, Fidel, 232

Cauca Valley, Colombia, 21–23

Cavuto, Neil, 44

CBS (TV network), 134

Central Intelligence Agency, 27, 227
   Latin American Division, 228–31, 233

need to revitalize, 233–35
and Watergate, 231–33
Chaudry, Iftikhar, 47, 48, 49
Chavez, Hugo, 106
Chechen terrorists, 80, 84–85, 260
China, threats against personnel or
  property in, 145
Chiquita Brands, 24–25, 139
choke points, 182
Chubb Corporation, 114, 236
CIA. *See* Central Intelligence Agency
Citigroup, Inc., 45
class attacks
  classes of people targeted by ter-
    rorists, 53
  on commercial aviation, 53–54,
    75–82
  on commercial targets, 54–60
  on hotels, 53–54, 91–95
  on tourists and tourist sites,
    53–54, 97–101
  on trains and subways, 53–54,
    83–90
close-protection specialists. *See*
  bodyguards
CMT. *See* Crisis Management Team
USS *Cole* (destroyer), 65
Colgate-Palmolive Company, 209,
  213, 217, 218
Colombia
  armed robbery activities in, 161
  evaluating security in, 21–23
  extortion activities in, 24–25,
    138–39, 143
  kidnappings in, 106, 107, 108,
    109, 116–17, 126–27, 131

lobbying against payments to
  extortionists, 139
roadside bombs in, 190
Colombian Revolutionary Armed
  Forces. *See* FARC
Columbia University, 227
commercial aviation, attacks on
  bombings, 78–80
  hijackings, 76–79
  liquid explosives, 39, 79
  missiles launched at, 80
communicating with kidnappers,
  122–23, 133–34
  See also negotiating with
    kidnappers
concierge/doorman as protection,
  162, 163, 167, 172, 283, 291
Conoco Inc., 210, 217
Conrads, Ernie, 208, 211, 216, 217,
  219
Constitutional Court building, 74
copy-cat strikes, 46
corporations and terrorism
  avoiding risks of both class and
    specific attacks, 53–54
  dealing with extortion, 137–44
  dealing with political instability,
    31–32
  dealing with threats against per-
    sonnel or property, 145–51
  handling kidnappings, 113–29
  interacting with corporate secu-
    rity, 207–10, 211–13, 215–20,
    243–45
  mistakes corporations can make,
    244–45

need for staff monitoring intelligence, 29–30, 32
See also counterterrorism strategies; Crisis Management Team; risk avoidance; travel guides for security measures
corruption in police departments, 118–19
Corzine, John, 203
Costa Rica, street crime in, 166
Counterspy (magazine), 234
counterterrorism/countercrime strategies, 170–77
Ackerman Principles, 17–18
advice on visiting a resort, 101
avoiding express kidnapping and carjacking, 156–57
avoiding kidnapping, 108–109, 181–88
avoiding pocket picking and grab-and-run thefts, 166
dealing with armed robberies, 159–60
dealing with extortion, 139–40
dealing with suspicions about home invasion/burglary, 170
finding a safe hotel, 94
learning how to be safe on the streets, 162
mistakes corporations can make, 244–45
for nonwhites, 165
reducing risks. *See* risk avoidance
ways airline passengers can protect themselves, 82, 257–63

ways commuters can protect themselves, 90
for women, 164
See also residential protection; risk avoidance; security enhancements; travel guides for security measures
credibility of corporate security director, 215–20
credit cards, 155, 166, 258, 275, 279
credit card fraud, 167
crime
armed robberies, 158–60
carjackings, 155–56
at entertainment venues, 167–68
express kidnappings, 155–60
extortions, 137–44
kidnappings, 105–11, 113–29, 131–35, 150, 181–89, 223–24, 283–84
residential crime, 169–77
street crime, 161–66
threats, 145–51
Crisis Management Team
dealing with express kidnappings and carjackings, 158
dealing with extortion, 142–43, 148
dealing with kidnappings, 113–14, 116, 118
Cuba, 228
cyber-criminals, 140–41

Dartmouth College, 224–25, 227
Days Inn hotel, 93

DDoS. *See* Distributive Denial of
Service
DEA. *See* Drug Enforcement
Administration
"declaration of war against the
Americans," 15
Delta Airlines, 82
Democratic Front for the Liberation
of Palestine. *See* DFLP
detached homes, safety in, 173–77
checklist for homes in high-risk
areas, 299–304
checklist for homes in moderate-
risk areas, 305–308
Deutsche Bank, 190–91
DFLP, 77
Diana (Princess), 201–202
dirty bombs, 45–46
Diskin, Yuval, 37
Distributive Denial of Service, 141
dogs
as security, 175
sniffer dogs, 147
domestics
aiding or preventing home invasions and burglary, 170
safety checklist for selecting,
289–90, 293, 299, 304,
307–308
Dominican Republic, 228, 229
kidnappings in, 120–21
doorman/concierge as protection,
162, 163, 167, 172, 283, 291
Dow Jones Industrial Average, 44
driver-bodyguards, 199–200, 202

drivers of armored cars, 191–92
driving course, protective, 160, 183,
191, 198
Drug Enforcement Administration,
211
drugs used in committing armed
robbery, 161, 167–68
Dulles, Allen, 227
DuPont, 209, 210, 213, 215, 217

Early Show (TV program), 134
Eastern Europe
extortion activities in, 139, 142
Mafia in, 139
racial crimes in, 164, 283
economic disruption as objective of
terrorists, 43–46
aimed at classes of people, 53
aimed at commercial targets,
54–60
aimed at specific targets, 60–64,
65–74
See also class attacks
Ecuador
government involved in kidnapping negotiations, 126
kidnappings in, 126–27, 132–34
EDS. *See* Electronic Data Systems
Egypt
attacks on commercial targets,
54–60
attacks on hotels, 92, 99, 253
attacks on tourism-related targets,
40, 56–58, 99, 100–101,
171–72, 254

future of terrorism in, 242, 243
home invasions/burglaries in, 171–72
tourist sites at risk, 57
Eisenhower, Dwight D., 225
El Al Israel Airlines, 76, 77
Electronic Data Systems, 29
el-Ghriba synagogue, 97, 254
ELN, 14, 107, 109, 110
El Salvador, 14
kidnappings in, 107
employees
at airports, 81–82
corporations dealing with threats against employees, 145–51
evaluating the director of corporate security, 215–20
exit interviews, 146, 148–49
hiring a corporate security director, 211–13
modifying behavior taught to protect against violence, 181–87
as source of threats, 146
and workplace-violence, 145, 150–51
See also preemployment screening
Entebbe, Uganda, 14
entertainment venues, criminal activities in, 167–68
Erickson Air-Crane Inc., 133, 134
escape, attempting to, 184
escorts. *See* bodyguards
ETA, 14, 85–87
and extortion, 137, 138

exit interviews, 146, 148–49
express kidnapping, 155–60
extortion, 137–44, 168

Fakhet, Serhane ben Abdelmajid, 87
Farabundo Marti National Liberation Front. *See* FMLN
FARC, 14, 22–23, 25, 190
and extortion, 137, 138
and kidnappings, 106, 107, 109–10
favelas, 162
Fawzi, Akram Mohamed, 100
Fayed, Dodi al-, 201–202
Fayed, Mohammed al-, 202
Federal Bureau of Investigation (FBI), 21, 95, 209, 213, 224, 233
and kidnappings, 118, 133
Federal Investigative Agency in Lahore, 256
firearms
reacting to gunfire, 262, 263, 266, 281
as security, 175–77, 198
FIS, 60–61
"fishing" done by extortionists, 139–40
Flannery, Jim, 23, 228–29, 230, 238–39
FMLN, 14
follow-car, 200
Food and Drug Administration, 207
Ford, Gerald, 234

France, 60, 78, 105
    attacks on trains and subways,
        83–84
"Friendship Express" train, 89, 252

Gama'a, 53–54, 55–60, 99, 243
gated communities, 171–73
    safety checklist for high-risk
        areas, 294–99
Gaza, 191
Geer, Jim, 209–10, 213, 215,
    216–17
Germany
    attack on Ramstein Air Base, 39
    attacks on airports, 39
    extortion activities in, 141
    roadside bombs in, 190–91
Ghazala Gardens Hotel, 99
GIA, 63–64, 72, 79, 84
Gibril, Ahmed, 78
Ging, John, 191
Glasgow, car-bomb attempt, 39–40,
    81, 251
Global Jihad
    Ackerman Principles to use
        against, 17–18
    character of, 37–41
    choices of targets. See airports,
        attacks on; commercial avia-
        tion, attacks on; governmental
        and military targets; hotels,
        attacks on; tourists, attacks on;
        trains
    choosing the eleventh of a month
        for attacks, 73, 74

future of, 241–45
objectives of, 43–46. See also
    economic disruption as objec-
    tive of terrorists; political chaos
    as objective of terrorists
See also al-Qaida; independent
    terrorist cells; regional affiliates
    of al-Qaida; terrorist cells with
    links to al-Qaida
governmental and military targets,
    21, 48, 49, 50–51, 65, 73–74,
    255, 256
grab-and-run thefts, 161, 165–66
Grand Hyatt, 93
GSPC, 72
Guantánamo Bay detention camp, 92
Guatemala, 228
    kidnappings in, 107, 123–24, 131
guns
    reacting to gunfire, 262, 263, 266,
        281
    as security, 175–77, 198

Halliburton Company, 72
Hameedi, Badr bin Abdullah al-, 70
Helmerich & Payne, Inc., 133, 134
Helms, Dick, 232, 236–38
heroism vs. reason, 18, 166
Herrhausen, Alfred, 190–91
Higgins, Anthony, 68–69
high profile, danger of, 109, 181,
    184, 269
hijackings
    nonsuicidal hijacking, 260–63
    by PFLP, 76–77

security measures for traveler, 257–63

suicidal hijackings, 263

TWA Flight 847, 21, 77, 243

Hijazi, Raid, 91–92

Hilton hotels, 99, 253

Hindi, Abu Issa al-, 45–46

Hizbollah, 21, 32, 77, 243

home invasions, 169–77, 285, 290, 294, 299, 305

home security measures, 171–77

checklist for gated communities in high-risk areas, 294–99

checklist for single-family homes in high-risk areas, 299–304

checklist for single-family homes in moderate-risk areas, 305–308

hostage recovery, 13–14, 123. *See also* negotiating with kidnappers

hostile countries, travel to, 278–80

hotels

attacks on, 53, 91–95

finding a safe hotel, 94

security measures for, 267, 270, 275–76

HSBC bank, 53, 71, 249

Hunt, Leamon, 192–93

Hussein, Saddam, 31

Huyser, Robert, 29

Ideal Staffing Solutions, Inc., 82

IIT. *See* Indian Institute of Technology

Ila, Sabir Abu al-, 57, 58–59

independent terrorist cells, 37, 39, 241–42

India, 38, 44, 89, 164, 275

attacks on commercial targets, 71–72

attacks on trains and subways, 83, 88–89, 252

Indian Institute of Technology, 72

Indonesia

attacks on governmental and military targets, 255

attacks on hotels, 92–93, 253

attacks on tourism-related targets, 15, 98, 101, 254

carjackings and express kidnapping activities in, 157

information (intelligence), critical need for, 17, 27–34, 53

instincts, following, 162, 163, 187, 188, 197, 259, 282

International Monetary Fund, 45

IRA, 14

Iran

future of terrorism in, 243

security analysis of, 28–29

Iraq

future of terrorism in, 242

as a high-risk area, 181

Iraq War, 34, 40, 44

roadside bombs in, 190

Islamic Army for the Liberation of Holy Sites, 98

Islamic Brigades of Pride, 99

Islamic Group. *See* Gama'a; JI

Islamic Salvation Front. *See* FIS

Israel, 13–14, 37, 55, 78, 199, 243, 257, 258

anti-Zionist attacks on, 58, 75–78, 80, 92, 98, 99, 243, 251
Israeli-Lebanese dispute, 31, 32
Italy
    killing of Leamon Hunt in, 192–93
    KR&E insurance not sold in, 33

Jacobs, Robert, 68
J & J. See Johnson & Johnson
JI (Jemaah Islamiyah), 38, 98
Jinks, Larry, 233
Johnson, Lyndon B., 228, 232
Johnson, Paul, 68
Johnson & Johnson, 209
Jordan
    attacks on hotels, 91–92, 93, 253
    future of terrorism in, 242
Justice Commandos, 14
JW Marriott hotel, 92–93, 253

Kahn-al-Khalili Bazaar, 100, 254
Keefe, Pat, 208–209, 210, 213, 216, 217, 218
Kennedy, John F., 50
Kenya, 275
    attacks on commercial aviation targets, 80, 251
    attacks on hotels, 92, 253
    carjackings and express kidnapping activities in, 156
Khalid, Leila, 77
Khomeini, Ruhollah (Ayatollah), 29
Khrushchev, Nikita, 225

Kidnap, Ransom, and Extortion insurance. See KR&E insurance
kidnappings, 61–62, 105–11, 113–29, 131–35, 137–38
    communicating with kidnappers, 122–23, 133–34
    corporations dealing with, 113–29
    death of victim, 131
    for economic gain (ransoms), 105–109, 111
    express kidnapping, 155–60
    handling tough cases, 131–35
    hostage recovery, 13–14, 123
    to induce terror (political kidnapping), 109–11
    and mutilations, 109, 128, 129
    negotiating with kidnappers, 13–14, 115, 120–30, 131, 133–34, 138, 150
    proof of survival in kidnapping negotiations, 128, 131
    rescue operations against kidnappers, 14, 62, 115
    responders and kidnappings, 114–18, 134–35, 223–24
    security measures for surviving an abduction, 283–84
    ways to discourage kidnappings, 108–109, 181–88
    wisdom of attempting to escape, 184
    See also ransoms for kidnappings
Kiyani, Ashfaq Parvez, 49, 51
KLM (airline), 82

KR&E insurance, 32–33, 114, 151, 236

Kuwait, invasion of, 31

Lal Masjid (Red Mosque), 48
Lashkar-e-Tayyaba. *See* LT
leapfrog technique, 200
leftist movements vs. nationalist groups, 15
Lehman, Bill, 234
Limburg (super-tanker), 65, 249
liquid explosives, 79
Lockerbie, Scotland, 78
Lockheed Martin, 68
locks, choosing the right one, 174–75, 287, 292, 296, 301–302, 304, 306–307
London bombings, 15, 39, 40, 83, 87–88, 90, 252
Look over My Shoulder, A (Helms), 232
Los Angeles Times (newspaper), 235
low profile as protection, maintaining, 108–109, 181, 187
LT, 38, 48, 71–72, 88–89, 241
Luna Caprese restaurant, 94–95
Luxor massacre, 59
luxury automobiles and carjackings, 156–57

Macri, Franco, 125–26
Macri, Mauricio, 125–26
Madrid bombings, 15, 83, 85–87, 252

Mafia, 139, 147, 219, 232
Mahjoub, Rifaat al-, 56
Mahsud, Baitullah, 38, 48
Manser, Amos, 224–25
Marriott hotels, 93, 94, 253
Martinez, Eugenio, 231–32
massacres
  al-Khobar massacre, 68
  Luxor massacre, 59
McGovern, George, 235
Merari, Ariel, 13–16
Mexico
  armed robbery of motorists in, 158–59
  carjackings and express kidnapping activities in, 155, 157, 158, 160
  extortion activities in, 140
  kidnappings in, 106, 118–19, 128, 131
  robberies in restaurants, 167
MIA, 53–54, 61–63
Miami Herald (newspaper), 233–34, 235
military targets. *See* governmental and military targets
Millennium Plot, 91–92
missiles, shoulder-launched, 80
Mohammed, Khalid Sheikh, 45, 98
Mohammed Reza Pahlavi (shah), 29
Mombasa, 80, 251
Monotheism and Holy War. *See* TJ
Montalbano, Bill, 233
Moscow Energy Institute, 165

motorists
  and armed robbery attempts,
    158–60
  and carjackings, 155, 156
Mubarak, Hosni, 55, 59, 60, 242
Muirhead-Smith, Edward, 69
Multinational Observer Force (in
  the Sinai), 192
Mumbai, attacks in, 83, 88–89, 252
Muqrin, Abd al-Aziz al-, 68
Museum of the Revolution, 226
Musharraf, Pervez, 44, 47–49, 50,
  65, 242, 255
mutilation and kidnappings, 109,
  128, 129

Nasrallah, Hassan, 31, 243
nationalist groups vs. leftist movements, 15
National Liberation Army. See
  ELN
nationals as target of kidnappers,
  107–108
National Security Council (Russia),
  237
National Socialist Party of Russia,
  165
Naval College in Lahore, 256
Nawar, Nizar bin Muhammad, 97–98
negotiating with extortionists
  different from dealing with kid-
    nappers, 138
  possible ways to handle, 148–49
negotiating with kidnappers, 13–14,
  115, 120–30, 133–34

asking for proof of survival, 128,
  131
different from dealing with extortionists, 138
impact of on family members,
  124–25
possible ways to handle, 150
proof of survival in kidnapping
  negotiations, 128, 131
See also communicating with
  kidnappers
New People's Army. See NPA
New York City
  1993 attack on World Trade
    Center, 55, 63–64, 79
  New York Stock Exchange, 44, 45
  9/11 attacks, 15, 43–44
  as target for future attacks, 45–46
New York Times, 132, 233
Niger Delta
  as a high-risk area, 181
  kidnappings in, 33–34, 105, 107,
    108, 199
9/11 attacks, 15, 43–44
  Air France attempt as a precursor,
    63–64
  Global Jihad choosing the
    eleventh of a month for attacks,
    73, 74
Nixon, Richard, 225, 232
nonsuicidal hijacking, security
  measures for travelers, 260–63
nonwhites, dangers for, 164–65
  security measures for nonwhite
    travelers, 283

Northrop Grumman, 68
North West Frontier Province. *See*
  NWFP
NPA, 137, 138
NWFP, 38, 48, 49, 51

Ortho Pharmaceutical Company,
  209
Overseas Security Advisory Council
  (OSAC), 215

packing, security measures for,
  258–59, 277–79
Pakistan, 44
  attacks on commercial targets, 65,
    249
  attacks on governmental and mili-
    tary targets, 48, 49, 50–51, 65,
    255, 256
  attacks on hotels, 93, 94, 253
  future of terrorism in, 241–42
  kidnappings in, 65
  reasons for attacks in, 45, 47–52
Pakistani Taliban, 38, 48
Pakistan People's Party, 49–51
Palestinian Authority, 191
Palestinian nationalists, 14, 21, 75,
  76, 77–78, 99, 260
Palumbo, Lou, 27, 236
Pan American Airways, 76–77, 78,
  79
Paradise Hotel, 92, 253
parking, safety checklist for, 286,
  291, 296, 301, 306
passengers, airline

screening passengers at airports, 81
security measures for air travel,
  257–63
ways to protect self, 82
Patriot Act (US), 139
Paul, Henri, 202
Pearl, Daniel, 65
pedestrians
  as victims of armed robbery, 161
  as victims of express kidnappings,
    158
people watching, importance of,
  185–87. *See also* surveillance
  recognition
Perot, Ross, 29
personal information, guarding,
  187–88
personnel, corporations dealing
  with threats against. *See*
  employees
Peru, 14
  attacks in, 91
PFLP, 76–79
PFLP-General Command, 78
Philippines
  demands for "war taxes" in, 137
  lobbying against payments to
    extortionists, 139
Philippines Airlines, 79
Phillips, Dave, 228–29, 230–31,
  233, 238
Pike Committee, 234
planning for trips, security measures, 257–58, 268–69, 272–73
pocket picking, 165–66

police
  and extortion, 142–43, 149
  and kidnappings, 118–20, 132,
    133, 199
political chaos as objective of ter-
    rorists, 43, 44, 45
  kidnappings to induce terror,
    109–11
  reasons for attacks in Pakistan,
    45, 47–52
political kidnappings. See
    kidnappings
political stability, assessing, 29–30,
    31–32
Popular Front for the Liberation of
    Palestine. See PFLP
Popular Party of Spain (PP), 85
PPP. See Pakistan People's Party
predictability, danger of, 181–82
preemployment screening, 146
  to avoid burglary/home invasions,
    170
  background investigations on
    employees, 17, 81–82, 146, 170
  need for at airports, 81–82
  safety checklist for selecting
    domestics, 289–90, 293, 299,
    304, 307–308
product-contamination threats, 140,
    143–44
proof of survival in kidnapping
    negotiations, 128, 131
property, corporations dealing with
    threats against, 145–51
"protection money." See extortion

protective details. See bodyguards
protective-driving courses, 160,
    183, 191, 198
Prudential Financial, Inc., 45
Puerto Rico
  murder of Alan Randall, 28
  risk assessment of, 28, 208
  smuggling weapons and drugs to,
    82
Puri, M. C., 72

QAP, 38, 68–70, 241
QIM, 38, 72–74, 241
QJI, 38, 51–52, 76, 93, 241, 242
Quantas, 82
Queen of Sheba Temple, 40, 101, 254

racial attacks, 164–65
  reducing risks of, 283
Radisson hotel, 92, 93
RAF, 190–91
Rahaman, Hazil Mohammed, 80
Rahman, Umar Abd-al-, 55, 63–64
railroads. See trains
Randall, Alan, 28
ransoms for kidnappings, 105–109,
    111
  for express kidnappings, 158
  protecting large ransoms, 126–27
  ransom delivery, 125, 127
  trying to lower kidnapper
    demands, 133, 134, 135
Rawalpindi, attacks in, 48, 49,
    255–56
Razel (construction firm), 73, 250

Reagan, Ronald, 21

reason vs. heroism, 166

recognizing surveillance. *See* surveillance recognition

Red Army Faction. *See* RAF

Red Brigades, 192–93

Red Mosque. *See* Lal Masjid (Red Mosque)

Rees-Jones, Trevor, 202

regional affiliates of al-Qaida, 37, 38, 39, 40, 44, 275. *See also* JI (Jemaah Islamiyah); LT; QAP; QIM; QJI; Taliban

Reid, Richard, 79–80, 251

religious zealotry, 54, 59, 62, 97, 243

remises, 158

Republican National Committee, 234

reputation, threats to corporations about, 137

rescue operations against kidnappers, 14, 62, 115

residential crime, 169–77

residential protection, 170–77

  security checklists for apartments in high-risk areas, 285–90

  security checklists for apartments in moderate-risk areas, 290–93

  security checklists for gated communities in high-risk areas, 294–99

  security checklists for single-family homes in high-risk areas, 299–304

  security checklists for single-family homes in moderate-risk areas, 305–308

resisting assault, 160, 183

responders and kidnappings, 114–18

  reasons not to have more than one responder, 134–35

  selecting best one, 223–24

restaurants

  bombing of, 94–95

  criminal activities in, 167–68

restraining orders, 149–50

risk analysis, importance of, 27–34, 53, 54

risk avoidance, 54

  awareness as a key to safety, 185–87

  guarding personal information, 187–88

  maintaining a low profile, 108–109, 181, 187

  surveillance recognition, 109, 181, 182–83, 185, 197, 198, 200

  unpredictability, 108–109, 181–82, 185

  use of armored cars, 109, 189–93

  use of bodyguards, 109, 195–203

  See also counterterrorism strategies; residential protection; security enhancements; travel guides for security measures

Risknet, 29, 264, 269, 273

  analysis of Algeria, 62

  analysis of Egypt, 57

finding a safe hotel, 94
using to learn which areas are safe in a city, 162
Riyadh, attacks in, 66–67, 68–70, 249, 255
roadside bombs, 72, 74, 190, 191, 250
Roleros (gang), 159
route variation to create unpredictability, 182
Russia
    Ackerman serving as advisor on business security, 237–38
    attacks on commercial aviation targets, 80
    attacks on trains and subways, 84–85
    and extortion, 137
    extortion activities in, 139, 147
    racial attacks in, 164–65
    security analysis report on a franchisee, 219–20
    threats against personnel or property in, 145
    See also Soviet Union

SAC. See Strategic Air Command
Sadat, Anwar, 55
Sadr, Muqtada al-, 243
safe areas in cities, knowing, 161–62, 167, 283
safe havens
    in apartments in high-risk areas, 288–89
    in gated communities, 297–98
    in the home, 177, 303–304

salafi-jihadi militants, 16
salafism, 37
Salafist Group for Preaching and Combat. See GSPC
Sanchez, Illich Ramirez, 83–84
Saudi Arabia
    attacks on commercial aviation targets, 251
    attacks on commercial targets, 53, 66, 67, 68, 69, 70, 74, 249
    attacks on governmental and military targets, 21, 255
    future of terrorism in, 242
    kidnappings in, 68
Sawt al-Jihad (Web site), 70
Schlumberger Ltd., 133
Schneider Electric, 69
scopolamine, 161, 167–68
screening passengers at airports, 81
Scroggs, Kenneth, 68
Sears Tower, 45
Secret Service agents, 196
security, corporate
    choosing a director of corporate security, 211–13
    corporations not paying as much attention as should, 243–44
    evaluating the director of corporate security, 215–20
    function of corporate security, 207–10
    mistakes corporations can make, 244–45
    See also corporations and terrorism

security analysis, corporations' need for, 17, 27–34, 53
security enhancements
armored cars, 185, 189–93
bodyguards, 185, 195–203
security measures
for the home, 170–77, 285–308
for travel, 257–84
self-generated groups of Islamic extremists. *See* independent terrorist cells; terrorist cells with links to al-Qaida
Semiramis InterContinental Hotel, 57, 59
Sharm al-Sheikh bombing, 100, 254
Sheraton Hotel, 65, 249
Sherpao, Aftab Ahmed Khan, 49, 256
Shia, 21, 52, 77, 181, 243
Shin Bet, 37
Shining Path, 14, 91
simultaneous exchange of ransom and hostage, 123–24
Singapore as a safe city, 161–62
single-family homes, 171–77
safety checklist for high-risk areas, 299–304
safety checklist for moderate-risk areas, 305–308
singletons and extortion, 137–38, 139, 140
skinheads, 164–65, 283
Socialist Party (Spain), 85
solo travel, security measures for
in high-risk areas, 267–72
to hostile countries, 278–80
in moderate-risk areas, 272–75
to the Muslim World, 275–78
by nonwhites, 283
to unstable countries, 281–82
by women, 282–83
Sonatrach, 72
Soviet Union
Ackerman in study program, 225–27
Soviet-Afghan War, 16, 242
See also Russia
Spain
attacks on trains and subways, 15, 83, 85–87, 252
lobbying against payments to extortionists, 139
"spiderman" burglars, 173
Sri Lanka, 260
STASI, 190–91
Strategic Air Command, 227
street crime, 161–66
armed robbery of motorists, 158–60
See also carjackings; express kidnapping
Street Man (Ackerman), 234
"street smarts," 197
Stroitransgas, 72–73, 250
subways. *See* trains
suicidal hijackings, security measures for travelers, 263
suicide-bombers, 21, 39, 48, 49, 65, 70, 71, 80, 83, 85, 86–87, 92, 93, 97–98, 99, 100, 249, 252, 253, 254, 255, 256, 275

Sunni, 37, 52, 60, 75, 79, 242, 243
Surete Quebecois, 144
surveillance recognition, 109, 181, 182–83, 185
    bodyguards trained in, 197, 198
    and leapfrog technique, 200
Swissair, 61, 76–77

takfiri doctrine, 37, 51–52, 67
Taliban, 37, 38
Taliban, Pakistani, 38, 48
Tamil separatists, 260
targets for terrorists. *See* airports, attacks on; commercial aviation, attacks on; governmental and military targets; hotels, attacks on; tourists, attacks on; trains
Tawhid wal-Jihad, al-. *See* TJ
taxis, 162
    judging safety in riding in, 157, 158, 162–63, 187, 188, 269, 270, 271, 273, 274
    taxi rides leading to express kidnappings, 157
    warnings for women, 163, 282
Taylor, Sean, 176–77
Tel Aviv University, Terrorism and Low Intensity Warfare Project, 13
Terrorism and Low Intensity Warfare Project (Tel Aviv University), 13
Terrorism Roundtables, 237
terrorist cells with links to al-Qaida, 30, 37, 38–39, 40, 44, 101. *See also* Gama'a; YSB

threats, dealing with, 145–51
time variation to create unpredictability, 182
TJ, 99–100
tourists, attacks on, 15, 40, 53, 56–59, 97–101, 171–72, 254
trains
    security measures for train travel, 272
    trains and subways, attacks on, 53, 83–90, 252
travel guides for security measures
    for air travel, 257–63
    for nonwhite travelers, 283
    for solo travel in high-risk areas, 267–72
    for solo travel in moderate-risk areas, 272–75
    for solo travel in the Muslim World, 275–78
    for solo travel to hostile countries, 278–80
    for solo travel to unstable countries, 281–82
    for travel with bodyguards, 263–67
    for women, 282–83
traveling alone. *See* solo travel, security measures for
Treaster, Joseph B., 132
trip planning, security measures for, 257–58, 268–69, 272–73
Trotsky, Leon, 226
Trujillo, Rafael Leonidas, 229
Tunisia, attacks on tourism-related targets, 97–98, 101, 254

"Tunisian." *See* Fakhet, Serhane ben
  Abdelmajid
Turkey
  attacks on commercial targets, 53,
    71, 249
  attacks on governmental and mili-
    tary targets, 255
TWA Airlines LLC, 76–77

United Airlines, 82
United Brands, 25
United Fruit Company, 25
United Kingdom, 105
  attack on British Consulate in
    Istanbul, 71, 255
  attacks on commercial aviation
    targets, 39–40, 79, 80, 81, 251
  attacks on trains and subways, 15,
    39, 40, 83, 87–88, 252
United Nations, 255–56
  attack on offices in Algiers, 74, 256
  UN Relief and Works Agency
    (UNRWA), 191
United Self-Defense Forces of
  Colombia. *See* AUC
United States
  attacks on airports, 40
  attacks on governmental and mili-
    tary targets, 40, 65, 255
  attacks on New York City, 15,
    43–44, 45, 63–64, 79
unpredictability, 108–109, 181–82,
  185
UNRWA. *See* United Nations
unstable countries, travel to, 281–82

Uribe, Alvaro, 25, 106, 190
US Consulate in Karachi, 65, 255
UTA, 78

validity of threats, 146–47
Vargas Lleras, German, 190
Venezuela
  armed robbery of motorists in,
    158–59, 195
  attacks on commercial aviation
    targets, 80, 251
  carjackings and express kidnap-
    ping activities in, 155, 158
  kidnappings in, 106, 195
Vinnell Corporation, 68
violent street crime, 161–66
  armed robbery of motorists,
    158–60. *See also* carjackings;
    express kidnapping
Virginia Tech killings, 46
Voice of Jihad. *See Sawt al-Jihad*
  (Web site)

"war taxes," 137, 139. *See also*
  extortion
Washington Beltway snipers, 46
Washington Post, 233
Watergate scandal, 231–32
Web sites, threats to corporations
  about, 140–41
Welch, Dick, 231, 234
Westinghouse, 208, 217, 219
women
  facing special dangers, 163, 164,
    168

security measures for women
 travelers, 282–83
Woolard, Ed, 215
workplace violence, 145, 150–51
World Bank, 45
World Trade Center
 1993 attack on, 55, 63–64, 79
 Air France attempt as a precursor
  of 9/11, 63–64
 9/11 attacks, 15, 43–44

Yarkas, Imad Eddin Barakat, 86
Yeltsin, Boris, 237
Yemen
 attacks on commercial targets, 66,
  70–71, 249

attacks on tourism-related targets,
 254
tourism in, 101
Yemen Soldiers Brigades. *See* YSB
Yousef, Ramzi, 79
YSB, 101

Zapatero, José Luis Rodriguez, 85
Zardari, Asif Ali, 49, 50
Zardari, Bilawal Bhutto, 50
Zarqawi, Abu Musab al-, 52, 76, 93
Zawahiri, Ayman al-, 48, 52, 55, 73
zealotry, 54, 59, 62, 97, 243
Zougam, Jamal, 86
Zubaydah, Abu, 91